Innovation and Tourism Destination Development

Tourism is a central part of regional development strategies in many localities around Europe, not just in traditional coastal or mountain resorts but also in areas without a strong track record with regard to visitor economy. In a globalizing world, destinations can no longer take their traditional visitors for granted and escape growing competitive pressures, because increasingly experienced, specialised and demanding travellers now have a vastly greater number of potential destinations to choose from. Both well-established and emerging tourist destinations are therefore under pressure to be innovative to increase their attractiveness in the globalizing visitor economy. This book focuses on the role played by tourist destinations—conceived as multi-layered and functional governance structures—in stimulating or complicating the development of new tourist experiences. The complex relationship between firm-level and territorial development dynamics is, of course, by no means confined to tourism development, and the book will therefore be of a more general relevance for research into innovation and spatial development dynamics.

This book was published as a special issue of *European Planning Studies*.

Henrik Halkier is professor of regional and tourism studies at Aalborg University, Denmark.

Marek Kozak is professor of regional policy and tourism studies at Warsaw University, Poland.

Bo Svensson is associate professor of political science at Mid-Sweden University, Sweden.

Innovation and Tourism Destination Development

Edited by
Henrik Halkier, Marek Kozak and Bo Svensson

LONDON AND NEW YORK

First published 2015
by Routledge

2 Park Square, Milton Park, Abingdon, Oxon OX14 4RN
711 Third Avenue, New York, NY 10017, USA

Routledge is an imprint of the Taylor & Francis Group, an informa business

First issued in paperback 2017

British Library Cataloguing in Publication Data
A catalogue record for this book is available from the British Library

ISBN 13: 978-1-138-92246-4 (hbk)
ISBN 13: 978-1-138-08286-1 (pbk)

Typeset in Times New Roman
by RefineCatch Limited, Bungay, Suffolk

Publisher's Note
The publisher accepts responsibility for any inconsistencies that may have arisen during the conversion of this book from journal articles to book chapters, namely the possible inclusion of journal terminology.

Disclaimer
Every effort has been made to contact copyright holders for their permission to reprint material in this book. The publishers would be grateful to hear from any copyright holder who is not here acknowledged and will undertake to rectify any errors or omissions in future editions of this book.

Contents

Contents

Citation Information

The chapters in this book were originally published in *European Planning Studies*, volume 22, issue 8 (August 2014). When citing this material, please use the original page numbering for each article, as follows:

Chapter 6
World Heritage and Tourism Innovation: Institutional Frameworks and Local Adaptation
Susanna Heldt Cassel and Albina Pashkevich
European Planning Studies, volume 22, issue 8 (August 2014) pp. 1625–1640

Chapter 7
Beyond the Transfer of Capital? Second-Home Owners as Competence Brokers for Rural Entrepreneurship and Innovation
Ingeborg Nordbø
European Planning Studies, volume 22, issue 8 (August 2014) pp. 1641–1658

Chapter 8
Innovation and Destination Governance in Denmark: Tourism, Policy Networks and Spatial Development
Henrik Halkier
European Planning Studies, volume 22, issue 8 (August 2014) pp. 1659–1670

Chapter 9
Tourism Lobbying in Bavaria: Between Ignorance, Parochialism and Opportunism
Markus Pillmayer and Nicolai Scherle
European Planning Studies, volume 22, issue 8 (August 2014) pp. 1671–1692

Please direct any queries you may have about the citations to
clsuk.permissions@cengage.com

INTRODUCTION

Innovation and Tourism Destination Development

HENRIK HALKIER*, MAREK KOZAK** & BO SVENSSON[†]

*Department of Culture and Global Studies, Aalborg University, Aalborg, Denmark, **Centre for European Regional and Local Studies (EUROREG), University of Warsaw, Warsaw, Poland, [†]The European Tourism Research Institute (ETOUR), Mid-Sweden University, Östersund, Sweden

Tourism is a central part of regional development strategies in many localities around Europe, not just in traditional coastal or mountain resorts, but also in areas without a strong track record with regard to visitor economy (Anastasiadou, 2006; Hall, 2008; Halkier, 2010a). Traditionally strategies for developing tourism have relied heavily on marketing the experiences currently available to new potential customers. However, in a globalizing world, destinations can no longer take their traditional visitors for granted and escape growing competitive pressures, because increasingly experienced, specialized and demanding travellers now have a vastly greater number of potential destinations to choose from (Weaver & Lawton, 2002; Hall & Page, 2006; Halkier, 2010b), and hence both well-established and would-be emerging tourist destinations are under pressure to be innovative to increase their attractiveness in the globalizing visitor economy. It is, therefore, hardly surprising that in the increasingly competitive market for leisure and business travel, more attention is now being given to innovation in experiences and services (Hall & Williams, 2008; Hjalager, 2010; Halkier, 2011), and that the growing awareness of tourism's economic growth potential has also lead policy-makers to search for more comprehensive approaches to the development of the sector, as evidenced in reports by, for example, the OECD (2006), UN's World Tourism Organization (UNWTO, 2005), and the EU (European Commission, 2006).

The academic literature on innovation in tourism is small but growing, and in a recent review Hjalager (2010) identified a number of gaps in the existing body of literature, including innovation processes in enterprises and organizations, and the interplay between these processes and the wider governance contexts in which they take place.

The contribution of this Special Issue of *European Planning Studies* focuses on the role played by tourist destinations—conceived as multi-layered and functional governance structures (Weaver & Lawton, 2002; Hall, 2008)—are playing in stimulating or complicating the development of new tourist experiences. The complex relationship between the firm-level and territorial development dynamics is, of course, by no means confined to tourism development, but has also been intensely debated in the general literature on, for example, clusters and regional innovation systems (Amin, 1999; Martin & Sunley, 2003; Asheim *et al.*, 2006; Olsen, 2012). Recent contributions have focused in particular on the relationship between local processes and global knowledge flows (Asheim *et al.*, 2007; Crevoisier & Jeannerat, 2009; Cooke *et al.*, 2010), a theme particularly pertinent in the context of an increasingly global industry like tourism—and hence, hopefully, the contributions of the current Special Issue will also be of a more general relevance for research into spatial development dynamics.

The relationship between the development of a tourist destination and innovation within individual enterprises is explored in the first article where Anders Larsson and Kristina Nilsson Lindström focus on the difficulties in creating synergies between tourism development strategies and potential providers of new attractive tourist experiences from private actors in other sectors of the economy. Adopting an evolutionary perspective, the authors examine how a destination with a relatively immature tourism sector, Orust on the west coast of Sweden, attempts to mobilize somewhat conservative leisure boat manufacturers to spur innovation in experience production, and the article identifies both obstacles for collaboration and some interesting possibilities for future intersectoral knowledge sharing.

The issue of crossing boundaries in innovative destination development is further developed in the article by Eva Gustafsson, Mia Larson and Bo Svensson which analyses an attempt to establish a regional destination brand, "Delightful Christmas" that covers both the Aare ski resort and the city of Östersund, Sweden. Focusing on the network dynamics of the process, the text explores how continuous efforts in a weakly resourced multi-project network eventually find it difficult to create a geographically innovative place brand that spans two well-established and adjoining—but in terms of experience offer rather different—tourist destinations.

The third article, by Bodil Stilling Blichfeldt and Henrik Halkier, focuses on the interplay between creating activities that may attract visitors and the wider issue of creating a place brand with extensive involvement of the local community. Set in a small rural town in North Jutland, Denmark, the analysis focuses on the relationship between stakeholders and branding strategies, and in particular aims to uncover the role of the signature food festival in aggravating or alleviating inherent tensions between different internal and external stakeholders and target groups.

In contrast to the relatively positive Danish experience, the article by Marek W. Kozak underlines the difficulties that can be faced by non-state actors in integrating their activities in official tourism development agendas. The article analyses the emergence of the Palaces and Gardens Valley project in the south-west of Poland which has transcended the traditional emphasis in Polish destination development on natural or cultural heritage and created a multidimensional and innovative product which, however, now may be faced with constraints on further development due to generally limited cooperation between public and private bodies.

The issue of heritage as a tool for destination development is pursued from a different perspective in the article by Susanna Heldt Cassel and Albina Pashkevich, who discuss the issues raised when an attraction receives World Heritage status and becomes part of a global brand. Focusing on Swedish experiences and the Great Copper Mountain in Falun in particular, the article explores the extent to which World Heritage status changes the preconditions for destination development in terms of product development, marketing and collaborative networks through new ways of interacting with local community stakeholders.

The theme of external sources of innovation in tourist destinations is pursued from a different angle by Ingeborg Nordbø in her analysis of the role of second-home owners as competence brokers for entrepreneurship and innovation in two destinations in rural Norway. The study demonstrates that many second-home owners are both interested in and, in practice, willing to contribute to the development of the destination in which their second-home is located, and that they have the skills and experiences required to further entrepreneurship, innovation and development in the host community.

The importance of governance structures for destination development policies is the focus of the article by Henrik Halkier on the difficulties of placing innovation at the centre of the tourism policy agenda. Despite stagnating numbers of international visitors, destination development initiatives and national tourism policies in Denmark have continued to rely on traditional efforts like collective marketing and local visitor information services, while giving limited priority to innovation-oriented measures that could renew the tourist experiences available. The article examines the role of governance structures in explaining the slow adoption of new destination development strategies and points in particular towards the continued domination of tourism-related policy networks by short-term sectoral and localist interests.

The importance of governance structures and processes is also stressed by the final contribution to the Special Issue by Markus Pillmayer and Nicolai Scherle which focuses on the role of lobbying in the development of tourism in Bavaria, Germany. Tourism in the region is characterized by a curious coexistence of diminishing competitiveness due to a persistent investment backlog on the one hand, and exceedingly ambitious tourism policies on the other. The article argues that in the case of Bavaria, more professional forms of tourism lobbying could act as a mediator between public and private actors and lead to more realistic long-term strategies for the development of the region as a tourism destination.

The guest editors hope that the articles, emanating from a workshop organized at Mid Sweden University in Östersund organized on behalf of the Regional Studies Association research network on *Tourism and Regional Development*, have helped to illuminate the interplay between innovation processes in tourism enterprises and organizations, and the wider governance contexts in which they take place. In particular, taken together, the articles would seem to suggest the importance of understanding the development of tourist destinations as a relational process, not just within the locality between public and private actors, but also set in a wider geographical context both in terms of visitors and governance structures.

References

Amin, A. (1999) An Institutionalist perspective on regional economic development, *International Journal of Urban and Regional Research*, 23(2), pp. 365–378.

Anastasiadou, C. (2006) Tourism and the European Union, in: D. Hall, M. Smith & B. Marciszewska (Eds) *Tourism in the New Europe: The Challenges and Opportunities of EU Enlargement*, pp. 20–31 (Oxford: CABI).

Asheim, B., Coenen, L. & Vang, J. (2007) Face-to-face, buzz and knowledge bases: Socio-spatial implications for learning, innovation and innovation policy, *Environment and Planning C: Government and Policy*, 25(5), pp. 655–670.

Asheim, B., Cooke, P. & Martin, R. (Eds) (2006) *Clusters and Regional Development* (Abingdon: Routledge).

Cooke, P., de Laurentis, C., Collinge, C. & MacNeill, S. (Eds) (2010) Trends and drivers of the knowledge economy, *Platforms of Innovation: Dynamics of New Industrial Knowledge Flows*, pp. 1–26 (London: Edward Elgar).

Crevoisier, O. & Jeannerat, H. (2009) Territorial knowledge dynamics: From the proximity paradigm to multi-location milieus, *European Planning Studies*, 17(8), pp. 1223–1241.

European Commission (2006) *Innovation in Tourism: How to Create a Tourism Learning Area. The Handbook.* Developing thematic, destination-level and regional tourism knowledge networks. (Brussels: European Commission).

Halkier, H. (2010a) EU and tourism development: Bark or bite? *Scandinavian Journal of Hospitality and Tourism*, 10(2), pp. 92–106.

Halkier, H. (2010b) Tourism knowledge dynamics, in: P. Cooke, C. d. Laurentis, C. Collinge & S. MacNeill (Eds) *Platforms of Innovation: Dynamics of New Industrial Knowledge Flows*, pp. 233–250 (London: Edward Elgar).

Halkier, H. (2011) Erhvervspolitik mellem det lokale og det globale? Dansk turismepolitik under forandringspres, *Økonomi & Politik*, 84(4), pp. 11–24.

Hall, C. M. (2008) *Tourism Planning: Policies, Processes and Relationships*, 2nd ed. (Harlow: Pearson Prentice Hall).

Hall, C. M. & Page, S. J. (2006) *The Geography of Tourism and Recreation. Environment, Place and Space*, 3rd ed. (London: Routledge).

Hall, C. M. & Williams, A. (2008) *Tourism and Innovation* (Abingdon: Routledge).

Hjalager, A.-M. (2010) A review of innovation research in tourism, *Tourism Management*, 30(1), pp. 1–12.

Martin, R. & Sunley, P. (2003) Deconstructing clusters: Chaotic concept or policy panacea? *Journal of Economic Geography*, 3(1), pp. 5–35.

OECD (Ed.) (2006) *Innovation and Growth in Tourism* (Paris: OECD).

Olsen, L. S. (2012) Territorial knowledge dynamics: Making a difference to territorial innovation models and public policy? *European Planning Studies*, 20(11), pp. 1785–1801.

UNWTO (2005) *The Future of Traditional Destinations—Is their Experience Relevant to Emerging Countries in Europe?* (Madrid: UNWTO).

Weaver, D. & Lawton, L. (2002) *Tourism Management*, 2nd ed. (Milton: John Wiley).

Bridging the Knowledge-gap Between the Old and the New: Regional Marine Experience Production in Orust, Västra Götaland, Sweden

ANDERS LARSSON & KRISTINA N. LINDSTRÖM

Department of Human and Economic Geography, and Centre for Tourism, School of Business, Economics and Law, University of Gothenburg, Göteborg, Sweden

ABSTRACT *Today many regions in the industrialized world have to deal with a transformation from traditional industry such as agriculture or manufacturing to service-oriented production such as tourism. Nevertheless, few studies highlight the possibilities and limitations of inter-sectoral knowledge sharing among stakeholders representing these sectors and hence there seem to be missed opportunities for mutual collaboration in the era of experience production. Using an evolutionary perspective, this article aims to analyse how the leisure boat manufacturing and the tourism sectors in the municipality of Orust on the Swedish west coast, combine knowledge from these two sectors as a way to spur innovation in experience production. The article shows how there are a number of limitations to sectoral knowledge interaction. Some of them can be linked to the conservative nature of the traditional industry, and to the immature nature of the tourism sector, others to the role of policy. However, at the same time as there being a number of obstacles for collaboration, the article reveals some interesting possibilities to form inter-sectoral knowledge sharing.*

1. Introduction

This article provides insights into the transformation typical for many regions in the industrialized world – a change from traditional agriculture or manufacturing to service-oriented production, often with a base in the tourism sector (Heldt Cassel & Pashkevich, 2011). More specifically, the article investigates the notion of tourism development in combination with local industry, highlighting the potential and the challenges faced in inter-sectoral knowledge interaction. The empirical focus is on the maritime heritage of

5

the Swedish west coastal community of Orust, and the development potential of marrying the leisure boat manufacturing sector with the tourism sector. Hence, in this context, the concept of industrial tourism is mainly referring to tourist visits to operational industries with a core activity that is non-tourism-oriented and where the motive of the tourist is based on an interest in the company, its management, its products and/or the production processes (Frew, 2008).

As the increasing demand for tourist products is becoming more diversified, there is also a growing interest in educational experiences as a complement to traditional relaxation and escape motives (e.g. Quadri-Felitti & Fiore, 2012). This has resulted in an increasing number of companies opening up their industrial productions for visitors (Otgaar et al., 2010). Mader (2003) argues that the potential to develop tourism is favourable if the industrial product has a strong local identity and brand within a luxury segment. These apply to the local leisure boat sector discussed here.

Regional transformation from traditional to experience-based production is multi-facetted and challenging. The need to gain knowledge about how to develop strategies for inter-sectoral cooperation is essential for sustainable regional growth. One fundamental challenge in regional tourism development is the fact that it needs strong linkages to the surrounding economy for it to work successfully (Telfer, 2001). However, at the same time that tourism development is increasingly used to enhance regional economies, its linkages to other traditional regional sectors tend to be weak (Hall, 2005). One reason for this is because tourism is traditionally considered a consumer activity, and as such, too often regarded subordinate to traditional industrial activities (Ionnides & Debbage, 1998). This causes a gap between the "old" (as in declining manufacturing and agricultural industries) and the "new" (as in tourism and other experience industries), and potentially missed opportunities to share and transmit knowledge between various regional stakeholders.

Nevertheless, inter-sectoral knowledge sharing is essential as a way to spur tourism innovation. Hjalager (2002) argues that to create innovation in tourism one has to look outside the core tourism sector. Ruhanen and Cooper (2004) also stress the competitive advantage for the tourism sector to form joint ventures with partners who have complementary skills and technologies, and to learn from others through benchmarking. Furthermore, linking the tourism sector to the wider regional context should be regarded as a strategy to a sustainable regional development path (Gill & Williams, 2011). One principal argument for this is that industrial tourism has the potential to create an increased interest in learning more about local business life (Otgaar et al., 2010). Furthermore, increased demand for local products not only sustains the local identity, e.g. branding and promotional strategies become more focused on local identity, but also supports local endogenous economic growth. Cross-sectoral collaboration also means connecting local stakeholders with new patterns of partnerships, which benefit the development of trust and mutual commitment (Hall, 2005).

With an attempt to contribute theoretically to the field of tourism geography, an evolutionary perspective frames the notion of regional economic development (e.g. Ionnides & Debbage, 1998; Gill & Williams, 2011). Hence, the current position, and the potential for future change of the regional economic landscape, is based on the historical co-evolution of firms, public authorities, policy-makers and individual entrepreneurs in a number of different fields. One particularly important area, in terms of changes, is innovation and knowledge exchange. For tourism it has especially important connotations since this sector is often identified as a potential new contributor to growth and sectoral restructuring, while at the same time it finds itself poorly integrated into traditional man-ufacturing-based regional economies (Hjalager, 2002).

The specific aim of the article is to analyse possibilities and limitations over time for innovation based on a combination of knowledge between the traditional leisure boat man-ufacturing and the tourism sectors of the economy. This is operationalized through the fol-lowing research criteria:

(a) What are the important events and conditions behind the development of knowledge and innovative capacity in the respective sectors including the policy arena?
(b) Are there limitations to sectoral knowledge interaction?
(c) Are there possibilities and potential windows of opportunity for collaboration between the sectors?
(d) One additional aim is to reflect on the role of policy.

Empirical data was collected by employing a multi-method technique, including semi-structured interviews with representatives of the leisure manufacturing sector and the tourism sector at local, regional and national levels; document reviews (e.g. National Strat-egy for Tourism Growth, regional development plans for maritime and industrial heritage and local strategies); and complementary statistical information.

Following this introduction the theoretical framework is presented. The third section is a presentation of the case study, followed by a discussion of the empirical findings. The article is finalized with a conclusion, including policy implications.

2. From Sectors as Knowledge Bases towards Territorial Dynamics of Knowledge Interaction

2.1 Sectoral and Territorial Modes of Knowledge Creation and Interaction

We commence by outlining a theoretical understanding of the dynamics of knowledge cre-ation and interaction in a territorial context, specifically the challenge of linking traditional manufacturing sectors with network, or systemic, service-based activities, i.e. tourism. This sectoral approach provides our study with an important set of concepts to understand the knowledge dynamics in traditional sectors. Regarding the tourism industry we draw on the territorial models and the importance of territorial governance and institutions to build and facilitate efficient knowledge interaction in a heterogeneous industry.

A renewed focus on innovation and knowledge in the regional economy appeared as a consequence of the interest in the transition problems of industrial regional economies of the 1990s (Hassink, 1992; Grabher, 1993b; Cooke, 1995). This has continued to gain inter-est, especially regarding science and technology-based manufacturing sectors such as pharmaceuticals and biotech (Zeller 2004; Moodysson & Jonsson, 2007; Moodysson et al., 2008). Consequently, theoretical advances have developed largely in accordance with a manufacturing logic based on the concept of innovation in relation to physical arte-facts.

On the other hand, the understanding of innovation in services has been hampered by its non-physical character (Gadrey et al., 1995). A number of factors distinguish service inno-vation from manufacturing. First, the view of service innovation as dependent on (and therefore second to) manufacturing; second, the heterogeneous nature of the service sector, and last but not least, the methodological problems of studying intangibles, and how they change over time (Howells, 2007). These are arguments for treating service innovation on its own merits. According to Bryson and Monnoyer (2004), one can identify the development of a distinct research area within service innovation, with promising fields for new research in developing the understanding of the integration between innovation in goods and services.

In this article, one specific issue of concern is that tourism does not correspond to the industrial-sectoral logic. First, the fact that tourism and destination development innovation involve, and hence influence, a wide range of conventional sectors of the economy makes it difficult to delimit according to sectoral borders and statistics (Roehl, 1998). Second, innovation is considered to be a technological input in industry, while in tourism it is measured by consumption (Smith, 1998). The third aspect relates to the specific link between tourism, destination development and the physical territory as its main resource. This calls for an alternative approach to the dynamics of knowledge creation and interaction between manufacturing and service-oriented sectors in a territorial context. In the following, we will make a comparison of sectoral and territorial perspectives regarding how innovation and knowledge integration is treated, concluding with a link to evolutionary theory discussing the dynamics of regional change.

The concept of sectoral innovation systems (SIS) is one of several approaches trying to apply a systemic view of innovation (Breschi & Malerba, 1997). According to (Malerba, 2005), a sector is defined as "a set of activities which are unified by some related product groups for a given or emerging demand and which share some basic knowledge". A sectoral innovation system is then characterized by its specific knowledge and technological domain; actors and networks and institutions (Malerba, 2002). It highlights the interplay between the three dimensions and that change is made through a process of co-evolution of its parts. One advantage of this approach is that it connects technology and social/institutional factors as inter-dependent forces that shape sectors in an evolutionary way. Furthermore, it brings forward the importance of institutional norms and rules that make knowledge exchange and innovation more efficient within sectors than between them. Since tourism is difficult to define as one or several physical products (Roehl, 1998; Smith, 1998), the SIS approach has its limitations when it comes to explaining innovation concerning the combination, dissolution or absence of sectoral borders. To understand contemporary experienced-based regional economies, there is a need to link technology, actors and institutions in potentially complementary activities based on something other than the traditional concepts of sectors and industries. Space is one dimension that can act as a uniting concept.

The relationship between innovation and geography has been studied through a number of different approaches with a common basic assumption that institutions and social interaction, supported by geographical proximity, play a basic role in creating successful knowledge-based development. In an overview Moulaert and Sekia (2003) identify three broad schools of explanation. One with focus on endogenous institutional factors, including the French *milleu innovateur* and the industrial districts approach (Crevoisier & Maillat, 1991). Second, with the emphasis on territorial learning and interaction as important drivers of innovation, the regional innovation systems approach focuses on the role of policy and governance (Braczyk *et al.*, 2004). And third, the Californian school of new industrial spaces introduced flexibility and complementarity in regions as a model to challenge the rigid Fordist system of large-scale production and regulation (Scott, 1988).

Malmberg (1997) and Malmberg and Maskell (2002) developed the regional innovation systems approach by pointing to the role of regions as spaces for interactive learning based on exchange and interaction of knowledge. Following the logic that the more unstandardized and tacit the knowledge, the more important is spatial proximity for actors to take advantage of and "decode" the information due to common cognitive maps. This initially endogenous argumentation was further developed to involve the combination of local "buzz" and global "pipelines" as equally important for knowledge generation and re-generation in clusters (Bathelt *et al.*, 2004).

The work of the "French proximity school" (Carrincazeaux *et al.*, 2008) formed the ground for a more multi-faceted view on proximity by questioning the often implicit view that proximity is only physical and always positive. Torre and Gilly (2000) distinguished between geographical and organizational proximity and argued that there is a trade-off between the two. Boschma (2005) draws on this work and questions the importance of geographical proximity in relation to other relative forms for innovation and knowledge interaction.

So far we have highlighted the specific characteristics of sectoral and territorial models, but to understand the potential for combining knowledge from traditional sectors and more open systems, we need to understand the change over time. How is it possible for regions to change from the old sector−industry logic towards a service and experience-based economy?

2.2 *Understanding Change and Dynamism using Path Dependence and Lock-in*

To understand the possibilities and limitations for inter-sectoral knowledge exchange, this article will use the theoretical concepts of "path dependency" and "lock-in" from the field of evolutionary thinking and apply these to the problems of linking knowledge bases. There is a wealth of conceptual discussion with an evolutionary base in economic geography to address this issue (Boschma & Frenken, 2006; Martin & Sunley, 2006; Grabher 2009; Boschma & Martin, 2010).

Path dependency highlights the fact that learning and knowledge development is a gradual and long-term process which builds on previous knowledge, events and structures (MacKinnon, 2008; Martin, 2010). The key point from a geographical perspective is that today's regional economic landscape, including innovative potential and institutional set-up, cannot be fully understood without applying a historical perspective. It addresses how the historical influence of a dominant technology in a specific regional setting might lead to considerable problems to change the industrial structure of a region due to the influence of these established technologies, its institutions and social networks of powerful actors. The concept of regional lock-in is used to describe a situation where the path-dependent development is strong enough to reinforce the traditional industrial structure at the expense of new innovative ideas. Actors are locked into a narrow path where social, technological and political relations have grown; as Grabher (1993a, p. 24) puts it, "from ties that bind to ties that blind". Such a situation will pose a major limitation to a cross-sectoral model of regional innovation and development. On a positive note, path dependency might also help a region to concentrate resources into a limited number of sectors, to continuously innovate and stay competitive (Martin & Sunley, 2006).

It is important to stress that we use path dependence and lock-in as a "lens" (Gill & Williams, 2011) through which to analyse knowledge interaction between sectors in one specific region over time. We see the historical legacy as a key forming factor but not as a deterministic power (Hudson, 2005; Strambach, 2008; Garud *et al.*, 2010).

Interestingly, the evolutionary concepts have gained limited attention in tourism geography. However, examples can be found in studies of actors and policy processes in relation to destination development (Bramwell & Cox, 2009; Gill & Williams, 2011). Their conclusion is that a path-dependence approach is useful to understand continuity and change and to what extent this has path-creating effects.

3. A Case Study of the Marine Experience Production in Orust

3.1 *Introduction to the Study Area*

Orust is Sweden's third largest island and a municipality in the county of Bohuslän on the west coast. Most of the municipality comprises countryside, with interspersed pockets of population – Henån, in northern Orust, being the largest agglomeration and the administrative centre. The municipality has just over 15,000 residents; however, as one of Sweden's most attractive tourist regions, this figure increases dramatically in the summer. Today Orust is well known for the manufacture of leisure boats. The island is home to a cluster of manufacturers and suppliers specializing in high performance motor and sailing yachts (Orust Municipality, 2012), who produce approximately 80% of the leisure sailing craft in Sweden (Figure 1).

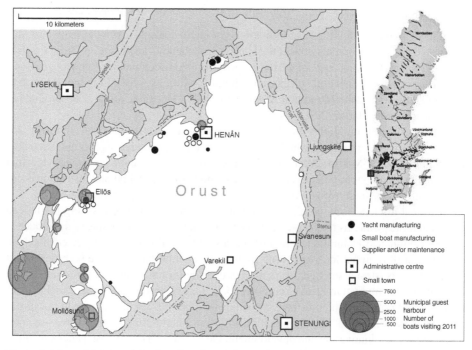

Figure 1. Map of Orust and the location of yacht manufacturers, suppliers and guest harbours.
Source: Orust Municipality.

The industry is small scale in nature. Apart from a few larger firms with up to 300 employees, most businesses have between one and ten. Today there are approximately 700 people directly involved in boatbuilding in the leisure boat manufacturing cluster, although it is estimated that, indirectly, it triples sector-related employment, making it the largest industrial sector in the municipality (Orust Municipality, 2012). However, the knowledge is very much based on craftsmanship skills, which is reflected in the low rates of staff with tertiary education (Fransson, 2009). Nevertheless, as the leisure boat manufacturing sector is facing the combination of global competition and financial crisis, the advent of new business opportunities is essential, and here tourism is considered a promising sector.

As already mentioned, Orust has a lure on tourists, mainly for its extraordinary coastline and archipelago and, hence, boat tourism is an important niche market. Nevertheless, the tourist industry in the region (as well in most parts of Sweden) is small scale and still in its infancy. One challenge is the extreme seasonal variation due to the climate, which produces a short visitor-high season between mid-June and mid-August. In spite of the lack of reliable data of the value of tourism in Orust, representatives of the municipality estimated an annual turnover of €20 million in 2010. The municipality estimates 2500 employment sites in the tourism sector, roughly employing 4700 (although most of the jobs are seasonal), 13 accommodation units offering 56,000 bed nights in 2011 and 18,000 overnight stays in public marinas, which is the most common ownership and management of (leisure craft) marinas in Sweden.

3.2 Development of Local Boat Manufacturing and Tourism

In spite of the observed lack of organized interaction between the sectors of leisure boat manufacturing and tourism, the two are interlinked. In fact, the birth of leisure boat manufacturing can be traced back to early coastal tourism in the mid-nineteenth century, when summer residents in coastal communities showed a growing interest not only to observe, but also to experience the open sea first hand. Taking visitors on board provided an opportunity for fishermen to earn some extra income. Eventually, the fishing boats were modified to fit the needs of the nautical tourists; and some of the summer residents even requested their own jig or cockboat. One could argue, therefore, that one of explanatory factors behind the leisure boat maritime heritage in Orust is due to the experience gained from a tourism demand some 150 years ago.

The first initiative in the modern era can be accredited to the local entrepreneur Harry Hallberg who, in the 1950s, was already experimenting with composite materials (reinforced plastics) in boat manufacturing. This later became the standard material for yachts (Blundel & Thatcher, 2005; Hallberg-Rassy, 2012). As a growing number of Swedes gained the privilege to go on coastal holidays (e.g. paid public holidays became a legal right in 1938), so increased an interest in boat life. Following the technological innovation of the plastic boat hull that was developed and flourished in the early 1970s, the market for leisure boats exploded. This created an advantage since the local players in Orust were early inventors in this field. It was the start of a successful period where high performance and craftsmanship could be combined with the scale efficiency and flexibility of the plastics.

Still, in Sweden today, every fourth leisure boat in use was produced in this era, and boating is a major Swedish leisure-time activity. In 2010 there were almost one million leisure boats, with approximately 15% of them located along the Swedish west coast. Apart from Sweden, key markets for the Swedish leisure boat manufacturers are Norway, Denmark, the UK and Germany.

A well-developed second-hand market and a weak economic climate have affected today's demand for new leisure boats. The boat manufacturers have experienced a serious downturn in recent years. Today the leisure boat manufactures of Orust face serious problems, and some have even gone bankrupt. However, as discussed below, the demand for additional products, for example, after-sale's services are increasing, and may possibly open up for alternative business when boat production is stagnating. In spite of this potential, the study respondents agree on the fact that the leisure boat manufacturers are relatively uninterested in developing new business opportunities in more experience-based production. Doubtless, the reasons for this are geared towards the scepticism of making an additional income out of such activities and the risk of revealing business secrets. At the same time, boat manufacturers are afraid of making additional investments in, for example, the education of guides and visitor centres (Angel & Rokotova, 2012). However, while the leisure boat sector generally has to face the fact that the golden era might be over, one could argue that the tourism sector in Sweden generally, and Orust in particular, has possibly just started theirs.

The gap between the manufacturing and service sectors in the region could, therefore, benefit from being bridged to maximize their combined potential. Here policy has played, and largely can still play, a significant role in facilitating cross-sectoral collaboration. In the following section, we discuss some examples of the national and regional policy contexts that form the framework for potential action.

3.3 Policy-related Response

Swedish spatial planning has been characterized by a two-level system established with the state on one level and local authorities having a high degree of autonomy on the other (Baldersheim & Ståhlberg, 2002). Regionalization in Sweden has changed this picture (Böhme et al., 2004), and Västra Götaland region is one of two Swedish test cases for devolving responsibilities to the regional level. This started in 1999 and is now formally established. The most important change is the increased regional authority over development issues, including economic development (Lindström, 2007).

As a result of the combined processes of Europeanization and regionalization, spatial planning today is increasingly finding itself facing a multi-level context. The traditional national–local relationship is gradually changing towards a European–national–regional–local multi-layered system. This has triggered new opportunities for regional actors to coordinate local initiatives and, therefore, formed the basis for a maritime strategy, which is currently being updated to become a cluster policy. Part of this work included Gothenburg which, together with the Swedish west coast, hosted the European Maritime Days in May 2012 (Commission of the European Communities, 2012).

Over the last five-year period, there have been a number of strategic attempts to coordinate the maritime heritage interests within the region. In this context, as tourism is included in most of these strategies, it is evident that the sector has gained legitimacy as an important economic sector in Sweden. Nevertheless, the ambiguity of the notion of maritime heritage sometimes tends to favour fishing over, for example, leisure boat production and tourism.

When scrutinizing strategic attempts made by the public tourism sector to approach other sectors, the National Strategy for Tourism Growth (Tourism, 2020) stands out. In 2010, the Swedish government allocated €6 million to tourism development. A share of €1.2 million has been appropriated to the county of Bohuslän, including Orust. The First National Tourism Strategy has clearly impacted upon regional and local policy through its ambitious goals of doubling the number of tourists and turnaround of the industry by 2020 (Svensk Turism, 2010). At the same time, all of Europe is facing an economic crisis that is fundamentally having an impact upon markets and industries. This has had a direct local effect on the leisure boat manufacturers who have witnessed plummeting sales in the last years. The National Strategy states that in order to reach its goals, "innovative cooperation" is essential for communities developing tourism.

In addition to the national tourism strategy, the regional strategy for maritime tourism 2009–2013 needs to be mentioned (West Sweden Tourist Board, 2009). Among other goals, the regional maritime tourism strategy aims at "engaging the leisure boat manufacturing sector in the development of maritime tourism" (ibid., p. 3). Now, after three years, it is evident that this goal is difficult to fulfil, mainly owing to a low degree of involvement from the leisure boat manufacturers.

It is clear that there are problems to navigate and organize cross-sector interaction in the system. One regional planner stated: "Our organization hesitates to contact local businesses directly. We risk creating a negative relation to local politicians." While from the local level there is a corresponding lack of overview of collaboration potential, as illustrated by a local municipality officer: "It might be our fault ... but we are part of the municipality association and they receive funding through the national growth agreements. There might be funding from the region ... but so far we have not received any."

This is not restricted to the different policy levels. Lack of coordination between policy and the business community is identified as a drawback. This specifically relates to national and EU funding opportunities, where the public authority participation is decisive on who is eligible to apply. The functional interactions regarding the specific case in this study are clearly affected by the lack of communication and trust among actors. There is, for example, no information service for visitors interested in the marine experience or the possible combinations with other attractions in the region. Several of the interviewees also pointed to the fact that missing collaboration and communication between businesses and public authorities seriously affected the potential for "package tourism". This is especially important in order to extend the short summer season with new innovative and less weather-sensitive offerings.

3.4 *Current and Future Plans*

A limited number of existing cross-sectoral events are highlighted in the interviews and the secondary data used in the study. The two most salient ones are the annual floating boat show "Open Yards" (Open Yards, 2012) and the "Coastal Conference".

In the mid-1990s the manufacturers initiated the start-up of the Open Yards annual floating exhibition in which to present their products. This has been a very successful event, growing year on year, although the format has changed little over its 18-year history. Nevertheless, in accordance with the respondents' understanding of the event, it is more of a sales market with limited potential to develop additional experience-based services and products. One of the reason for this is the boat manufacturers' lack of time and interest when busy selling their products.

Another existing event with the purpose of integrating representatives from the leisure boat sector, tourism sector and the public sector is the annual "Coastal Conference" initiated by the West Sweden Tourist Board. It was first organized in 2005 as an external event during the annual leisure boat fair in Gothenburg. However, the conference only attracted limited attention among the leisure boat manufacturers. So in 2007, to increase the interest and the potential arenas for collaboration, the event became an integrated part of the fair. Nevertheless, it is still a problem to catch the interest of the boat manufacturers. As one respondent states, it is difficult "to attract the boat people enough to make them leave their stands, it is like they are afraid of missing an opportunity to make business if they leave".

In addition, several respondents mention the boat manufacturer Najad. Before its bankruptcy in 2009, the firm initiated a number of innovative development efforts with the aim of broadening the scope towards a more experience-based product. One possible explanation put forward in interviews is that Najad were then owned by a UK group and, therefore, had the opportunity to act outside of the traditional family business logic in the local area. As illustrated by one national industry representative: "In general, the leisure boat manufacturers are very traditional, and Orust is no exception." Before they went bankrupt, Najad were very innovative focusing on more than just the technological aspect and having the slogan "The Najad way of life".

In spite of the abrasiveness of the leisure boat manufacturers, the non-manufacturing respondents share a number of interesting ideas on how to develop leisure boat maritime tourism in the region. It is evident that there are both potential and partly ongoing processes. Perhaps the most developed vision on how to marry tourism with the maritime heritage in the region is the notion of a maritime experience centre, where the modern plastic boat heritage would constitute a significant part of the centre. However, since this is a very costly investment, this is still more of a vision for the region. One of the representatives of the Västra Götaland region interviewed in the study explains about the project:

> We are doing a pre-study, a kind of a vision how to develop the Bohuslän museum to twice its size, with up to 40 leisure boats and the history around them, particularly focusing on the plastic era, that is modern time.

Another idea brought up during interviews is the notion of learning from the car manufacturing industry and developing a centre for innovation, where the boat manufacturers and the car manufacturers in the region could share knowledge and learn from each other. In spite of a number of interesting ideas where the leisure boat manufacturers are partly involved, the majority of the ideas brought up in the interviews more directly involve the leisure boat sector. Such ideas involve company visits, and after-sales follow ups, but these are often rejected as difficult due to lack of infrastructure, knowledge, skills and the risk of revealing industrial secrets (Angel & Rokotova, 2012). Nevertheless, most of the respondents who do not represent the leisure boat manufacturing sector refer to other industrial sectors that are successful in opening up their production, claiming that the limitation is the boat manufacturers' attitude rather than other obstacles. As illustrated by one national boat association representative' words:

> It is like they only have energy to produce and deliver boats, everything else is not their business. But we believe both opening up the production and after-sales is

really exciting ... and we believe that in the end it would lead to an increased demand for boats.

It is clear from our interviews that the manufacturing industry identity of the yacht makers plays an important part in the lack of collaborative options, as formulated by a national boat association representative:

[The boat manufacturers] view themselves as an industry, the fact that they close for four weeks each July in accordance with traditional industrial holiday dates ... these are the exact same weeks when tourism has its absolute peak in the region. The biggest hurdle is the fact that they do not see themselves as being in the experience business at all.

This traditional view has led to a conservative approach to new opportunities even within the narrower sector. Recent market trends are pointing towards a bigger service and experience content in the purchase of yachts in this luxury segment. So far the Orust firms have shown limited interest to combine services with its products. It is actually one of their German competitors in the cheaper large-scale segment that has established a rental and service point in Orust. The local firms are changing; but it seems that the pace is rather slow.

In spite of the need to develop inter-sectoral projects, it is evident that it is crucial to establish a dialogue between the various stakeholders. There is a lack of arenas in which to meet and discuss, share knowledge and to develop a mutual understanding for the two sectors. As argued by one of the representatives of the tourism sector: "We have the contacts [referring to the boat manufacturers], but we have to create the venues and to explain the point of involving in such cooperation."

Furthermore, in spite of the growing number of relevant national and regional strategies for the development of maritime tourism with its base in the local maritime heritage of leisure boat manufacturing, the interviews highlight the importance of the local policy level. It is evident from discussions with the respondents that the various stakeholders play important roles. Nevertheless, the municipality of Orust has a gate-keeping role and needs to take initiative in creating cross-sectoral collaboration between the leisure boat manufacturing sector and the tourism sector.

4. Discussion

4.1 Path-influencing Events, Actors and Contexts

Figure 2 summarizes the major path-influencing events for the case study. One clear pattern is the historical legacy of the leisure boat manufacturing sector and the lack of major innovative events since the mid-1990s. Furthermore, one can observe a development where events and actors on the regional and national scale have increased its influence in relation to the local.

Starting with a theoretical evolutionary concept of path dependence and lock-in, as well as the SIS approach, is useful to understand and explain how the incremental knowledge creation process in the leisure boat manufacturing industry has created a world-leading cluster in one specific segment. Until the end of the last decade, this proved to be a very successful path to follow, but in the wake of a global financial crisis, sales have

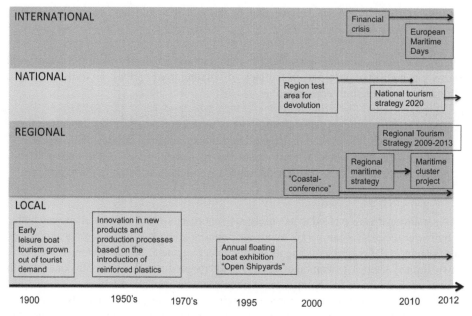

Figure 2. Major path-influencing events in the yacht manufacturing experience. *NB*: The time dimension is not linear.
Source: Authors' compilation from interviews and documents.

fallen to record low levels. Today, the strong local path that focuses on production and technology has created a political and social lock-in situation. This might seriously limit openness to new cross-sectoral business opportunities.

Tourism, on the other hand, has a long history in the area, but there is no direct evidence of a sectoral path-dependent development. The heterogeneity of activities under the tourism industry label does not fit easily into the theoretical model of clearly identifiable sectors and their paths. On the contrary, tourism in the region is characterized by the same small-scale, network-based, heterogeneity of activities with seasonal variations, as experienced by most actors in the business (Ionnides & Debbage, 1998). In the context of this research, cross-sectoral integration can be seen as almost a "natural state-of-mind" in the tourism industry. From a traditional industrial perspective, this might be interpreted as a problem, but in terms of innovation potential the heterogeneity and network organization are creating a useful opportunity for new cross-boundary development.

In terms of scale it is possible to identify a shift in initiative from the local business arena to the multi-scalar policy arena, a situation that can both bring opportunities for cross-sectoral innovation in Orust and reveal barriers and limitations. In the following, we will look more closely at enabling and disabling factors in the interaction between tourism and other sectors in general, and more specifically in our case.

4.2 *Opportunities*

Hall (2005) summarizes a number of synergies potentially generated through cross-sectoral collaboration. Regional development of industrial tourism creates leverage in both tourism and manufacturing sectors as it stimulates the development of new value-added production. If this is done successfully, it will benefit the export market of the region, and the attraction of external resources. Furthermore, regional development of the traditional sector into experience-based production creates direct relationships between the producers and the consumers, and thereby potentially greater local economic return.

These arguments are acknowledged in current tourism policies at regional and national levels. The gain for both industry and the regional economy are straightforward in theory, but at least two parties should be prepared to collaborate towards the same goal. In the Orust case, it seems to boil down to the fact that successful tourism and manufacturing industry collaboration depends on two or more partners being able to see the same opportunity and identify a commercial potential. The local leisure boat manufacturers have, so far, been unwilling to participate in the policy process unless there has been a short-term specific commercial potential. Rather cynically, the current crisis may be the external shock that changes the lock-in state (Martin, 2010) of the leisure boat sector. There are signs of mergers and take-overs in the sector that may eventually lead to a more open attitude towards broadening the scope of activities and redefine the self-image of the sector.

Previous research in the field shows that industrial tourism creates opportunities both for companies and for the region, many of which are considered mutually beneficial. Otgaar *et al.* (2010) identify that industrial tourism has the potential to benefit the boat building industry as a marketing instrument because it exposes potential customers to the product and creates an interest in it through, for example, a company visit. Furthermore, it generates direct sales through factory sales, both in regular products and souvenirs. The opportunity to meet the customer can be used as a market investigation instrument. Opening up the production for visitors in various ways may also create value for the employees in terms of pride or demand for decent working conditions as the production becomes public. This may have the knock-on benefit of raising the attractiveness of the industry as a place to work.

Manufacturers who use the international boat fairs as their main interface towards new customers have so far neglected the marketing aspect of local tourism integration. As stated earlier, there are plans to construct a leisure boat experience centre in the region, supported by public money. This is an example of an opportunity to attract new and related activities and potential customers to the local area. So far the boat manufacturers have shown only limited interest and the current ideas do not include Orust as an alternative site.

4.3 *Limitations*

In spite of the potential for regions and industries to engage in industrial tourism, there are a number of barriers that have to be dealt with when developing regional strategies for industrial tourism. In this context, Otgaar *et al.* (2010) stress the role of policy-makers. The public sector must be willing to invest in and support the industries' development of tourist attractions, financially as well as policy-wise. This is a limitation that policy-makers and public authorities have identified, and today there are a number of regional, national and EU strategies to facilitate cross-sectoral integration. The problem for Orust in particular and for localities in general is that a multi-level policy structure can be perceived as very complex from a bottom-up perspective, leading to a situation where small firms and local planners do not have the knowledge and overview needed to take decisions.

One of the most important challenges tends to be to changing attitudes towards industrial tourism. Short-term profit thinking and the perception that there is nothing interesting to show to visitors are common among actors in the leisure boat industry (Alebaki *et al.*, 2012). In the sectoral innovation system approach (Malerba, 2002), innovation and knowledge creation is seen as a constant change process based on a common technology, product and market. This view is in line with the construction of the self-image of the leisure boat firms as being a manufacturing activity within a very specific product niche and market segment. So far it has proved to be virtually impossible to influence the industry "from outside". One further important aspect is the small-scale local structure of the industry that has created an additional dimension of local competitiveness and lack of trust.

The other side of this coin is the fuzzy boundary of tourism activities in the light of sectors. This is one important image-related limitation to a possible interface between traditional product sectors and non-material sectors such as tourism. If you cannot define yourself with a physical product, you run the risk of obscurity in a region that has a traditional industrial view of economic development and innovation. One example is the current update of the regional maritime strategy (Region Västra Götaland, 2011) in Västra Götaland where a cluster concept is used to identify important fields for future innovation in the maritime sector. Coastal tourism is one of seven key fields identified, but is the only one not defined by a specific technology or function. To facilitate a more cross-sectoral interaction, it is important that the different parts of the regional economy, including services, are valued and taken into account based in their own potential. The case in this study has shown that this is far from a simple and straightforward task.

The leisure boat manufacturing sector and the tourism sector in the coastal community of Orust have long traditions; however, the evolutionary perspective in this study shows weak interaction over the years. In spite of its potential to collaborate in the development of networks and new arenas for meeting the growing demand for innovative experience-based products and services (Quadri-Felitti & Fiore, 2012) it is evident that a number of structural, cognitive and political lock-in situations block such cross-sectoral knowledge sharing in the region (Grabher, 1993b).

5. Conclusions and Policy Implications

Tourism is purported to be a key economic contributor in a growing number of societies throughout the world. Sweden is no exception to the trend. In the recent "Vision 2020" the government identified tourism as a new leading industry with the ambitious goal to double its number of visitors and economic turnaround within less than 10 years (Svensk Turism, 2010). A transformation is, therefore, necessary to reach such a target in regions with a long tradition of manufacturing as the main contributor to the economy. The mind-sets of business people and public/regional authorities, and the policies that they devolve, need to shift towards a more service-oriented and consumption-driven production view as part of a wider economy increasingly involved with cultural values (Britton, 1991; Pratt, 1997).

In this article we have applied an evolutionary, path-dependency lens as an analytic tool (cf. Gill & Williams, 2011) when investigating the conditions for such a transformation. Based on our case study, we can conclude that there is only limited current potential for innovation based on knowledge interaction between the "old" leisure boat manufacturing sector and the "new" experience tourism production-consumption system in Västra Götaland. An overall result is that the restructuring of a regional economy from a predominantly manufacturing base to one based on services, or in our case the combination of the two, is far from an easy and quick task. In terms of policy, one major challenge is linked to the difference between manufacturing and service activities, i.e. their relation to technology and physical products as well as the definition of sectoral borders and not the least their self-image.

In his classic work *The Tourist*, MacCannell (1976, 1999) states that any firm, regardless of business type, can develop tourist attractions as an additional industrial activity. One key condition for this to become a reality is an understanding for the potential of opening up manufacturing activities to visitors, and thus recognizing the value of experience components in developing business. In the (tourism) literature most examples of industrial tourism are from the food and wine sectors (Hall & Mitchell, 2001; Hjalager & Richards, 2002; Alebaki *et al.*, 2012) and the car sector (Otgaar *et al.*, 2010). These are sectors successful in developing industrial tourism, mainly because of their regional or local influence due to size and share of business life, but also because they realize and use experience as an integrated part of their product image. The situation in Orust shows that the potential opening up of sectoral borders has to fight the social-cognitive lock-in that so far has characterized the conservative leisure boat sector.

Further, the tourism industry consists of a large and fragmented collection of businesses, producing something that is primarily defined as an experience in a "non-factory" environment, i.e. consumers visit and take part in the production (Debbage & Daniels, 1998; Smith, 1998). Even in this study based on one single case, tourism covers a wide array of actors and sectors such as museum and heritage, accommodation, yacht-exhibitions, food and drink, tourist guides, private and public transportation, advertising and media, to mention a few. This heterogeneity is the strength of the industry when integration is successful, and at the same time its weakness if the parts act alone. Our conclusion is that tourism needs to be acknowledged as a "serious" economic sector with long-term impact and not a "quick fix" to regional recovery when the old industry does not deliver any more. Here policy obviously plays a key role in facilitating and supporting tourism innovation as a platform for knowledge interaction. It is telling that a regionally powerful and shrinking automotive sector has already seen policy support for "Open Arena" platforms for knowledge interaction for several years (Alänge *et al.*, 2005).

Clearly there are both technological and institutional issues yet to be solved to get the established industry "on the train" towards cross-sectoral innovation. But this is only one side of the argument. The historical development of the Swedish unitary state administration has created a situation with a strong local independence and self-governance in terms of both financial and political power. This evolutionary path is currently facing the impact of both regionalization and Europeanization simultaneously. Two effects are important to develop here.

First, we have identified the problem of overlapping and unclear functions in the new multi-level governance structure. There is evidence of collaboration problems due to unclear roles and uncoordinated activities on local, regional, national and European levels. Second, and probably more problematic, is the strategic role of municipalities. Their high level of local independence has resulted in a situation where many regional initiatives are dependent on local regulations and financial support for its implementation. At the same time there is a competitive situation between municipalities, not the least in trying to attract visitors. This is definitely an area where regional policies and regional funding might impact on the collaborative spirit of local actors.

Furthermore, it is crucial that these initiatives can bring value addition to the involved partners. Overall there seems to be "project fatigue" where meetings and application processes are seen as important networking and learning events, but ultimately did not lead to more or new resources. This is, of course, of key importance when creating a real interest among actors in the business world. It might also act as a real, or sometimes imagined, barrier to the involvement of private actors in joint innovation projects.

At the time of writing (Spring 2012), the region is in the middle of a process that might change these conditions. The view of separate sectors is challenged by a cluster initiative proposing a maritime innovation platform spanning a number of sectors, including coastal tourism and shipbuilding. This is well in line with the conclusions from this research. We see a growing understanding among a wide range of actors that collaboration is necessary and needs new arenas as well as coordination. From a policy point of view, there may be an opportunity to take the lead by facilitating cross-sectoral meeting platforms.

Acknowledgments

We would like to thank two anonymous referees for valuable comments. This research was funded by the Foundation for Economic Research in West Sweden.

References

Alänge, S., Fogelberg, H., Lundqvist, M., Mellby, C. & Thorpenberg, S. (2005) Project open arenas. The evolution of the Lindholmen and innovatum "Arenas" and their role for innovation in vehicle technology. In *Visanu – National Programme for Development of Innovation Systems and Clusters*. Visanu Report 2005: 8. Available at http://publikationer.tillvaxtverket.se/Download.aspx?ID=820 (accessed 30 September 2012).

Alebaki, M. I., Iakovidou, O. I. & Menexes, G. C. (2012) Current State and Potential of Wine Tourism In Northern Greece: Weighing Wine-makers' Perceptions. Paper presented at the Second Advances in Hospitality and Tourism Marketing and Management, Corfu, Greece, 31 May–3 June.

Angel, S. & Rokotova, Y. (2012) Yacht-shipyard tourism in Orust: A pre-study. *HUI Research*, Stockholm [in Swedish].

Baldersheim, H. & Ståhlberg, K. (2002) From guided democracy to multi-level governance: Trends in central-local relations in the Nordic countries, *Local Government Studies*, 28(3), pp. 74–90.

Bathelt, H., Malmberg, A. & Maskell, P. (2004) Clusters and knowledge: Local buzz, global pipelines and the process of knowledge creation, *Progress in Human Geography*, 28(1), pp. 31–56.

Blundel, R. & Thatcher, M. (2005) Local responses to globalisation: The case of volume yacht manufacturing in Europe, *Journal of Entrepreneurship and Regional Development*, 17(6), pp. 405–429.

Böhme, K., Richardson, T., Dabinettte, G. & Jensen, O. B. (2004) Values in a vacuum? Towards an integrated multi-level analysis of the governance of European space, *European Planning Studies*, 12(8), pp. 1175–1188.

Boschma, R. (2005) Proximity and innovation: A critical assessment, *Regional Studies*, 39(1), pp. 61–74.

Boschma, R. & Frenken, K. (2006) Why is economic geography not an evolutionary science? Towards an evolutionary economic geography, *Journal of Economic Geography*, 6(3), pp. 273–302.

Boschma, R. & Martin, R. (2010) The aims and scope of evolutionary economic geography, *Papers in Evolutionary Economic Geography*, No. 10.01 (Utrecht: Utrecht University).

Braczyk, H.-J., Cooke, P. & Heindrich, M. (2004) *Regional Innovation Systems. The Role of Governance in a Globalized World*, 2nd ed. (London: Routledge).

Bramwell, B. & Cox, V. (2009) Stage and path dependence approaches to the evolution of a national park tourism partnership, *Journal of Sustainable Tourism*, 17(2), pp. 191–206.

Breschi, S. & Malerba, F. (1997) Sectoral innovation systems: Technological regimes, Schumpeterian dynamics and spatial boundaries, in: C. Edquist (Ed.) *Systems of Innovation: Technologies, Institutions and Organisations*, pp. 130–156 (London: Pinter).

Britton, S. (1991) Tourism, capital, and place: Towards a critical geography of tourism, *Environment and Planning D*, 9(4), pp. 451–478.

Bryson, J. & Monnoyer, C. (2004) Understanding the relationship between services and innovation: The RESER review of the European service literature on innovation, 2002, *The Service Industries Journal*, 24(1), pp. 205–222.

Carrincazeaux, C., Lung, Y. & Vicente, J. (2008) The scientific trajectory of the French school of proximity: Interaction- and institution-based approaches to regional innovation systems, *European Planning Studies*, 16(5), pp. 617–628.

Commission of the European Communities. (2012) *The European Maritime Day*. Available at http://ec.europa.eu/maritimeaffairs/maritimeday/ (accessed 13 March 2012).

Cooke, P. (Ed.) (1995) *The Rise of the Rustbelt* (London: UCL Press).

Crevoisier, O. & Maillat, D. (1991) Milleu, industrial organization and territorial production system: Towards a new theory of spatial development, in: R. Camagni (Ed.) *Innovation Networks: Spatial Perspectives*, pp. 13–34 (London and New York: Belhaven).

Debbage, D. & Daniels, P. (1998) The tourist industry and economic geography: Missed opportunities, in: D. Ionnadies & K. G. Debbage (Eds) *The Economic Geography of the Tourist Industry. A Supply-Side Analysis*, pp. 17–30 (London and New York: Routledge).

Fransson, U. (2009) Shift in competences and the dynamics of the labour market: The case of the leisure boat manufacturing sector in Orust, in: *Occasional Papers* 2009: 5. Department of Human and Economic Geography, University of Göteborg [in Swedish].

Frew, E. A. (2008) Industrial tourism theory and implemented strategies, in: A. G. Woodside (Ed.) *Advances in Culture, Tourism and Hospitality Research*, Vol. 2, pp. 27–42 (Bingley: Emerald Publishing Group).

Gadrey, J., Gallouj, F. & Weinstein, O. (1995) New modes of innovation: How services benefit industry, *International Journal of Service Industry Management*, 6(3), pp. 4–16.

Garud, R., Kumaraswamy, A. & Karnøe, P. (2010) Path dependence or path creation? *Journal of Management Studies*, 47(7), pp. 760–774.

Gill, A. & Williams, P. (2011) Rethinking resort growth: Understanding evolving governance strategies in Whistler, British Columbia, *Journal of Sustainable Tourism*, 19(4–5), pp. 629–648.

Grabher, G. (1993a) Rediscovering the social in the economics of interfirm relations, in: G. Grabher (Ed.) *The Embedded Firm: On the Socioeconomics of Industrial Networks*, pp. 1–31 (London: Routledge).

Grabher, G. (1993b) The weakness of strong ties: The lock-in of regional development in the Ruhr area, in: G. Grabher (Ed.) *The Embedded Firm: On the Socioeconomics of Industrial Networks*, pp. 255–277 (London: Routledge).

Grabher, G. (2009) Yet another turn? The evolutionary project in economic geography, *Economic Geography*, 85(2), pp. 119–127.

Hall, M. (2005) Rural wine and food tourism cluster and network development, in: D. Hall, I. Kirkpatrick & M. Mitchell (Eds) *Rural Tourism and Sustainable Business*, pp. 149–164 (Clevedon: Channel View Publications).

Hall, C. M. & Mitchell, R. (2001) Wine and food tourism, in: N. Douglas & R. Derrett (Eds) *Special Interest Tourism: Context and Cases*, pp. 307–329 (Brisbane, Australia: John Wiley).

Hallberg-Rassy. (2012) From shed to famous boatyard: Company history. Available at http://www.hallberg-rassy.com/oldSiteIndex.php?p=/company/company.shtml (accessed 30 September 2012).

Hassink, R. (1992) *Regional Innovation Policy: Case-Studies from the Ruhr Area, Baden-Württemberg and the North East of England* (Utrecht: Koninklijk Nederlands Aardrijkskundig Genootschap).

Heldt Cassel, S. & Pashkevich, A. (2011) Heritage tourism and inherited institutional structures: The case of Falun Great Copper Mine, *Scandinavian Journal of Hospitality and Tourism*, 11(1), pp. 54–75.

Hjalager, A.-M. (2002) Repairing innovation defectiveness in tourism, *Tourism Management*, 23(5), pp. 465–474.

Hjalager, A.-M. & Richards, G. (Eds) (2002) *Tourism and Gastronomy* (London: Routledge).

Howells, J. (2007) Service and innovation: Conceptual and theoretical perspectives, in: J. Bryson & P. Daniels (Eds) *The Handbook of Service Industries*, pp. 34–44 (Cheltenham: Edward Elgar).

Hudson, R. (2005) Rethinking change in old industrial regions: Reflecting on the experiences of North East England, *Environment and Planning A*, 37(4), pp. 581–596.

Ionnides, D. & Debbage, K. (1998) Neo-Fordism and flexible specialization in the travel industry, in: D. Ioannides & K. Debbage (Eds) *The Economic Geography of the Tourism Industry. A Supply-side Analysis*, pp. 99–122 (London: Routledge).

Lindström, A. (2007) Territorial governance in transition, *Regional and Federal Studies*, 17(4), pp. 499–508.

MacCannell, D. (1976, 1999) *The Tourist: A New Theory of the Leisure Class* (Berkley, CA: University of California Press).

MacKinnon, D. (2008) Evolution, path dependence and economic geography, *Geography Compass*, 2(5), pp. 1449–1463.

Mader, T. (2003) *Produzierende Betriebe als Touristische Attraktionen im Ruhrgebiet. Grundlagen, Erscheinungsformen, Probleme. Magisterarbeit* (Heninrich-Heine-Universität Düsseldorf. Hamburg: Diplomica GmbH).

Malerba, F. (2002) Sectoral systems of innovation and production, *Research Policy*, 31(2), pp. 247–264.

Malerba, F. (2005) Sectoral systems of innovation: A framework for linking innovation to the knowledge base, structure and dynamics of sectors, *Economics of Innovation and New Technology*, 14(1–2), pp. 63–82.

Malmberg, A. (1997) Industrial geography: Location and learning, *Progress in Human Geography*, 21(4), pp. 573–582.

Malmberg, A. & Maskell, P. (2002) The elusive concept of localization economies: Towards a knowledge-based theory of spatial clustering, *Environment and Planning A*, 34(3), pp. 429–449.

Martin, R. (2010) Roepke Lecture in Economic Geography – Rethinking Regional Path Dependence: Beyond Lock-in to Evolution, *Economic Geography*, 86(1), pp. 1–27.

Martin, R. & Sunley, P. (2006) Path Dependence and Regional Economic Evolution, *Journal of Economic Geography*, 6, pp. 395–437.

Moodysson, J. & Jonsson, O. (2007) Knowledge collaboration and proximity. The spatial organization of biotech innovation projects, *European Urban and Regional Studies*, 14(2), pp. 115–131.

Moodysson, J., Coenen, L. & Asheim, B. T. (2008) Explaining spatial patterns of innovation: Analytical and synthetic modes of knowledge creation in the Medicon Valley life-science cluster, *Environment and Planning A*, 40, pp. 1040–4056.

Moulaert, F. & Sekia, F. (2003) Territorial innovation models: A critical survey, *Regional Studies*, 37(3), pp. 289–302.

Open Yards. (2012) Welcome to Open Yards on Orust 2012. Available at http://www.oppnavarv.nu/ (accessed 15 February 2012).

Orust Municipality. (2012) Business in Orust 2012. Available at http://www.orust.se/genvagar/omorust/orustinenglish/businessinorust.4.50ae254f10d976361078000431html (accessed 30 September 2012).

Otgaar, A., van den Berg, L., Berger, C. & Xiang Feng, R. (2010) *Industrial Tourism: Opportunities for Cities and Enterprise* (Euricur Series. Farnham: Ashgate).

Pratt, A. C. (1997) The cultural industries production system: A case study of employment change in Britain, 1984–91, *Environment and Planning A*, 29(11), pp. 1953–1974.

Quadri-Felitti, D. & Fiore, A. M. (2012) Experience economy constructs as a framework for understanding wine tourism, *Journal of Vacation Marketing*, 18(1), pp. 3–15.

Region Västra Götaland (2011) Maritime Strategy for Västra Götaland. Available at http://www.vgregion.se/upload/Regionkanslierna/regionutveckling/Publikationer/2011/Maritime_Strategy_VastraGotaland-web1.pdf (accessed 30 September 2012).

Roehl, W. (1998) The tourism production system, in: D. Ioannides & K. Debbage (Eds) *The Economic Geography of the Tourist Industry*, pp. 53–76 (London/New York: Routledge).

Ruhanen, L. & Cooper, C. (2004) Applying a knowledge management framework to tourism research, *Tourism Recreation Research*, 29(1), pp. 83–87.

Scott, A. J. (1988) *New Industrial Spaces* (London: Pion).

Smith, S. (1998) Tourism as an industry: Debates and concepts, in: D. Ioannides & K. Debbage (Eds) *The Economic Geography of the Tourist Industry*, pp. 31–52 (London: Routledge).

Strambach, S. (2008) Path dependency and path plasticity: The coevolution of institutions and innovation – the German customized business software industry. In *Working Papers on Innovation and Space, 2008–02.* Marburg: Philipps University, Department of Geography.

Svensk Turism (2010) *National Strategy for the Swedish Tourism Industry*. Stockholm: Svensk Turism AB [in Swedish]. Available at http://www.strategi2020.se/ (accessed 20 March 2012).

Telfer, D. J. (2001) Strategic alliances along the Niagara wine route, *Tourism Management*, 22(1), pp. 21–30.

Torre, A. & Gilly, J.-P. (2000) On the analytical dimension of proximity dynamics, *Regional Studies*, 34(2), pp. 169–180.

West Sweden Tourist Board (2009) *Business Plan for Development of Maritime Tourism 2009–2013* [in Swedish]. Göteborg: Västsvenska Turistrådet AB. Available at http://www.vastsverige.com/documents/vastsvenska-turistradet/marinturism.pdf (accessed 20 March 2012).

Zeller, C. (2004) North Atlantic innovative relations of Swiss pharmaceuticals and the proximities with regional biotech arenas, *Economic Geography*, 80(1), pp. 83–111.

Governance in Multi-Project Networks: Lessons from a Failed Destination Branding Effort

EVA GUSTAFSSON*, MIA LARSON**,† & BO SVENSSON‡

*School of Business and IT, University of Borås, Borås, Sweden, **Department of Service Management, Lund University, Campus Helsingborg, Helsingborg, Sweden, †Centre for Tourism, School of Business, Economics and Law, Gothenburg University, Gothenburg, Sweden, ‡ETOUR, Mid-Sweden University, Östersund, Sweden

ABSTRACT *This article describes and analyses the process in which the establishment of a Christmas market led to an attempt to establish a regional destination brand named "Delightful Christmas". Our focus is on the network dynamics of the process, in particular its multi-project network characteristics. Empirical findings are based on qualitative data from personal interviews, participant observation and documentation in an action research approach. The process is analysed as a so-called project network (Hellgren & Stjernberg, 1995) involving different actors having different aims in event and destination brand development, thus creating a process with actors of existing, but resource-lacking, dependencies. Despite the disagreements between actors, the common beliefs and hopes for the integrated destination theme remained and innovative work continued for about three years in an environment where conditions were difficult due to insufficient financial resources, project coordination and long-term strategic planning. Conclusions concern the dynamics of a complex multi-project network organization and how its failure can be explained.*

1. Introduction

Seasonal Christmas markets have been established in European cities since the late Middle Ages. In the second half of the twentieth century, they became more and more like events and were popular destinations for excursions (Kammerhofer-Aggermann *et al.*, 2003). Destination development in relation to Christmas markets is a process of using the market as a tool to make a place or region an attractive and worthwhile place to visit. Some Christmas markets, such as the Christmas market in Dortmund, can be regarded as "hallmark events" (Richie, 1984), i.e. major events that are regularly arranged (usually annually) at a place and have become so closely linked to the place image and branding that the place and the event are inseparable in most people's mind (Andersson *et al.*, 2009). Thus, hallmark events are not necessarily large events in terms of visitors and turnover, but strong in association to place identity (Getz, 2005). Successful Christmas markets, therefore, can be regarded as vital in developing strong destination brands during the Christmas season, particularly when they are developed into hallmark events.

Considering the increasing amount of Christmas markets in the western world, competition is increasing. Previous studies have shown that event-goers look for new, different and exciting experiences (Formica & Uysal, 1998; Faulkner *et al.*, 1999). Innovative elements combined with the traditional elements of Christmas markets can, thus, be expected to motivate visitors to attend. The challenge for the organizers of Christmas markets is accordingly to innovate and reinvent some parts of the event, at the same time as developing permanent, unique characteristics, into a strong event brand—a brand that also can connect to the destination brand.

Event organizing and destination branding is a highly cooperative endeavour among many actors, which makes it problematic to regard it as an isolated project (Elbe, 2002; Larson, 2002, 2009b). To develop successful events and connect them into a bundle of events and activities forming a destination brand is about managing and supporting creative processes and collaboration in a network of projects. These kinds of innovation networks are often highly dynamic, and changing and the cooperative work is often carried out in an emergent process (Larson, 2009a).

Challenges in destination network collaboration evolve from the different outlooks or interests the different actors have, which often leads to conflicts and collaboration difficulties. A compromise between different interests is difficult but a precondition to successful long-term destination development (Jamal & Getz, 1996; Nordin, 2007). Certain collaboration difficulties could be derived from collaboration between public and private organizations and their different logics (Palmer, 1996; Nordin, 2007) such as long-term versus short-term interests. For instance, Nordin (2007) found that different actors in the destination development of Åre had different opinions of the development, such as too fast or too slow, wrong or right direction and/or targeted to the wrong or right target group. Also, different outlooks can be attributed to some actors having commercial interests, whereas others have non-commercial interests connected to a community. Moreover, when creating a regional destination brand, the geographical distance between actors can be an issue since the individual place identities, adopted by actors operating in different places, are dissimilar.

This article focuses on the processes of establishing a Christmas market as a way of kick-starting the winter season in the ski-resort of Åre, and how that ambition, on its way to realization, expanded into a regional branding process, overflowing into the neighbouring town Östersund. The purpose is to describe and analyse how a new destination development project aimed at creating a successful hallmark event at the same time as building a new destination brand is initiated and implemented by a network of actors. Thus, the network of actors, their interests, expectations, actions and interactions are in focus. The action research approach adopted in the study made it possible to follow the project and its processes in detail, which in turn led to an understanding of the complexity of such a project. The results of the article discuss why these complexities and problems occur and suggest how they can be dealt with.

The next section set the theoretical framework for this study, drawing inspiration from writings on project networks and destination governance, followed by a methodological section. The empirical sections analyse the project processes with a focus on the actors involved, their relations and how that shaped the process of theme-based destination and event development. Finally, the conclusions summarize the most notable findings and identify what went wrong and why, drawing lessons for future potential efforts in other settings.

2. A Governance Approach to Destination and Event Development

In the case study, event development and themed destination branding deal with linkages and joint activities performed by actors in two separate destinations. The empirical focus is thus new since research predominantly illustrates the centrality of one tourism destination, whether it is at the local, regional or national level. Here, there are two destinations that, for the first time, attempt to perform joint activities and develop a mutual seasonal destination brand.

There are many different types of events, e.g. cultural, arts and entertainment, sports and business and trade events (Getz, 2005). A Christmas market, such as the one in Åre, can be placed within several of these characterizations, although the core of it emanates from the cultural dimensions of the Christmas traditions. Such an event can be part of a strategic development of a destination to reposition or strengthen the destination brand and thereby attract more visitors (Getz, 2005). It can also be used to involve the locals in the tourism development process (Moscardo, 2007) and to ingrain a local touch to the tourism product that increases the authentic elements of the tourism experience (Cohen, 1988). Thus, to create an attractive destination image when developing event tourism, it is important to pay respect to the traditions of the place (Larson & Fredriksson, 2007).

There are many definitions and typologies of destinations: urban and rural, coastal and alpine, event and culture, to mention a few commonly used labels in everyday and scholarly usage of the term destination (see Buhalis, 2000). Even if different people use the same destination for different activities and generally a mix of activities, the above-mentioned types are closely related to some distinct activities that usually are important reasons for travellers to visit. Events can be said to be a particular kind of attraction at a certain destination that is occasional in character and sometimes tightly close to the destination image and brand (Getz, 2005).

Gnoth (2007) defines a destination brand as a "name, sign or symbol representing the core values of a place offered for tourism consumption". The brand represents the benefits of various services that are promised to tourists (Gnoth, 2007). The branding process is an expression of a destination to position itself (Kavaratzis, 2005; Avraham & Ketter, 2008) and events are often tools in the branding process (Blichfeldt & Halkier, 2013). Further, it has been suggested that destination branding is a long-term effort by many actors involved in communicating and producing the experience of a destination (Ritchie & Crouch, 2003). The development of a seasonal destination brand, such as the Christmas theme Åre and Östersund planned to develop (involving a number of Christmas activities, events and other arrangements such as decorations in the towns), is affected by the preconditions given by the settings where it takes place. When the settings are geographically set in several places, in destinations having separate destination brands and destination networks, and where there is an explicit ambition to change the destination brand during a particular part of the season, the destination branding process is bound to be particularly challenging.

A destination can be understood as "a place in which tourists, residents, stakeholders and enterprises interact and transactions take place, as well as planning, the development of industry and regional infrastructure and other aspects, and where there is an emphasis on tourism within the region" (Laws et al., 2011, p. 7). Network approaches have often been used to understand public–private relations and governance structures in tourism destinations (see Palmer, 1998; Tyler & Dinan, 2001; Pforr, 2002; Scott et al., 2008; Laws et al., 2011). Dredge (2006) emphasizes the need to take into account both public–private networks and business networks (networks of producers) when studying tourism development. Obviously, destination development involves multiple processes, among them the development of events, which is our focus.

The concept of governance can help us a bit further in conceptualizing our study object: the processes of event establishment and destination branding. The multi-actor complexity of destinations and destination development is one of the core arguments for a governance approach (Laws et al., 2011). The list of potential stakeholders is long, including governments (at different levels), different branches of the tourism industry, different special interest groups, residents, destination management organizations (DMOs) and visitors. Modelling how these actors interact, reach consensus (or not) and solve joint problems (or not) may, therefore, be of interest. Rhodes (1997, p. 15) states that "governance refers to self-organizing, inter-organizational networks characterized by interdependence, resource exchange, rules of the game and significant autonomy from the state". In other words, governance is about managing networks (Kooiman, 1993; Scharpf, 1997).

Larson (2002, 2009b) expanded on the idea of interaction between actors in networks in connection with studies of event organizing and marketing, and developed a metaphor for an event network—the "political market square" (PSQ). The metaphor focuses on the political aspects of interaction, i.e. on interests, conflicts and power, and highlights simultaneous processes that characterize change dynamics in the PSQ (Larson, 2002, 2009b). Larson's PSQ model has a number of implications. First, the boundaries of a network may be ambiguous, unless there is a formalized network where "access" is strictly controlled by a gate-keeper. Interactions are based on the actors' more or less mutual interests leading to "interaction" processes, which may be of a "consensual" or "conflicting" nature. Owing to the dynamics of interaction, interests and expectations may change over time; thus conflict can be turned into consensus or vice versa. Whether or not there are several changes of actors' power positions over time, the "change dynamics" of the PSQ can be characterized as turbulent or stable (resulting in change or stagnation). Turbulence is also triggered by the entries, exits or replacement of actors.

Collaboration in a PSQ is maintained through the commitment of individual actors (Larson, 2002, 2009a). Lawler and Yoon (1996) define commitment as the attachment an individual feels to a collective entity. Individual members' commitment towards the collective cause is affected by how well they trust each other, i.e. how well they believe that another actor's ability, intentions and motives coincide with one's own interests (Lewicki et al., 1998). This is confirmed by a study of stakeholder collaboration conducted in a festival context (Yaghmour & Scott, 2009). These authors identify governance and trust as the two most important of nine collaborative characteristics for achieving festival outcomes. Yaghmour and Scott also stress the significance of the initial legitimization process for obtaining a positive collaborative environment. Legitimacy building relates to processes that network actors undertake to justify themselves as an accepted and respected actor (Suchman, 1995). Suchman (1995, p. 574) defines legitimacy as "a generalized perception or assumption that the actions of an entity are desirable, proper, or appropriate within some socially constructed system of norms, values, beliefs, and definitions". Thus, a network having a high degree of legitimacy tends to attract many actors such as investors.

The contribution of the concept of governance and networks in our context is that it brings attention to interdependencies and resource exchange between actors in a network and in particular between public and private actors. Palmer (1996) stresses the importance of bridging the gap between the bureaucratic culture of public administration and the marketing culture adopted by private tourism firms in tourism governance. The regular interactions between the actors are often caused by their need to negotiate shared purposes and exchange resources such as funding, information, trust and expertise. There are certain resource dependencies between the actors in the destination that are important dynamic factors which need to be understood (Nordin & Svensson, 2007). What the crucial relations are may vary between processes within the same destinations. Obviously, stakeholders have different interests in different issues, and thereby take different roles and bring different resources into the process, depending on the issue in process.

The multi-actor complexity with its resource dependencies also between public and private actors is also true for the theme-based destination brand and the Christmas event described and analysed in this article. Processes around event management are dependent on their destination context. In our case, the complexity increases since the processes spans across two destinations that might differ in leadership, stakeholder constellations, community involvement, role of government and rules of conduct and tourism development priorities.

3. A Project Perspective of Destination and Event Governance

One suggestion on how to understand the complexity of organizing destination branding and event development is to see it as project networks. According to Hellgren and Stjernberg (1995) a project network is

> a web of relationships in which no single actor can act as a legitimate authority for the network as a whole. The network is open in that there are no absolute criteria for how the boundaries of the network are identified and controlled. It is also temporary, dynamically mutable and can be partially reconstructed from one project to the next.

Despite the temporal, dynamic and open structure of project networks, often having a vague goal, the actors do gather around a mutual vision or mission (Christensen & Kreiner, 1997). Our study shows that a new concept is needed to describe a situation where actors in a project network gather around several disparate visions or goals, which makes collaboration, and thus success, harder. Therefore, we will introduce the multi-project network concept.

Each actor involved in organizing an event or being part of developing a destination brand operates within a single project either as a permanent or temporary organization. In this project, a work group perform tasks within limited time frames in which some kind of transformation occurs (Lundin & Söderholm, 1995). Lundin and Söderholm

(1995) developed four sequential concepts that describe actions in a temporary organization: action-based entrepreneuralism; fragmentation for commitment building; planned isolation and institutionalized termination. They state that different kinds of actions dominate in the different phases of the lifecycle of the organization. In the first phase—the action-based entrepreneurialism phase—entrepreneurial actions are needed. It is important to convince interest groups and, therefore, "mapping by rethorics" is a basic mode here to initiate the project. Mapping by rethorics entails convincing arguments in favour of the task and the existence of the temporary organization. It is a way to make a particular situation appear real, tangible and less ambiguous to interest groups and, thus, harder for opponents to criticize (Lundin & Söderholm, 1995, p. 446). Thereby, the project can become legitimized. For temporary organizations, fragmentation for commitment building is particularly important in its development phase. For unique tasks, such as creating a new hallmark event or a new destination brand, it is important to discuss what kind of knowledge is needed and what actors should be included. The third phase, in which the project is executed, is dominated by planned isolation. In this phase, the temporary organization tries to screen off from its environment to execute the task as intended. Therefore, external changes and influences are seen as disturbances that have to be eliminated. The last phase Lundin and Söderholm refer to is institutionalized termination, i.e. when the temporary organization is dissolved. This phase gives the actors the opportunity to summarize experiences and learn for future projects. Hence, to successfully manage projects such as the development of a new event and destination brand demands specific actions in the different stages of the project.

A typical problem for permanent organizations operating many projects at the same time is the so-called "resource allocation syndrome" in multi-project organizations (Engwall & Jerbrant, 2003). We find this discussion useful in analysing our case study since the involved actors all have many other projects and operations to deal with at the same time as they aim to develop a new Christmas market and themed Christmas destination brand. According to Engwall and Jerbrant (2003), multi-project management is about allocating resources. An organization is often overwhelmed with issues concerning prioritization of projects and the distribution of resources. Resource redistribution to increase the resource for one project often brings negative effects on other projects in the portfolio. Projects compete with each other to secure the limited resources for their own projects. A reason behind the resource allocation syndrome is, for example, failure of project scheduling, which enhances resource demand among ongoing projects. Another reason is overcommitment, i.e. when organizations carry too many projects in terms of their available resources. Clark and Wheelwright (1992) call this the "canary cage approach" to portfolio planning, i.e. every new project is thrown into a cage without any analysis of the effects of the other projects already in the cage. Moreover, opportunistic project management behaviour is another reason behind the resource-allocation syndrome. To obtain the best resource, project managers try to obtain higher priority for their project than others and, thus, political games occur in between projects.

4. Methodology

The studied project stems from two separate ideas formed through contacts with the research organizations involved (Centre for Tourism and European Tourism Research Institute). On the one hand, the Swedish Airport authority (Swedavia) raised the question whether the establishment of a regular event with international reach could be used as a tool to generate airline traffic during off-season weeks in otherwise busy locations. This question was put to our research team. On the other hand, Åre Destination, the DMO in the mountain resort of Åre, were discussing the establishment of a two-month Christmas market, running from mid-November to mid-January as a way of attracting international visitors during the early part of the ski season. This idea perfectly matched the question from Swedavia; hence, the Åre Christmas market was used as a case to test the question raised by Swedavia. The research team followed the process and supported it with feedback from observations and research input in general, in an interactive process.

Thus, the study can be defined as an action research project. The action research methodology consists of a four-step process of planning, acting, observing and reflecting on results generated from a particular project (Dick, 2000, cited in Thompson & Perry, 2004). The methodology can be used by a group of people who work together to improve their work processes (Altrichter et al., 2000, cited in Thompson & Perry, 2004). However, the researchers involved are also interested in analytical generalization (Yin, 1994). These two objectives can sometimes conflict with each other, which was distinguished in the project work in this study since there were some sceptical comments on why the research would be funded instead of the practical work.

The research team were active participants of the project and arranged several formal meetings with the project's stakeholders. At the meetings, the researchers' observations and reflections were presented, and the researchers took an active part in the discussions on strategies for pursuing the project. In addition to these formal meetings, there were a number of informal meetings with members of the research team and the project members. These meetings have all been documented and are part of the empirical base for this article. There are meeting protocols to account for those meetings that our research team could not attend.

In addition to the empirical data generated from the action research approach, two series of semi-structured interviews were conducted; in total 14 interviews that lasted between 60 and 100 minutes each. The first series of interviews were carried out one month after the first Åre Christmas market had ended and the second series of interviews about one month after the second market. The interviews aimed at factual information (who did what, when and why) rather than the individuals' attitudes and beliefs. However, in the accounts on relationships, dependencies and explanations, the individual interviewee's interpretation was asked for. All interviews were recorded and then transcribed, and we used computer software (NVivo) for the qualitative content analysis (Bryman & Bell, 2011) of them. To present the empirical findings, a project story in five parts has been constructed and triangulates with the rest of the empirical data (meeting protocols and field notes of observations and interactions). The project story presented below serves as the basis for the subsequent analysis.

Despite the factual focus of the interview questions, the material showed that, in some respect, the parties involved had very different understandings of what had been going on. These contradicting interpretations further stress the complexity in multi-level projects; however, for the purpose of this article we have limited our use of the empirical data to the consensus accounts, i.e. where actors tell the same story of what has taken place.

5. The Project Story: From Good Ideas to Failures

Why a project fails despite good intentions and enthusiastic support might have more than one explanation. Some explanations are obvious and hence acknowledged by all stakeholders involved; others are less obvious and might not be recognized by the participating actors. The literature on event management tends to focus on "the good ones" and eventually presents strategies or guidelines that will foster success (i.e. Shone & Perry, 2001). Ultimately, stories on failure are equally important to understand. In the following section, we present the project story in five parts. As stated above, the story is based on the interviews accounts and it aims for an objective and politically neutral representation of the events, rather than a representation of conflicting interpretations, individual beliefs or personal motives.

5.1 *The Project Story Part I: Setting the Scene—The Christmas Project Network and its Stakeholders*

The Åre mountain resort's decision to establish a Christmas market is the initial spark of the processes under study here. Our interviewees all agree that the idea came from the village business association, Åre Destination, and that it was seen as an attempt to kick-start the winter season a couple of weeks earlier than usual, i.e. a couple of weeks before Christmas. The extension of the winter season was in line with the relatively recent all year round ambitions in Åre, while the winter season is largely run and dictated by the ski-lift owner Skistar. In the Christmas market case, the interests of the destination and Skistar appear to go hand-in-hand: both had a strong interest in stretching the winter season. It soon became obvious, however, that while Skistar supported the idea of a Christmas market, they were not prepared to put any significant resources into the event. In the first project meeting, the Skistar representative made it clear that they considered a Christmas market to be an issue for the destination since it concerned the village rather than their core product, i.e. alpine skiing. As members of Åre Destination, yes they were involved to the extent their membership suggested, but not as the most resourceful independent actor in the village.

After some time the Christmas market idea found its way into the regional organization, Jämtland-Härjedalen Tourism (JHT), who were already involved in the project idea through the airport company Swedavia.[1] Initially, in response to the question about funding from Åre, JHT said that funding to individual destinations was impossible since they only funded projects that involved more than one destination. When the Christmas market project was transformed into a broader Christmas theme, "Delightful Christmas", also involving Östersund, JHT, funded the project.

As a destination, Östersund profiles itself as the Winter City ("Vinterstaden") and uses that brand all year round, despite the fact that summer tourism is bigger. During the period studied, tourism development in Östersund was largely managed by the municipality, with the Tourism and Congress Bureau as its front body. Private tourism in town was loosely organized, except for a group of hotels who had limited cooperation through a network. A DMO, Destination Östersund AB, was formed in late 2011.

5.2 *The Project Story Part II: Starting Point—The Åre Destination Network*

Destination development and marketing of Åre as an all-year-round destination dates back to the opening of Holiday Club in 2004. Since Holiday Club Åre aimed to attract tourists off-season they invested heavily in marketing. When the tourists eventually came, the local business network in Åre began to realize that it was possible to attract tourists for reasons other than skiing. In 2004, there were several actors involved in the marketing of Åre and the ski-resorts close by, but none of them were doing the off-ski season. The people at Holiday Club made it clear for the local business society that they were not able to develop and market the destination Åre off-season by themselves. Therefore, it was decided to pool the resources in the region and Åre Destination was funded as a joint-stock company to establish Åre as one of the top year-round destinations in Europe. Åre Destination is owned by the local Åre business society, with two actors singled out as key owners: Holiday Club and Skistar. As the largest players in Åre, Holiday Club and Skistar invest heavily in development and marketing of their own products, and through their participation in Åre Destination, they also support the Åre Destination as such. In practice, Åre Destination has appointed Skistar as responsible for the marketing of the winter season, whereas Åre Destination is responsible for the remaining part of the year. This arrangement has been explained to us by the representatives of Åre DMO as the best solution since Skistar had the experience and the network.

5.3 *The Project Story Part III: From Plan to Action—The First Åre Christmas Market*

The formal Christmas project network, working on the destination brand Delightful Christmas and the Åre Christmas market, consisted, apart from the research team, of representatives from Åre DMO, Swedavia and Östersund, but it took some time and many discussions back and forth before the Östersund group fully embraced the idea. During the first one and a half years, the group discussed at length the overall concept of the Christmas brand and the Åre Christmas market as part of it. As one interviewee put it "we were very good at talking". Writing up the project planning and marketing activities were done separately and posed few problems.

Skistar's annual reception for British tour operators provided a marketing opportunity and the project group arranged a Christmas public relations (PR) theme at the airport for the arriving guests. According to the notes, the Christmas project group had five meetings in 2009. In September, with December only three months away and the work on the market still not in progress, it was decided that the implementation of the Christmas market was to be outsourced. As a consequence, the whole Christmas project as such was outsourced, including the development of the regional Christmas brand. On the initiative of Åre DMO, Fieldwork, a well-known PR firm that they had worked with before, was engaged. For the Åre part of the Christmas project, the instructions to Fieldwork were straight-forward: Åre DMO needed events that would not be dependent on the weather, and Fieldwork should commence by organizing the Christmas market in Åre. For the Christmas project as a whole, Fieldwork was hired to design a communication platform (what later became the Delightful Christmas) and further look into what other events could fit the concept.

Fieldwork Åre office was located in the same building as Åre DMO, which facilitated close cooperation between the two and a regular exchange of ideas and updates on the project progress. At this point, when the operative work in the Christmas project had become "all Åre people" as one Östersund interviewee put it, JHT engaged an event entrepreneur in Östersund to work with the Christmas project half-time. The event entrepreneur was knowledgeable in the Östersund destination brand and he described his role as that of an observer. He understood his task in that he should keep himself and other actors in Östersund updated on the project progress through regular briefings by Fieldwork.

The first Åre Christmas market in 2009 was small scale and had about 10,000–11,000 visitors. According to the visitor survey performed by a PhD candidate in the project, most of them were there for the World Cup event, but once there, the visitors appreciated what was offered. There were market stalls, and a variety of family activities. The Åre square was nicely decorated with Christmas lighting and most shops had engaged in the Christmas theme. In the follow-up meeting of the event, the stakeholders were all enthusiastic and pleased by the Christmas-cottage-homely atmosphere that had been created by Fieldwork and Åre DMO.

5.4 *The Project Story Part IV: The Åre Christmas Market—Not Genuine Enough?*

The first version of the Christmas market had the local, cosy atmosphere achieved through lighting and the presence of market stalls selling local products. However, most of the products were not local at all; they were brought in from other parts of Sweden or from abroad. According to the local Sami organization representative, the local Sami producers were approached too late so they had no time to produce the goods that were asked for. Instead they had to make a quick fix and use what they had in store in the Sami shop. The local Sami organization could only "fill" one stall; so Fieldwork had to turn to other Sami actors to fill the market space. Except for the local Sami organization and their one stall, the local businesses were not involved in the first Christmas market. According to Fieldwork, the time schedule simply was too tight to involve more people.

For the second version of the Christmas market, the local businesses were better prepared and also motivated to participate to a larger extent. Over the year they had regular meetings within the Åre DMO with the Christmas market being part of the agenda. The Fieldwork representative communicated with all Åre DMO members about upcoming activities. Local companies individually did what they could in terms of Christmas decorations to contribute to the Christmas theme.

Our interviewees in Åre have all pointed out that the Åre Christmas market was carried out twice despite lack of resources. Åre DMO and Fieldwork took advantage of what was already there, mainly the activities of Skistar on the Lucia weekend, and they added a Christmas theme to this sport event by including a Lucia procession on skis, more lighting, decorated shops and market stalls. After having launched two Christmas markets, Åre DMO came to the conclusion that the market itself should not be the core product because it did not fit well enough with the image of Åre. During a brain-storming session, it was concluded that the Christmas market was too common to be attractive. Åre is unique for its surrounding mountains, light and darkness, snow and ice, and these aspects needed to be included in the event in order to be successful. However, such an event would take a lot of funding and up till then, Åre DMO had not managed to find a sponsor willing to invest in such a project.

5.5 *The Project Story Part V: Delightful Christmas—The Creation of an Umbrella Logo*

The communication platform that Fieldwork developed was conceptualized under the brand "Delightful Christmas". The logo was simple showing the brand name in the form of a hallmark to illustrate the umbrella concept that could host a variety of smaller events and activities in both Åre and Östersund. To communicate the Delightful Christmas concept, ÅRE DMO and Fieldwork set up a weekly Saturday meeting point at the Åre square where they informed passers-by about the concept, its purpose and what should take place in the time to come. English-speaking native friends of the people developing the brand approved the combination "Delightful" and "Christmas" but there was no formal testing of the concept and no referral among the stakeholders since the schedule was too tight for that.

During the Åre Christmas market the brand, Delightful Christmas, was communicated through several channels, e.g. a pile of Christmas gifts shown in one of the booths, where Delightful Christmas was part of the package as the sender of the gifts. On the Internet, the Delightful Christmas concept was supposed to be visualized in an animated movie done by Fieldwork. However, due to the lack of resources, the Delightful Christmas web site was not developed other than the text shown below:

Welcome to Åre Östersund Sweden

During the month of December the people of Jamtland join together in creating a glorious Christmas atmosphere with everything from concerts, Christmas markets, and exotic Swedish traditions to colorful action filled events, savory food experiences and some of Europe's best skiing. (Retrieved from www.adelightfulchristmas.com)

All in all, there were at least eight different actors involved in the process of coordinating the regional activities during the first part of December: Fieldwork, ÅRE DMO, Skistar, JHT tourism, the Östersund World Cup Biathlon group, the Jamtli market group and Östersund municipality. Not everyone was involved in the creation of new events, but all of them were stakeholders with an interest to influence what was going to happen during this period. As the Östersund representative said: "Many calendars have to be synchronized to make this work."

For the presentation material of Delightful Christmas, Fieldwork put together a portfolio of photographs that could be seen as relating to the Delightful Christmas brand, e.g. pictures from the first Christmas market, the Jamtli market and from sports events. The destination Östersund people expressed some doubts that they would put their established brands under the umbrella, but they did not stop the work of Fieldwork either. Fieldwork had developed the Delightful Christmas theme in quite a discreet way so as not to dominate the regional marketing. The first year Delightful Christmas was used in advertising in local and regional press only. Year two it was also used in the PR to Norwegian tourists.

6. Analysis

The Christmas branding project originated in the Åre Destination with the idea of growing a local hallmark Christmas market. However, as shown in Part I of the project story, the project quickly expanded into a network of six stakeholders: Åre Destination, Skistar, JHT, Swedavia, Östersund municipality (fronted by the Tourism and Congress Bureau) and the research team.

The constellation of stakeholders was the result of a political process that had two significant outcomes. First, it changed the original idea of the main purpose of the network from developing a local hallmark Christmas market to developing a regional Christmas destination brand. Second, it reduced the power and influence of the initiating actor (Åre Destination). Thus, the entrance of new powerful actors in the PSQ shifted the power positions (see Larson, 2002) in the network and forced the initiating actor to redefine its initial purpose. Moreover, the actors brought with them their already existing networks, which, in turn, had established mechanisms for, e.g. gate-keeping (Larson, 2002), views on the market and conventions for trust and commitment. We explore these in more depth in the following.

Part II of the project story shows the consequences of multi-project network in terms of distribution of power and influence (Larson, 2002, 2009a), and access to external and internal resources (Nordin & Svensson, 2007). Unlike the Christmas project network, the distribution of power and influence in the Åre Destination network was a consequence of resource possessions. The biggest private actor, Skistar, acted on behalf of the Åre Destination simply because "they were the best suited" as one respondent put it. Nevertheless, Skistar had to watch the interest of its owners and in this role Skistar was gate-keeper and set the boundaries for external relations with sponsors in a two-way direction. From the Åre DMOs "external" perspective, through a number of big, successful sports events, Skistar had set the standard for what sponsors could expect in return, in terms of visitors and media coverage. From the Åre DMOs' "internal" perspective, Skistar's sponsor contacts were "theirs"; these sponsors were not to be contacted even though formally they had been recruited by the Åre DMO and not Skistar. As a consequence, when the idea of a Christmas market came up, the Åre DMO people knew they could not follow the established Åre model for external partnerships. Hence, the Christmas market had to be conceptualized differently from the typical Åre (heavily sponsored) event.

Throughout the progress of the project there were discussions and disagreements on the amount of "commerce" that was to be allowed as part of the Christmas market. These kinds of disputes are common for public–private collaborations (Palmer, 1996; Nordin, 2007). Representatives for Åre DMO promoted the Christmas market as a local, genuine event while other stakeholders thought differently and pointed at Rovaniemi as the good example.[2] However, for Åre DMO, the concept of "local" was a key element, which can be explained in that Christmas markets typically are local in character, for example with market stalls selling locally produced products. By adopting this approach the Christmas market is connected to authentic elements of the destination (Cohen, 1988) and can, thus, be marketed as such. Another explanation for the focus on "local" we find in the network itself. Åre DMO hindered private funding for a commercial Christmas market to be considered as a viable choice, thereby restricting access to the network (Larson, 2002, 2009a). By deciding on the local, non-commercial character for the Christmas market the most resourceful actor, Skistar, was provided with legitimate reasons not to participate apart from giving "moral support". In practice, Skistar became the gate-keeper in the network, restricting actors in the wider networks of potential cooperation partners from entering and, as a consequence, external funding and sponsoring was hindered.

Part III shows the problems of moving from talk to action in the initial project phase. Instead of focusing on mapping by rethoric (Lundin & Söderholm, 1995) to increase the external legitimacy (Suchman, 1995) of the project (resulting in, e.g. sponsoring), the actors spent a long time on building consensus within the network (Larson & Wikström, 2001) and make sense of the project work internally. In the initiating phase of the project, Fieldwork was given access to the Christmas project network when the actors perceived an urgent need to shift it from planning to action. Skistar had the resources required to take on the event itself, but their obligations were strictly tied to the winter season. The choice of Fieldwork was hard to dispute on rational reasons since Fieldwork had the local knowledge and they were experts in event marketing and event branding. Rational reasons apart, the presence of Fieldwork meant a shift in power that had to be balanced; Åre DMO and Fieldwork formed a strong Åre coalition that had the power to sidestep JHT's interest of using the Christmas project for regional development. To prevent this from happening, JHT included a new actor in the network, whose engagement was a highly political move by JHT—a coalition building process (see Larson, 2002) to strengthen the power position in the network. The Öster-sund-based entrepreneur had competences very similar to that of Fieldwork but he was not engaged to contribute to the project as such and take part in the operative work. His role was that of an observer who should function as the gate-keeper towards the market of potential visitors.

Destination Östersund had for a long time worked in a proactive way towards the market of regional visitors and managed to establish an increasing share of this for its events. How the Christmas project approached the regional market of potential visitors was highly rel-evant for destination Östersund, hence the gate-keeping function of their recruit. In addition to the changed dynamics in the network as such, Fieldwork's inclusion in the Christmas project further reinforced the position and relative influence of Skistar in the Åre DMO network. Fieldwork had working relationships with Skistar and hence was unli-kely to act in a way that would jeopardize their business with them. So by including Field-work, the agenda and interests of Skistar was watched as well and, thus, the power position of Skistar was strengthened.

Although Fieldwork organized the Åre Christmas market, they did not manage to create a market for it. The visitors came to Åre for the World Cup event, and once there they visited the Christmas market as well. Thus, the market was not a prime motive for visiting Åre. Given the time frame, it is no surprise; to establish a market in such short notice is not done easily. However, the major reason is probably best sought in the network itself. Gate-keeping mechanisms towards potential cooperation partners as well as towards the poten-tial market of visitors were upheld and reinforced by the internal coalitions of the network.

Part IV describes the end of the Christmas market as the core of the Delightful Christ-mas theme and the reasons behind the closure according to Åre DMO. Having carried out two Christmas markets, it was concluded that the Christmas theme itself did not attract enough numbers of new visitors. In other words, the product was not attractive enough and one of the explanations was that it was not genuine and unique. The local Sami com-munity could have been an actor to provide that, but they were approached too late by the event organization to be able to fully contribute. Moreover, Fieldwork and the Sami organ-izations had different views on how to expose the Sami people on the market, which led to Fieldwork excluding the Sami organization in the market planning.

We, therefore, believe that the main reason for the failure of the market lies in the network relations itself, i.e. the gate-keeping processes excluding valuable actors as con-tributors or sponsors. We address the lack of legitimacy (Suchman, 1995) for the project network as the major obstacle, which led to lack of funding for further development of the Christmas market. Moreover, the failure to produce a unique local market can be explained by the lack of commitment of small local companies. Not until the second year did Åre DMO and Fieldwork try to involve these local businesses, which meant the legitimacy of the Christmas project was questioned. In this case using a community approach to governing the network (Hall, 2011) could have improved these relationships. The Åre Christmas market is still happening, but on a small scale and without the initial ambitions of becoming a hallmark event tied to it.

As described in Part V, Fieldwork was engaged to implement the Åre Christmas market but they were also given the task (monitored by the Östersund representative) to develop a communication platform, which integrated all Christmas activities in the region into a regional Christmas brand. Also, here, the gate-keeping processes in the network restricted sponsors from entering and contributing to developing the brand. Both destinations agreed initially on a common interest in the Delightful Christmas idea and that they were mutually interested in closer cooperation between the destinations. Some resource dependencies were identified, such as Östersund's temporary need for accommodation capacity during major events, and Åre saw the potential in adding attractiveness to its pre-season programme with the events and attractions of Östersund. However, there was also a conflict potential in the fact that Östersund already had an established Christmas market based on local and regional products, attracting mainly regional visitors. There was no overt conflict in the process but it was obvious that the incentives for closer cooperation were not clear and the destination branding network faded away.

The concept of Delightful Christmas was scarcely used by tourism actors in the region and only a few fully embraced the idea, all of them related to the Åre DMO. The Östersund people did not oppose the concept as such, but they did not use it in relation to their already existing destination brand such as the Jamtli market. The brand was developed quickly and

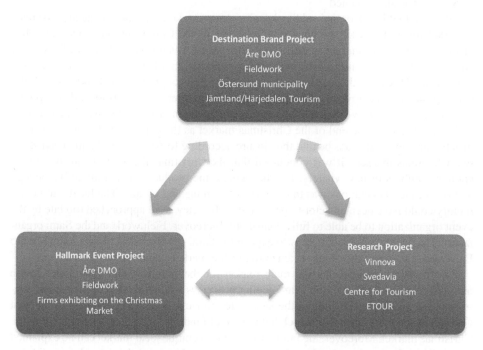

Figure 1. The decoupled project network forming a multi-project network.
Source: Authors elaboration.

very little was done to analyse the appropriateness of the concept. Moreover, there were only limited efforts to build commitment for the brand among companies and organizations in the region resulting in poor interest.

7. Conclusions

Tourism can be regarded as a network industry par excellence, i.e. that destinations consist of networks of tourism suppliers, which together create the tourism product. Research on tourism networks is about collaboration and trust, network marketing, communication in tourism destination networks, network forms of governance, networks and social capital and networks as representations of complex systems (Scott *et al.*, 2008, pp. 15–23).

In our study, it is obvious that it spans across some of these categories since aspects of the different areas are relevant. What remains is the network approach to processes at hand. The clustering of events into a seasonal theme is closely related to the preconditions given by the destination settings it takes place. The emerging event network is, to some extent, given by the network organization of destinations, which is particularly true if we are talking of a major event with an explicit ambition to change the destinations' image and performance during a particular part of the season.

Since the destination process of Delightful Christmas included a number of events, the multi-project network character of the process at hand is even more obvious. While networks have different objectives and goals, they are also interconnected in ways that will be elaborated on below. It has been illustrated that the actors in the Delightful Christmas network had their own idea about what it should be. All involved agreed that the Delightful Christmas should add new dimensions to the regional destination brand that would eventually attract more visitors. One key aspect for this to happen was to expand the destination Åre brand beyond the already established ones, namely skiing and sports events. However, there were different ideas on what the brand should include and who. The Christmas market was a central part of the project that all actors agreed needed to be expanded as a start to developing the brand. This was somewhat intricate since the market stakeholders saw the branding of a broader theme as a way of realizing the market, which very much made the whole branding process seem a construction with little bearing on other events in the region.

The study shows how these tasks, to develop the brand and to organize the Christmas market, decoupled from each other and formed two separate project networks, having separate purposes and, in the case of the Christmas market, restricted access into the network. Moreover, another project network can be distinguished, connected to the Christmas theme development project: the research project. Thus, the original project network consisting of actors having a mutual purpose to expand the season in the region of Östersund and Åre evolved into "a multi-project network" consisting of three networks (Figure 1): the destination brand development project (Delightful Christmas), the hallmark event development project (Christmas market) and the knowledge development project.

The project networks were linked to each other although over time became more and more loosely coupled. Funding was an issue for all these purposes. The research was already funded through sources external to the region, but nevertheless it was obvious that other actors considered it unfair that research, but not the actual operative work with the market and brand, could be funded. In a way, competition between the different purposes became apparent (Engwall & Jerbrant, 2003); for instance there was less interest to participate in activities performed by the researchers. From the researchers' perspective, this was to some extent a failure since the research purpose was to be a proactive partner by bringing research-based knowledge and observations into the process. However, knowledge, as a resource, could not compensate for the lack of funding in the process.

According to many actors, the main obstacle for the network to succeed was the lack of funding. Traditionally, events in Åre are sponsored through private funding, while events in Östersund mostly have a substantial part of financial support from the municipality. As pointed out by Fieldwork, events need public funding simply because the community is a large part of the core product. And besides Holiday Club and Skistar, there were no large local actors that could contribute to financing. Skistar "are not allowed to invest money in activities outside the opening season of the ski lifts" as one interviewee put it. So, the funding of the project relied on Åre DMO, Östersund municipality and the regional tourism organization JHT, organizations which have obligations to fund many other projects—too many in terms of their available resources. Thus, the Christmas project was "a victim of" the "canary cage approach" to project portfolio planning as it was added as a new project without much analysis or consideration of other already ongoing projects (Clark & Wheelwright, 1992).

As already stated, both Fieldwork and Åre DMO have other projects to work with besides the Christmas market, and there were not enough resources to allocate one person as the locomotive for the event. The local coordination and anchorage improved from year one to year two of the market, but still the organizations suffered from overcommitment since they carried too many projects and tasks at the same time (Engwall & Jerbrant, 2003).

The local organizations that had the potential to be forceful actors in this event were not well organized. For instance, the local Sami organization, which would be able to bring in valuable authentic elements to the Christmas market, was split up between those who strongly oppose any forms of "traditional" Sami culture to be exposed and those who see some value in showing parts of the cultural heritage. On the part of the Sami people, there were also the problems of coordination of moving the animals, producing the crafts asked for and to prioritize between the different arenas that need Sami representation. For the business Sami people, it is more lucrative to be part of something like the Lisebergs Christmas market in Gothenburg than to have a stall in Åre. On the part of Åre DMO, even though they were engaged, not all local businesses in the village were organized through it or cared about what was going on.

Another problem in the Delightful Christmas project concerned the division of work in the network as such. Fieldwork was given the responsibility for the communication platform and for the events in Åre. In Östersund, more actors needed consideration; not least the already ongoing and established events that already had some hallmark characteristics and did not see the upside of the Delightful Christmas theme. This somewhat skewed the situation where Åre wanted to establish something new and Östersund to strengthen without disturbing what is already ongoing, which meant the two destinations entered the branding process with different expectations. It is obvious that during the entrepreneurial phase of the branding project, key actors—Destination Åre and JHT—should have legitimized the project by being more careful to "map the rhetoric" of it, to get stakeholders involved (Lundin & Söderholm, 1995). Moreover, it is obvious that the branding process would have required more of a community approach to governance (Hall, 2011), i.e. to put more effort into anchoring it among stakeholders within the local community.

The third network, the research network, what happened with that? One might say that it lost its role in the process as the involved stakeholders lost their interest in the process. The proactive dimension of the research approach, the provision of knowledge and reflections along the way, could not prevent the real processes from eroding. What started out as a mutual learning process among researchers and practitioners could not survive the harsh realism at hand. In the longer term, we hope and believe that the knowledge generated is relevant in other places, at other times, where grand event ideas and destination brand themes are emerging.

Notes

1. At this stage its name was the state authority Luftfartsverket, later corporatized into Swedavia.
2. Rovaniemi in northern Finland has for many years branded itself as the hometown of Santa Claus and a two-month Christmas season.

References

Andersson, T. D., Larson, M. & Mossberg, L. (2009) *Evenemang—Från Organisering till Utvärdering* (Lund: Studentlitteratur).

Avraham, E. & Ketter, E. (2008) *Media Strategies for Marketing Places in Crisis* (Oxford: Butterworth-Heinemann).

Blichfeldt, B. S. & Halkier, H. (2013) Mussels, tourist, and community development: A case study of place branding through food festivals in rural Northern Jutland, Denmark, *European Planning Studies*. doi: 10.1080/09654313.2013.784594

Bryman, A. & Bell, E. (2011) *Business Research Methods*, 3rd ed. (Oxford: Oxford University Press).

Buhalis, D. (2000) Marketing the competitive destination of the future, *Tourism Management*, 21(1), pp. 97–116.

Christensen, S. & Kreiner, K. (1997) *Projektledning—att Leda och Lära i en Ofull–komlig Värld* (Lund: Academia Acta).

Clark, K. B. & Wheelwright, S. (1992) *Revolutionizing Product Development: Quantum Leaps in Speed, Efficiency, and Quality* (New York: The Free Press).

Cohen, E. (1988) Authenticity and commoditization in tourism, *Annals of Tourism Research*, 15(3), pp. 371–386.

Dredge, D. (2006) Policy networks and the local organisation of tourism, *Tourism Management*, 27(5), pp. 269–280.

Elbe, J. (2002) *Utveckling av Turistdestinationer Genom Samarbete* (Uppsala: Uppsala Universitet, Företagsekonomiska Institutionen).

Engwall, M. & Jerbrant, A. (2003) The resource allocation syndrome: The prime challenge of multi-project management? *International Journal of Project Management*, 21(6), pp. 403–409.

Faulkner, B., Fredline, E., Larson, M. & Tomljenovic, R. (1999) A marketing analysis of Sweden's Storsjöyran festival, *Tourism Analysis*, 4, pp. 157–171.

Formica, S. & Uysal, M. (1998) Market segmentation of festival visitors: Umbria jazz festival in Italy, *Festival Management and Event Tourism*, 3(1), pp. 175–182.

Getz, D. (2005) *Event Management and Event Tourism* (New York: Cognizant Communication Corporation).

Gnoth, J. (2007) The structure of destination brands: Leveraging values, *Tourism Analysis*, 12(5/6), pp. 345–358.

Hall, C. M. (2011) A typology of governance and its implications for tourism policy analysis, *Journal of Sustainable Tourism*, 19(4/5), pp. 437–457.

Hellgren, B. & Stjernberg, T. (1995) Design and implementation in major investments—a project network approach, *Scandinavian Journal of Management*, 11(4), pp. 377–394.

Jamal, T. & Getz, D. (1996) Does strategic planning pay? Lessons for destination from corporate planning experience, *Progress in Tourism and Hospitality Research*, 2(1), pp. 59–78.

Kammerhofer-Aggermann, U., Hiebl, E., Keul, A. G., Bachleitner, R. & Screuer, M. (2003) Weinachtsmärkte: Zentren der sehnsuchte und des tourismus, *Tourismus Journal*, 7(3), pp. 329–354.

Kavaratzis, M. (2005) Place branding: A review of trends and conceptual models, *The Marketing Review*, 5(4), pp. 329–342.

Kooiman, J. (1993) *Modern Governance: New Government-Society Interactions* (London: Sage).

Larson, M. (2002) A political approach to relationship marketing: Case study of the Storsjöyran festival, *International Journal of Tourism Research*, 4(2), pp. 119–143.

Larson, M. (2009a) Festival innovation: Complex and dynamic network interaction, *Scandinavian Journal of Hospitality and Tourism*, 9(2/3), pp. 288–307.

Larson, M. (2009b) Joint event production in the jungle, the park, and the garden: Metaphors of event networks, *Tourism Management*, 30(3), pp. 393–399.

Larson, M. & Fredriksson, C. (2007) Destinationsutveckling genom evenemang: satsningar på sportarenor och multikoncept, in: M. Bohlin & J. Elbe (Eds) *Utveckla Turistdestinationer—Ett Svenskt Perspektiv*, pp. 177–194 (Uppsala: Uppsala Publishing House).

Larson, M. & Wikström, E. (2001) Organising events: Managing conflict and consensus in a political market square, *Event Management*, 7(1), pp. 51–65.

Lawler, E. J. & Yoon, J. (1996) Commitment in exchange relations: Test of a theory of relational cohesion, *American Sociological Review*, 61(1), pp. 89–108.

Laws, E., Richins, H., Agrusa, J. & Scott, N. (2011) *Tourist Destination Governance. Practice, Theory and Issues* (Oxford: CABI).

Lewicki, R. J., McAllister, D. J. & Bies, R. J. (1998) Trust and distrust: New relationships and realities, *Academy of Management Review*, 23(3), pp. 438–458.

Lundin, R. A. & Söderholm, A. (1995) A theory of the temporary organization', *Scandinavian Journal of Management*, 11(4), pp. 437–455.

Moscardo, G. (2007) Sustainable tourism innovation: Challenging basic assumptions, *Tourism and Hospitality Research*, 1(8), pp. 4–13.

Nordin, S. (2007) När det offentliga och privata möts—exemplet Åre, in: M. Bohlin & J. Elbe (Eds) *Utveckla Turistdestinationer—Ett Svenskt Perspektiv*, pp. 219–233 (Uppsala: Uppsala Publishing House).

Nordin, S. & Svensson, B. (2007) Innovative destination governance. The Swedish ski resort of Åre, *Entrepreneurship and Innovation*, 8(1), pp. 53–66.

Palmer, A. (1996) Linking external and internal relationship building in networks of public and private sector organizations: A case study, *International Journal of Public Sector Management*, 9(3), pp. 51–60.

Palmer, A. (1998) Evaluating the governance style of marketing groups, *Annals of Tourism Research*, 25(1), pp. 185–201.

Pforr, C. (2002) The makers and the shakers of tourism policy in the northern territory of Australia: A policy network analysis of actors and their relational constellations, *Journal of Hospitality and Tourism Management*, 9(2), pp. 134–151.

Rhodes, R. A. W. (1997) *Understanding Governance: Policy Networks, Governance, Reflexivity and Accountability* (Buckingham: Open University Press).

Richie, J. R. B. (1984) Assessing the impact of hallmark events: Conceptual and research issues, *Journal of Travel Research*, 23(1), pp. 2–11.

Ritchie, J. R. & Crouch, G. I. (2003) *The Competitive Destination. A Sustainable Tourism Perspective* (Oxford: CABI).

Scharpf, F. W. (1997) *Games Real Actors Could Play: Actor-Centered Institutionalism in Policy Research* (Boulder, CO: Westview Press).

Scott, N., Baggio, R. & Cooper, C. (2008) *Network Analysis and Tourism. From Theory to Practice* (Clevedon: Channel View Publications).

Shone, A. & Perry, B. (2001) *Successful Event Management: A Practical Handbook* (London: Continuum).

Suchman, M. C. (1995) Managing legitimacy: Strategic and organizational approaches, *Academy of Management Review*, 20(3), pp. 571–610.

Thompson, F. & Perry, C. (2004) Generalising results of an action research project in one work place to other situations: Principles and practise, *European Journal of Marketing*, 38(3/4), pp. 401–417.

Tyler, D. & Dinan, C. (2001) The role of interest groups in England's emerging tourism policy network, *Current Issues in Tourism*, 4(2/4), pp. 210–252.

Yaghmour, S. & Scott, N. (2009) Inter-organizational collaboration characteristics and outcomes: A case study of the Jeddah festival, *Journal of Policy Research in Tourism, Leisure and Events*, 1(2), pp. 115–130.

Yin, R. K. (1994) *Case Study Research, Design and Methods* (Thousand Oaks, CA: Sage).

Mussels, Tourism and Community Development: A Case Study of Place Branding Through Food Festivals in Rural North Jutland, Denmark

BODIL STILLING BLICHFELDT & HENRIK HALKIER

Tourism Research Unit, Aalborg University, Aalborg, Denmark

ABSTRACT *Rural areas are facing prospects of marginalization and peripherality in an age of globalization where the attention of governments and media focuses increasingly on the (lack of) competitiveness of urban and metropolitan regions in Europe. Many rural areas have, therefore, searched for ways to improve their position vis-à-vis other localities by mobilizing local resources and employing policy tools that are believed to foster indigenous social and economic development, including place branding. Unsurprisingly, using food as a means to profile rural localities has become widespread, with branding efforts revolving around local food festivals that commodify local cultural resources. The article attempts to illuminate the challenges faced by branding processes in rural areas through a case study of Løgstør, a small rural town in North Jutland, Denmark, which builds its branding efforts around an annual mussel festival. The analysis focuses on the relationship between stakeholders and branding strategies, and in particular aims to uncover the role of the food festival in aggravating or alleviating inherent tensions between different stakeholders and target groups. It is argued that in the case of Løgstør making a food festival pivotal, a signature event for the place branding efforts has been created, which appeals to both external and internal audiences, and that this may hold wider lessons for place-branding initiatives in other small towns across Europe.*

1. Introduction

Rural areas are facing prospects of marginalization and peripherality in an age of globalization where the attention of governments and media focuses increasingly on the (lack of) competitiveness of urban and metropolitan regions in Europe (European Commission, 2008). Many rural areas have, therefore, searched for ways to improve their position vis-à-vis other localities by mobilizing local resources and employing policy tools that are

41

believed to foster indigenous social and economic development (Pike *et al.*, 2006; Kneafsey, 2007).

Unsurprisingly, using food as a means to profile individual localities has become widespread (Ilbery & Saxena, 2009; Sims, 2009), and thus food has become an integrated part of attempts to apply place branding practices—originally primarily used in cities or tourist destinations (Blichfeldt, 2005; Therkelsen & Halkier, 2010)—in the context of rural areas and towns (Vik & Villa, 2010). Specifically, food festivals have come to play an important role in many rural development and branding strategies that revolve around the commodification of local cultural resources (Jenkins *et al.*, 1998; Hall *et al.*, 2003; Kneafsey, 2007).

Although food festivals may be characterized as niche events, these events are increasing in numbers across the globe, built around e.g. wine, beer, seafood, meat products, particular vegetables or special dishes (Griffin & Frongillo, 2003; Hall & Sharples, 2003; Einarsen & Mykletun, 2009). Many of these festivals attract quite a number of visitors, especially relative to the often small host communities, by offering visitors a series of experiences they apparently cannot get elsewhere and thus a "reason to go". Such festivals serve a multitude of purposes: to provide (to some extent voluntary) work for local residents; to enhance place images in the eyes of potential settlers and/or business; and to celebrate group and place identity (De Bres & Davis, 2001). This multi-functionality makes food festivals well suited to be integrated into wider efforts to position localities through place-branding activities, which may also be used to appeal to a wide range of target groups (Kotler *et al.*, 1999; Hankinson, 2007; Therkelsen & Halkier, 2008; Getz & Andersson, 2010). As argued by Kavaratzis and Ashworth (2005, p. 512) "the city is simultaneously a place of residence and a place of work for the people that live in it, a destination for the people that visit it (or plan to do so), a place of opportunity for the people who invest in it".

This is reflected in the general literature on place branding that has highlighted potential difficulties in accommodating different stakeholders and target groups within place branding (Kavaratzis & Ashworth, 2005; Therkelsen & Halkier, 2010).

(a) Should attraction of, e.g. tourists, be given priority over creation of identity within the community itself?
(b) Through which communicative and/or physical means should these strategies be pursued?
(c) How are different stakeholders involved in the process of designing and implementing a place brand?

In some cases particular combinations of interests and actor strategies may create a relatively consensual process, and it is therefore interesting to explore how these generic conflicts are played out in the context of relatively small communities, where two alternatives scenarios would seem to present themselves. Either the urgency of the task of branding small peripheral communities with no or relatively low public profile could lead to short-term "boosterism", which has a focus on maximizing the appeal to external place users while running the risk of neglecting diverging interests and/or internal community building. Or, the smallness of the place branding and the geographical and social proximity of key stakeholders form the basis of a relatively harmonious branding process, leading to a focus on activities building local pride rather than attraction of additional place users from outside.

A third option—that several small places engage in joint place-branding activities on the basis of perceived similarities—is not being considered in the current article due to the nature of the empirical case study, but while inter-local coalitions will, undoubtedly, add to the complexities of stakeholder relations, the coalitions could also facilitate focusing of branding efforts on the (presumably relatively few) commonalities between the localities involved.

This article attempts to illuminate the challenges faced by branding processes in small rural communities/towns through a case study of Løgstør, a small rural town in North Jutland, Denmark, which builds its branding efforts around an annual mussel festival. The analysis focuses on the relationship between stakeholders and branding strategies, and in particular aims to uncover whether the role of the food festival is aggravating or alleviating inherent tensions between different stakeholders and target groups. The text proceeds in three steps. In the following two sections, the theoretical and methodological approach, including the case study area, will be presented. Thereafter, the findings pertaining to the place-branding process and the mussel festival in which a multiplicity of actors and objectives intertwine are presented. On the basis of this the conclusion discusses the implications of the case study for the understanding of branding processes in small rural towns/communities and the potential role of food festivals as vehicles of branding.

2. Theoretical Framework

The study takes its point of departure in the existing literature on place branding and food festivals, both of which are reviewed below.

The term "place branding" refers to the efforts of cities, regions, countries, tourist destinations—indeed any place—to position itself in the competition for tourists, visitors, investors, residents, resources, etc. (Avraham & Ketter, 2008). Place branding is often perceived as the application of marketing and branding techniques by those who market a place (often a destination marketing organization (DMO) or local government). As a result, place branding is often defined as DMO's communication about the place in question to various target groups. However, as Kavaratzis and Ashworth (2005, p. 508) remind us "the boundaries of the brand construct are, on the one side the activities of the firm and on the other side the perceptions of the consumers. The brand becomes the interface between these two".

Place branding is, therefore, not only about what "the firm" (or DMO or local politicians) does, but it also incorporates consumers' (or local residents', local businesses', tourists', potential residents', investors', etc.) perceptions of the place. Accordingly, a strong place brand is one that key target groups are aware of and hold strong, unique and favourable associations to. Accordingly, the core ideas underlying place-branding theory and practices are:

(a) that places compete with each other for a series of valuable resource
(b) that it draws upon place identity.

Place identity (i.e. the meanings that various groups of people, such as residents, business people, policy-makers and tourists attach to the place) is thus at the heart of place branding. However, this identity is not a fixed and given entity but must be seen as negotiated, (re)constructed and "used" in a variety of ways (Massey, 1991; Blichfeldt, 2005). Moreover, place brands address multiple groups of stakeholders (e.g. local residents and tourists), have high levels of complexity and intangibility, incorporate multiple identities and represent various communities (Ashworth & Voogd, 1990; Dematteis, 1994; Hankinson, 2004; Blichfeldt, 2005; Kavaratzis & Ashworth, 2005).

Focusing on the supply side, Allan (2007) argues that place branding draws upon a series of key stakeholders (i.e. tourism, private sector, people, government, culture, education, government, investment and immigration) who all need to (both collaboratively and individually) invest in and communicate what is happening in the place. This diversity has important implications because both the ends and means of place branding must, therefore, be seen as the result of a more or less open political process through which the profile of the specific place brand emerges (Therkelsen & Halkier, 2008, 2010). In the following we outline two of the key dilemmas facing place-branding initiatives, namely the relationship between external and internal target groups, and between different types of branding activities.

With regard to target groups, place branding has often been interpreted as a more comprehensive form of place promotion (Morgan & Pritchard, 2001; Keller, 2003), aiming to attract more tourists, investors or residents to a particular area by increasing awareness and positive connotations among external audiences. This view has, however, increasingly been challenged by an interpretation stressing the importance of the internal audience, i.e. the role of place brands in building or sustaining identity within the branded community (Kavaratzis & Ashworth, 2005; Hankinson, 2007)—although it should be stressed, of course, that the two audiences can be highly interrelated as, for example, tourism impacts upon place identity and might even create "the materiality and social meaning of places" (Britton, 1991, p. 452) while place identity and particularly historically and culturally significant artefacts and heritage shape tourism.

Similarly, place-branding initiatives can employ different types of activities in order to bring their message across. Often the emphasis has been on creation of a new communications platform with logo, slogans and brand values (Short, 1999; Jensen, 2007) but recently increased importance has been given to the creations of tangible objects or activities that manifest the place vis-à-vis the community and potential external visitors/users through, e.g. signature buildings or events that link a particular activity with a specific location, such as Bilbao's Guggenheim Museum or the Cannes Film Festival (Gomez, 1999; Kotler et al., 1999; Arcodia & Robb, 2000; Eckstein & Throgmorton, 2003).

The empirical focus on the present article is on a specific form of signature event as part of place branding, namely a food festival. According to Janiskee (1980, p. 97) festivals are "formal periods or programs of pleasurable activities, entertainment, or events having a festive character and publicly celebrating some concept, happening or fact" and hence potentially useful in relation to place-branding initiatives, whether focusing on internal community building and/or external attraction of, e.g. tourists. In the tourism literature the role of food as a potential driver of travel is widely recognized (Hall et al., 2003; Blichfeldt & Therkelsen, 2010; Halkier, 2012) as is the potential for using food as a central part of place-branding activities (Boniface, 2003; Lee & Arcodia, 2011).

However, during the last decades, linkages between local identity and festivals have become a topic subject to research (Smith, 1993; Boyle, 1997; Davila, 1997; Getz, 1997; Waterman, 1998; De Bres & Davis, 2001; Rotherham, 2008). For example, Hill (1988) argues that festivals may serve the aim of building "pride of place"; Hall (1992) argues that they may assist in development and/or reinforcement of community identity and Getz (1997, p. 7) claims that they may even qualify as "celebrations of the community itself". Research devoted to the study of food festivals (Hjalager & Corigliano, 2000; Hall & Mitchell, 2008; Hall & Sharples, 2008) suggests that food festivals may be particularly intertwined with senses of place and pride due to their grounding in local produce and local culinary traditions.

As suggested by previous studies (Einarsen & Mykletun, 2009), success of such festivals depends on strong networks, entrepreneurship and public planning. These events may also give locals the opportunity to partake as hosts and as guests, thus both generating income and providing recreational and leisure activities for locals (Long & Perdue, 1990; De Bres & Davis, 2001).

Interestingly, the effects of festivals may, furthermore, be particularly important in smaller places, and Aldskogius (1993) found that in smaller places a larger proportion of the community both produces and attends festivals. This makes local citizens important stakeholders in, e.g. a local food festival, but of course events may celebrate some parts of the community, while neglecting, or even deliberately excluding, other parts (Getz & Andersson, 2010) and, thus, like in place branding, studies of the links between stakeholder involvement and decisions about event profiling remain important.

All in all it is clear that signature events like local food festivals are not only well suited to contribute to the branding of a particular locality, but also that they face some of the same key challenges as place branding in general, namely the potential tension between internal and external audiences, and the need to manage complex stakeholder relations. It is, however, also important to stress that food festivals in small localities would seem to have the potential to transgress some of the traditional dilemmas by providing a vehicle for extensive community involvement in activities that, at least potentially, may appeal to tourists, and other external place users, by creating a setting for unique and pleasurable experiences.

3. Methodology

If the aim is to uncover not only behaviour but also the lines of reasoning that guide behaviour, we need to adopt a research strategy that enables us to produce rich and thick data on the topic at hand. The research strategy that is probably best at generating rich and thick data is case study research (Yin, 1981, 1984; Eisenhardt, 1989). Case study research focuses on "how" and "why" questions about a contemporary phenomenon in its real-life context (Leonard-Barton, 1990). In the same vein, Yin (1984, p. 23) defined case study research as "an empirical inquiry that investigates a contemporary phenomenon within its real-life context; when the boundaries between phenomenon and context are not clearly evident; and in which multiple sources of evidence are used". Furthermore, a key characteristic of the case study method is the use of multiple sources of evidence (e.g. observations, qualitative interviews, questionnaires and internal as well as external secondary data) in order to (a) triangulate sources of evidence and (b) produce rich and thick data.

Single-case studies are often criticized for generating large amounts of data that are context-bound to such an extent that they do not produce knowledge that transcends the case in question (Blichfeldt, 2009) and hence, they may lack external validity. However, this problem may be minor insofar as one studies the kinds of cases that Teddlie and Yu (2007) categorize as typical. According to Seawright and Gerring

(2008) a typical case is one that is representative for the population of cases and thus, in our situation, it would typically represent all place-branding activities in rural areas involving food festivals as signature events. Unfortunately, it is almost impossible to know at the time when one chooses which case to work with whether it is, indeed, typical, as one only knows enough about it to determine this after case study research has been conducted. Muslingebyen Løgstør was, however, deemed a typical case on the basis of extensive reviews of the literature on food festivals and, especially, by applying the criterion that Patton (1990) labels "theoretical sampling" according to which a case is chosen because it is deemed "theoretically useful" and is thus likely to refine, enrich and extend extant theory (Eisenhardt, 1989).

In accordance with Yin's (1981) recommendations, the case study accounted for in this article draws on a variety of sources of evidence. First, the article draws on interviews within the "inner circle" of the festival organization. Second, official festival documents, media coverage of the festivals and the official website (and other marketing materials) of Muslingebyen Løgstør were analysed. Third, participant observations were conducted during the 2010 and 2011 festivals. Furthermore, during participation in the festival, photography was used extensively and hundreds of pictures were analysed and used as supplements to interviews and participant observations. Moreover, a series of interviews as well as more informal conversations with both hosts and guests were undertaken during the festival.

As mussels are a food product that many people (at least in the Danish context of this case study) do not eat, 20 interviews were also conducted with people who did not attend the festival. Furthermore, during one of the festivals the researcher participated in a "mussels cooking class" and a guided "mussels tour" at the local museum to experience how local actors apply storytelling to the mussels concept. As for the interviews and conversations that were done at the festival, the goal was to obtain accounts of "how those being studied feel about and understand events"; in this case the mussel festival event (Neuman, 2003, p. 185).

In situ interviews and conversations included a variety of stakeholders, e.g. tourists, one-day visitors, local visitors, volunteers, organizers and local businesses (accommodation, restaurants, cafes, shops, etc.). In total, around 50 interviews and more informal conversations were conducted—supplemented by around 200 photos and various souvenirs, programmes, flyers, folders, etc.

In the next sections, we present the key findings that emerged during analysis.

4. The Town, the Brand and the Festival

Løgstør is a market town situated in the rural parts of the North Jutland region in Denmark (see Figure 1). Until the end of 2006, Løgstør was the administrative centre of a local government area, but following a major reform of local government it was incorporated in a larger municipality, "Vesthimmerland", within which competition between localities appear to continue unabated. Løgstør is located on the coast of Limfjorden, an extensive saltwater bay, and although fishery is less important for the local economy than in the past, the common mussel is the most important catch for local fishermen.

Apart from fishery, the town also has a factory that processes mussels, and at present about 90% of the mussel production/harvest is exported. Apart from traditional mussel fisheries, mussel farming has recently been introduced in the area, and local actors have no doubt that mussels will continue to be important to the area.

The town markets itself as "The Town of Mussels" and heavily emphasizes mussels in its place-branding efforts. For example, the first thing one sees when visiting the town's official website (targeting tourists, potential settlers, business, etc.) is a logo in which some of the letters are substituted by mussels, as illustrated by Figure 2.

Furthermore, most of the local restaurants emphasize mussels in their communication, or, as one of the restaurant websites proclaims "of course, mussels are on the menu". Accordingly, only a few fast food restaurants (i.e. pizza parlours, etc.) do not have mussels on the menu. Furthermore, the town's largest visitor attraction, "Limfjordsmuseet" focusing on fishing and seafaring, is heavily involved in the festival and also offers "from bay to table" outdoor cooking classes for children, and collaborates with local chefs on a series of "mussels cooking classes". Importantly, in the Løgstør case

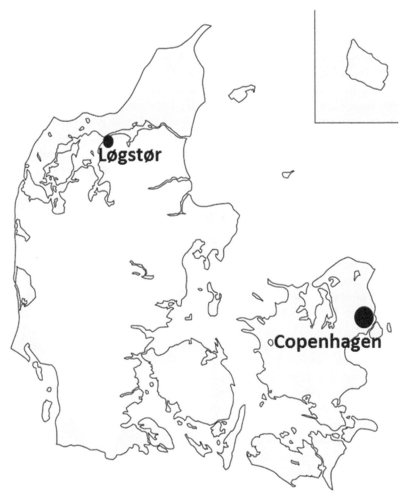

Figure 1. Map of Denmark with Løgstør.

Figure 2. The official Løgstør website.
Source: Løgstør—http://www.muslingebyen.dk/.

branding, emphasizing mussels is not only evident in the communication of the tourism DMO but used by a wide range of actors: the festival organizers, local restaurants, the "Limfjordsmuseum", etc. Previous research (Hankinson, 2004; Blichfeldt, 2005; Kavaratzis & Ashworth, 2005) has questioned the use of branding techniques in a destination context, primarily because DMOs cannot control the "product" a place offers to its guests, but merely has the capacity to emphasize certain elements in its communication and hope that the products offered by various stakeholders (e.g. restaurants, accommodation, attractions, etc.) and the relevant communication align with the brand elements.

Yet a striking feature of the branding of Løgstør as "The Town of Mussels" is that the mussel theme is adopted by a wide range of local stakeholders as well as by those responsible for the festival, thus suggesting that many stakeholders' products and communication draw on the same values and the same basic story. Accordingly, although Løgstør may have multiple identities (Dematteis, 1994; Hankinson, 2004), the identity as "Muslingebyen" (i.e. The Town of Mussels) is a core identity that the vast majority of stakeholders emphasize in their communication (Figure 3).

The first picture shows the sacks of mussels that are to be served during the peak event; in the background volunteers prepare for the cooking of the mussels. The next picture shows some of the people lining up for free mussels. The last two pictures show people, who have had their bowls of mussels (the white bowls held by the two buys and the pregnant lady).

The signature events of the Løgstør place brand, the "Mussel Harvesting Festival" in April and the main "Mussel Festival" in July, have taken place each year since 2005. The Mussel Festival is a four-day event (Thursday to Sunday in the second week of July) with a programme that includes a series of concerts, open galleries and artists' workshops, and various forms of maritime experiences such as sailing trips, which incorporate storytelling about the bay and the town, rental of small traditional boats, "open ship" events, etc. The festival also relies a great deal on the arts, and local artists were heavily involved in the mussel festivals from the very start in 2005, when local artists were asked to decorate a number of mussel sculptures which still dominate the sea front area and are part of the townscape.

Figure 3. The peak event.
Source: Blichfeldt's 2010 images.

Nonetheless, the primary event at both festivals is that mussels are served to all attendants free of charge, with usually between 1500 and 2000 people. Although 2000 attendants may not seem much, for a small place like Løgstør (4412 inhabitants) this event is crucial for the town and, indeed, its place-branding efforts.

In 2010, the mussel festival gained substantial media coverage and, furthermore, the organizers were very pleased with approximately 5000 attendees. Because of very bad weather, the 2011 festival was attended by a lower number of guests, but it still received significant media coverage (Figure 4).

Even though the festival incorporates arts, music, gastronomy, maritime elements, etc. mussels are the concept that ties the various elements of the festival together, and thus the festival aligns well with Janiskee's (1980) argument that festivals are public celebration of a "certain concept" and, indeed, clearly supports the overall place branding of Løgstør as "Muslingebyen".

5. Branding Løgstør through a Food Festival

The process of branding Løgstør by means of a food festival began in 2004 when a local painter invited a number of other residents to an informal discussion about the problems experienced in the town at that time, i.e. vacant stores and shops, dramatically decreasing housing prices and few new residents. In this first, informal meeting local artists, the mana-

Figure 4. Mussel sculptures in the city centre.
Source: Blichfeldt's 2010 images.

ging director of the town's largest production company—a person who had just moved to the area and who had experience in events—and representatives from the town fair, the local jazz festival, the local trade association, the local restaurants and the local tourist organization discussed whether "something could be done" to make the area more attractive (Andersen & Damgaard, 2010).

These people soon decided that the theme for this first, informal meeting should be whether it was possible to identify "something" that was unique for the town, and they reached consensus about mussels being both unique to the area and something that could be used to brand the town. Kearns and Philo (1993, p. 36) argue that turning a place into a tourist site often involves the "conscious and deliberate manipulation of culture", and with regard to the Løgstør mussel festivals this seems to be the case; the festivals did not start as local bottom-up celebrations but instead originate from a deliberate decision to communicate this aspect of the place to external audiences in order to brand the place. Compared to traditional conceptions (Long & Perdue, 1990; De Bres & Davis, 2001; Hall & Sharples, 2008) of specialized festivals and events in rural areas as something that is started by a few "dedicated souls" with a special interest in a particular theme (e.g. jazz music, knitting or folk dance) the Løgstør case stands out because the festivals were started by a series of people that

(a) represented all key stakeholders in the town;
(b) deliberately sought a theme that could brand the town and make it stand out from other towns;
(c) did not have any particular theme or festival in mind; and

(d) had a clear idea that the purpose was not "just" to make "yet another" festival or event, but to do something that would strengthen the place brand.

Accordingly, this group of people did not set out to make a festival; instead, they strove to "do something" that would positively affect the brand equity of the place Løgstør. Andersen and Damgaard (2010) argue that the main purpose of the mussel festivals is "to attract newcomers/new residents to a town with a dramatically decreasing of the population". In the same vein, one of the organizers explains that the reasons why the organizers spend a great deal of time and resources on the mussel festivals are as follows:

It has to do with getting people to come here and experience what we have to offer—and perhaps what we have to offer is also more unique than we tend to think ourselves—and for them to think that this is a nice place. And when they have visited us a number of times, they might start thinking about that small house in Fjordgade [the name of one of the streets close to the sea front—translates roughly into "Bay Street"] that is for sale.

Or as this was phrased by another festival organizer:

The festival and things like that are a means to an end, but the end goal is settlement—and the support from the local population is the precondition.

As evident in all these explications of the aim of the mussel festivals, the purpose is through the generation of (often one-day) tourist visits to make people aware of Løgstør and to form strong, unique and favourable associations to the Løgstør brand. Given the fact that the festivals do pull guests to the destination, the festivals seem to fulfil this purpose. However, what is especially interesting is that the mussel festivals—from the very start—first and foremost were place-branding initiatives targeting external audiences and not celebrations of community identity. Furthermore, from the very start the organizers drew on branding knowledge and competencies and the branding vocabulary (to "brand" Løgstør, to identify and use something that is "unique", to create "awareness" and to facilitate memorable "experiences") is present in both the interviews and in the various speeches, etc. that were given at the festival.

Accordingly, the mussel festivals are far more than simply food festivals in rural areas as they are both perceived and enacted as place-branding efforts, the purpose of which is to strengthen the equity of the Løgstør brand. Moreover, the ease with which local stakeholders from the public and private sector came together with representatives of the cultural and artistic communities around a common brand and an associated signature event would seem to suggest a high level of consensus, at least amongst these key actors.

It is, however, interesting to note that the organizers of the festival are aware of the fact that what is decisive for positive place brand equity is not that people visit the destination, but instead that they have positive and memorable experiences during the stay and henceforth, form positive, favourable and unique associations to Løgstør. As such, the festival organizers are aware that they (as DMOs) can (only) make people come to the destination, whereas the experiences people have at the destination heavily depend on both local businesses (e.g. accommodation, restaurants and shops) and on the ways in which local residents interact with the guests.

A central mantra of the festival organizers (and one that was repeated both during the interviews and in the official speeches during the festival) is, "In Løgstør, we don't have tourists. We only have guests."

This mantra is interesting as it clearly states the roles and obligations of the host community. Furthermore, these roles and obligations are not enacted as something only those directly involved in the festivals and/or in the tourism/hospitality sector should take on. On the contrary, the expression "we" means that all actors in Løgstør (including the residents) are to take on the role as a host in relation to the guests (and potential residents) that the festivals pull in.

Consequently, the festivals are also manifestations of a place-branding strategy according to which the notion of hospitality does not only encompass the commercial hospitality offered by those who directly profit from tourists, but also the more informal encounters between the tourists and the local residents in non-commercial contexts. Fortunately, the way in which the food festival has been organized leaves plenty of room for this kind of informal encounter, as local citizens both make a major contribution to the event by acting as volunteers in a wide range of activities (putting up tents and other facilities, cooking and serving mussels, cleaning up after the event, etc.) and, of course, also make up a significant part of the audience participating in the festival.

The third important group of stakeholders in the mussel festival consists of the participants in the signature event. The interviews and informal conversations carried out during the festival revealed that festival visitors are rather heterogeneous in terms of length of stay, type of accommodation, etc. Some visitors are one-day or short break tourists who drive to Løgstør to experience the festival; other guests are tourists who are already in the area staying in holiday houses or at caravan sites and coming to Løgstør for one or two days to experience the event. Another group of visitors are (predominantly Danish, Swedish and Norwegian) tourists, who sail around the Limfjord during the holidays and port at different coastal towns for shorter periods of time, often planning their multiple-stop vacation to incorporate a stop-over at Løgstør during the mussel festival.

The observations of the various groups of guests that the festival attracts are in line with the organizers' and the media's perceptions of who the guests at the festival are (Nordjyske Stiftstidende, http://www.nordjyskestiftstidende.dk/vesthimmerland/forside.aspx). Furthermore, all guests interviewed during the festival knew about the festival "before" they came to Løgstør. As this case study predominantly draws on data that are qualitative in nature it is not possible to verify that the mussel festival qualifies as "reason to go" for "all" guests. However, the interviews suggest that the festival is "reason to go" for "some" tourists. For example, a woman living in another area of Denmark (i.e. Zealand) explained why she was at the festival as follows: "My husband has tried this before and I'm very interested in food and very fond of shell fish, so here we are."

To visitors such as the woman quoted above, the mussel festival qualifies as a reason to go, thus making people who would otherwise not visit Løgstør come to the town. This is a feature that sets the mussel festival aside from "the ordinary town fair" as such fairs rarely attract additional faraway visitors, although tourists who are already in the area may "swing by". In the case of Løgstør, visitors especially seemed to be motivated by the fact that it focuses on mussels: to learn about mussels and to have freshly made mussels, both at the Friday night free mussels event and at the restaurants, were peak experiences for nearly all visitors the researcher talked to (albeit not a reason to go for all of them).

As mentioned previously, the study also includes a series of interviews with people that did not attend the festival. These interviews revealed that many people do not eat mussels and if they do so, only few of them (i.e. 3 out of 20 interviewees) prepare and cook mussels at home, and thus this group remained excluded from the event due to their gustatory preferences. In contrast, the *in situ* interviews and conversations suggest that the vast majority of guests at the festival both cook and eat mussels. For example, most participants in the mussel cooking class were highly experienced "mussel cooks" and predominantly participated in the cooking class to meet experts (i.e. the chef) and to get inspiration so that they could refine their own preparation of mussels at home. As another example, observations at the restaurants in the area suggest that mussels and mussel soup were the dishes ordered by most guests.

Furthermore, many visitors define themselves as people with a special interest in food and particularly in foods such as mussels, or as one visitor put it:

> We love mussels but I think that is because we have travelled so much and especially our travelling in France has made us appreciate gastronomy and seafood such as mussels. That is also why we eat mussels at home—because we've been inspired to do so when we've been in France.

As indicated by the quote above, it seems that a substantial number of the visitors at the festival are people who take a special interest in food, especially in "food as gastronomy" and people who define themselves as less neophobic (i.e. less afraid of novel and unfamiliar food) and more neophylic (i.e. attracted to novel food stuff) than "most people". Although highly tentative in nature, the empirical study thus indicates that the guests at the mussel festival may resemble Park *et al*.'s (2008) guests at a wine and food festival insofar an element of "social status" qualifies as a rather important motivational factor.

The festival is, however, also visited by locals and some of these guests are more motivated by the fact that the festival is something that locals support than by the gastronomic dimension, or as one of the locals (who smilingly referred to herself as a "tourist from Løgstør") said:

> It's my impression that everybody supports the mussel festival. When I look around I see many townspeople that I know. But this is also what Løgstør has become known for and it's not like something that is invented; this is about what Løgstør is and always has been. And it is the biggest event in town and something that pulls people in from outside.

Although the local resident quoted above rarely eats mussels and does not work as a volunteer at the festival, she still sees the mussel festival as something that locals ought to support. As such, although the cooking and eating of mussels are not part of her identity as a Løgstør resident, she acknowledges mussels as a "celebration of the community" (Getz, 1997) and as an integral part of both place identity (i.e. what Løgstør "is") and place image (i.e. what Løgstør is "known for"). Accordingly, it seems that the mussel festivals do provide a "pride of place" (Hill, 1988) for local residents—not so much because the locals find the mussel theme personally relevant, but because they are proud of the awareness of, and visits to, Løgstør that the festivals create, and thus the signature events of Løgstør's place-branding initiative would seem to have made itself worthy of resident support.

6. Conclusion

In Section 3, the attempt to brand the town of Løgstør by using the mussel festivals as a signature event was classified as "a typical case" (Teddlie & Yu, 2007; Seawright & Gerring, 2008) that represents other place-branding initiatives in rural areas revolving around food festivals. The Løgstør case is both clearly and explicitly positioned within the group of festivals, the purpose of which is to "do" place branding whereas it is not—nor was it ever intended to be—a means for community self-celebration. On the contrary, as one of the organizers pointed out, Løgstør has a town fair that serves that purpose. The success (or not) of a festival, the aim of which is to celebrate community identity is likely to be measured by the extent to which local residents define this festival as a celebration and/or the extent to which it enhances community identity. In the same vein, a festival with a destination-branding background is mostly measured by the number of tourists it pulls in, the money spent by these tourists, the actual experience or satisfaction that these tourists have, etc. The mussel festivals are successful insofar as they enhance brand equity for the town of Løgstør, i.e. if they create awareness of, and visits to, Løgstør and if the end result of these visits is that guests form favourable, strong and unique associations to the Løgstør brand; associations that may spur positive word-of-mouth communication and increase guest re-visits as well as settlement in the longer run.

The research undertaken demonstrates that the Løgstør initiative built around the mussel festival signature events has managed to transgress several traditional dilemmas in place branding. First, communicative efforts and tangible place-making have been integrated, thereby strengthening the credibility of the brand with target audiences. Second, by organizing the appeal to the prioritized external audience in a way that involves large numbers of local residents, it has indirectly helped to strengthen community identity and pride, although this was not originally a central aim of the Løgstør initiative. The key to addressing these perennial dilemmas effectively would appear to be found in a fortunate combination of political-organizational conditions and strategic choices. On the one hand, the ease with which key stakeholders came together in the early stages of the initiative is striking and suggests that, unlike in larger cities (see, e.g. Therkelsen & Halkier, 2010), the combination of social and spatial proximity within the local elite may have been crucial in setting things in motion. On the other hand, the choice of a signature event which could legitimately claim to be rooted in the locality and would allow ordinary citizens to become involved in a variety of ways quickly made what originally had all the hallmarks of a top-down initiative a much more inclusive activity. In short, in the case of Løgstør, using a food festival as a signature event has proved to be helpful in giving lasting momentum to local place-branding activities.

To what extent can this success be replicated in other small rural towns? Three factors would seem to be important here, namely:

(a) that the locality was big enough to be able to mobilize the social and economic resources needed to establish a signature event with the potential to reach external audiences

(b) that it was possible to build the event around a theme which was appealing to potential visitors without being divisive within the host community, and last but not least

(c) that the signature event allowed community involvement which not only added to local identity and pride but also gave the event a more authentic character in the eyes of external visitors.

As mentioned at the beginning of the article, rural areas face prospects of marginalization and peripherality, and many rural areas search for ways to improve their position vis-à-vis other localities by mobilizing local resources and employing policy tools that could foster social and economic development. So what can other rural areas learn from the case of Løgstør?

First and foremost, the lesson to be learnt from this single case study is that, if rural areas wish to engage in commodification of local cultural resources to improve their position and foster development, it is imperative that they choose to focus on stories and events that both appeal to internal and external audiences. The strength of the Løgstør initiative seems to stem from the fact that the choice to focus on mussels appeals to both sets of audiences, and thus the key criterion when seeking to mobilize local resources by means of festivals—and particularly food festivals—should be that the resources emphasized both appeal to the community itself and to external audiences. On a more general node, the case study also demonstrates that applying policy instruments such as place branding that were originally conceived and applied in much larger and/or urban contexts may actually also work in the context of small rural towns, provided due diligence is exercised with regard to the process, strategies and design when branding places that are off the beaten track.

References

Aldskogius, H. (1993) Festivals and meets: The place of music in "summer Sweden", *Geografiske Annaler Series B*, 75(2), pp. 55–72.

Allan, M. (2007) Place branding, *The Journal of the Medinge Group*, 1(1), pp. 1–16.

Andersen, M. L. & Damgaard, E. (2010) Musling og Branding. Available at http://www.lemvigmuseum.dk/Musling%20og%20branding%20%202008.pdf (accessed 22 July 2010).

Arcodia, C. & Robb, A. (2000) A future for event management: A taxonomy of event management terms, in: J. Allen, R. Harris, L. K. Jago & A. J. Veal (Eds) *Events beyond 2000: Setting the Agenda*. Proceedings of conference on event evaluation, research and education, pp. 154–160 (Sydney: Australian Centre for Event Management).

Ashworth, G. J. & Voogd, H. V. (1990) *Selling the City: Marketing Approaches in Public Sector Urban Planning* (London: Bellhaven Press).

Avraham, E. & Ketter, E. (2008) *Media Strategies for Marketing Places in Crisis* (Oxford: Butterworth-Heinemann).

Blichfeldt, B. S. (2005) Unmanageable place brands? *Place Branding*, 1(4), pp. 388–401.

Blichfeldt, B. S. (2009) Innovation and entrepreneurship in tourism: The case of a Danish caravan site, *Journal of Tourism and Cultural Heritage*, 7(3), pp. 415–431.

Blichfeldt, B. S. & Therkelsen, A. (2010) *Food and tourism: Michelin, moussaka and McDonald's*. TRU Progress working paper no 8, Aalborg University, Aalborg, Denmark.

Boniface, P. (2003) *Tasting Tourism: Travelling for Food and Drink* (Aldershot: Ashgate).

Boyle, M. (1997) Civil boosterism in the politics of local economic development, *Environment and Planning, A*, 29(11), pp. 1975–1997.

Britton, D. (1991) Tourism, capital and place: Towards a critical geography of tourism, *Environment and Planning, D*, 9(4), pp. 451–478.

Davila, A. (1997) Negotiating culture and dollars, *Culture and Power*, 4(1), pp. 71–98.

De Bres, K. & Davis, J. (2001) Celebrating group and place identity: A case study of a new regional festival, *Tourism Geographies*, 3(3), pp. 326–337.

Dematteis, G. (1994) Urban identity, city image and urban marketing, in: G. O. Baum (Ed.) *Managing and Marketing of Urban Development*, pp. 103–117 (Berlin: Dietrich Reimer Verlag).

Eckstein, B. & Throgmorton, J. A. (2003) *Story and Sustainability: Planning, Practice and Possibility for American Cities* (Cambridge, MA: MIT Press).

Einarsen, K. & Mykletun, R. J. (2009) Exploring the success of the gladmatfestival (The Stavanger Food Festival), *Scandinavian Journal of Hospitality and Tourism*, 9(2/3), pp. 225–248.

Eisenhardt, K. (1989) Building theories from case study research, *Academy of Management Review*, 14(2), pp. 532–550.

European Commission (2008) *The European Rural Development Policy: Facing the Challenges* (Brussels: European Commission).

Getz, D. (1997) *Event Management and Event Tourism* (New York: Cognizant Communication Corporation).

Getz, D. & Andersson, T. (2010) Festival stakeholders: Exploring relationships and dependency through a four-country comparison, *Journal of Hospitality and Tourism Research*, 34(4), pp. 531–556.

Gomez, M. V. (1999) Reflective images: The case of urban regeneration in Glasgow and Bilbao, *International Journal of Urban and Regional Research*, 22(1), pp. 106–121.

Griffin, M. R. & Frongillo, E. A. (2003) Experiences and perspectives of farmers from upstate New York on farmers' markets, *Agriculture and Human Values*, 20(2), pp. 189–203.

Halkier, H. (2012) Networking and food knowledge dynamics. Towards an understanding of factors and strategies in bringing regional food to international tourists, in: M. Mair (Ed.) *Culinary Tourism*, pp. 67–80 (Vienna: Springer Verlag).

Hall, C. M. (1992) *Hallmark Tourist Events: Impact, Management and Planning* (London: Belhaven Press).

Hall, C. M. & Mitchell, R. D. (2008) *Wine Marketing: A Practical Approach* (Oxford: Butterworth-Heinemann).

Hall, C. M. & Sharples, L. (2003) The consumptions of experiences and the experience of consumption? An introduction to the tourism of taste, in: C. M. Hall, L. Sharples, R. D. Mitchell & N. Macionis (Eds) *Food Tourism around the World: Development, Management and Markets*, pp. 1–24 (Oxford: Butterworth-Heinemann).

Hall, C. M. & Sharples, L. (2008) Food events, festivals and farmers' markets: An introduction, in: C. M. Hall & L. Sharples (Eds) *Food and Wine Festivals and Events around the World*, pp. 1–22 (Amsterdam: Elsevier/Butterworth-Heinemann).

Hall, C. M., Mitchell, R. D. & Sharples, E. (2003) Consuming places: The role of food, wine and tourism in regional development, in: C. M. Hall, L. Sharples, R. D. Mitchell & N. Macionis (Eds) *Food Tourism around the World: Development, Management and Markets*, pp. 25–59 (Oxford: Butterworth-Heinemann).

Hankinson, G. (2004) Relational network brands: Towards a conceptual model of place brands, *Journal of Vacation Marketing*, 10(2), pp. 109–121.

Hankinson, G. (2007) The management of destination brands: Five guiding principles based on recent developments in corporate branding theory, *Brand Management*, 14(3), pp. 240–254.

Hill, K. T. (1988) *Festivals* (New York: John Wiley).

Hjalager, A. M. & Corigliano, M. A. (2000) Food for tourists—determinants of an image, *International Journal of Tourism Research*, 2(4), pp. 281–293.

Ilbery, B. & Saxena, G. (2009) Evaluating "best practice" in integrated rural tourism: Cases examples from the England–Wales border, *Environment and Planning, A*, 41(9), pp. 2248–2266.

Janiskee, R. (1980) South Carolina's harvest festival: Rural delights for day tripping urbanites, *Journal of Cultural Geography*, 1(fall/winter), pp. 96–104.

Jenkins, J., Hall, C. & Troughton, M. (1998) The restructuring of rural economies: Rural tourism and recreation as a government response, in: R. Butler, C. Hall & J. Jenkins (Eds) *Tourism and Recreation in Rural Areas*, pp. 43–68 (Chichester: John Wiley).

Jensen, O. B. (2007) Culture stories. Understanding cultural urban branding, *Planning Theory*, 6(3), pp. 211–236.

Kavaratzis, M. & Ashworth, G. J. (2005) City branding: An effective assertion of identity or a transitory marketing trick? *Tijdschrift voor Economische en Sociale Geografie*, 96(5), pp. 506–514.

Kearns, G. & Philo, C. (1993) *Selling Places: The City as Cultural Capital, Past and Present* (Oxford: Pergamon Press).

Keller, K. L. (2003) *Building, Measuring, and Managing Brand Equity*, 2nd ed. (Upper Saddle River, NJ: Prentice Hall).

Kneafsey, M. (2007) Tourism, place identities and social relations in the European rural periphery, *European Urban and Regional Studies*, 7(1), pp. 35–50.

Kotler, P., Asplund, C., Rein, I. & Haider, D. H. (1999) *Marketing Places Europe: How to Attract Investments, Industries, Residents and Visitors to Cities, Communities, Regions and Nations in Europe* (London: Prentice Hall).

Lee, I. & Arcodia, C. (2011) The role of regional food festivals for destination branding, *International Journal of Tourism Research*, 13(4), pp. 355–367.

Leonard-Barton, D. (1990) A dual methodology for case studies: Synergistic use of a longitudinal single site with replicated multiple sites, *Organization Science*, 1(3), pp. 248–266.

Long, P. T. & Perdue, R. (1990) The economic impact of rural festivals and special events: Assessing the spatial distribution of expenditures, *Journal of Travel Research*, 29(1), pp. 10–14.

Massey, D. (1991) The political place of locality studies, *Environment and Planning, A*, 23(2), pp. 267–281.

Morgan, N. & Pritchard, A. (2001) *Advertising in Tourism and Leisure* (Oxford: Butterworth-Heinemann).

Neuman, W. L. (2003) *Social Research Methods: Qualitative and Quantitative Approaches* (Boston, MA: Allyn and Bacon).

Park, K.-S., Reisinger, Y. & Kang, H.-Y. (2008) Visitors' motivation for attending the South Beach wine and food festival, Miami Beach, Florida, *Journal of Travel and Tourism Marketing*, 25(2), pp. 161–181.

Patton, M. Q. (1990) *Qualitative Evaluation and Research Methods* (Thousand Oaks, CA: Sage).

Pike, A., Rodriguez-Pose, A. & Tomaney, J. (2006) *Local and Regional Development* (Abingdon: Routledge).

Rotherham, I. D. (2008) From haggis to high table: A selective story of festivals and feasts as mirrors of British landscape and culture, in: C. M. Hall & L. Sharples (Eds) *Food and Wine Festivals and Events around the World*, pp. 47–62 (Amsterdam: Elsevier/Butterworth-Heinemann).

Seawright, J. & Gerring, J. (2008) Case-selection techniques in case study research: A menu of qualitative and quantitative options, *Political Research Quarterly*, 61(2), pp. 294–308.

Short, J. R. (1999) Urban imagineers: Boosterism and the representation of cities, in: A. E. G. Jonas & D. Wilson (Eds) *The Urban Growth Machine. Critical Perspectives, Two Decades Later*, pp. 37–54 (New York: State University of New York Press).

Sims, R. (2009) Food, place and authenticity: Local food and the sustainable tourism experience, *Journal of Sustainable Tourism*, 17(3), pp. 321–336.

Smith, S. (1993) Bounding the borders, claiming space and making place in rural Scotland, *Transactions of the Institute of British Geographers*, 18(3), pp. 291–308.

Teddlie, C. & Yu, F. (2007) Mixed methods sampling: A typology with examples, *Journal of Mixed Methods Research*, 1(1), pp. 77–100.

Therkelsen, A. & Halkier, H. (2008) Contemplating place branding umbrellas. The case of coordinated national tourism and business promotion, *Scandinavian Journal of Hospitality and Tourism*, 8(2), pp. 159–175.

Therkelsen, A. & Halkier, H. (2010) Branding provincial cities: The politics of inclusion, strategy and commitment, in: A. Pike (Ed.) *Brands and Branding Geographies*, pp. 200–212 (Cheltenham: Edward Elgar).

Vik, J. & Villa, M. (2010) Books, branding and boundary objects: On the use of image in rural development, *Sociologia Ruralis*, 50(2), pp. 156–170.

Waterman, S. (1998) Carnivals for the elites? The cultural politics of arts festivals, *Progress in Human Geography*, 22(1), pp. 54–74.

Yin, R. K. (1981) The case study crisis: Some answers, *Administrative Science Quarterly*, 26(1), pp. 58–65.

Yin, R. K. (1984) *Case Study Research* (Thousand Oaks, CA: Sage).

Innovation, Tourism and Destination Development: Dolnośląskie Case Study

MAREK W. KOZAK

EUROREG, University of Warsaw, Warsaw, Poland

ABSTRACT *There is more to success in destination development than just natural or cultural heritage and assets. Increasing globalization and changes in the realm of tourism, both in supply and demand, helped to identify and recognize new development factors. Skilful application of various drivers and mobilization of stakeholders around well-defined development objectives may bring unique results in terms of creating a multidimensional, complex and innovative mega-product. Until now, public administration has been unable to identify timely innovative features and the high promotional and social potential in the Palaces and Gardens Valley project. Instead, the main drivers behind its success have, therefore, to be sought outside public policies, among new development factors utilized by private sector and non-governmental organizations. However, in the long run, recently intensifying close cooperation of public and private bodies is a condition of further development of the project in question.*

1. Introduction

Changes in contemporary tourism require increasingly innovative approaches to attract visitors. The more "upper shelf" tourism is involved, the higher and more complex are expectations, which go beyond simple tourism businesses and services, requiring networks of partners: business sector, local governments and non-governmental organizations (NGOs). Traditionally, it was expected that local government interconnected with destination marketing organizations would take a lead. The author suggests that, in many cases, successful initiatives will be taken more and more often by NGOs with specific skills and knowledge in tourism.

The aim of this article is to analyse specific innovation in the management of local assets (cultural heritage) in Jelenia Góra county (part of the Dolnośląskie region, Poland) to discuss the relationship between private entrepreneurship and public policy in the development/revitalization of a tourist destination. Until now, this relationship has not been copied elsewhere in Poland, although there are similar opportunities in other regions and localities. Increasing interests from other regions and institutions suggest that there is a great potential for creative imitation.

Apart from secondary sources, two main research methods are used: visits *in situ* (2010–2011) and communication (verbal and written) with the CEO of the Foundation of the Palaces and Gardens of the Jelenia Góra valley (the Foundation) being the key stakeholder.

Against widespread beliefs, not only in Poland, that natural or cultural assets are key factors for tourism development (see reviews by Boo, 1990; Lijewski *et al.*, 2002; Zaręba, 2006), the author suggests that in destination development/management, an increasing role is being played by networks that are organized under strong leadership, as a pre-condition of innovation in tourism. Of course, heritage matters as a core attraction, but it is not a sufficient driver. The same can be said about natural assets in the area.

This article is structured along the list of questions covering key spheres, which are important for understanding the Palaces and Gardens Valley Project:

- What are the concepts of innovation and heritage tourism and what sort of innovation can help develop heritage tourism in particular?
- What are the key features of the area in question and what tourism development activities were undertaken?
- What is the role of tourism policies in the area's development? What role have they played, particularly in case development?
- What were the features and drivers of local innovativeness?
- And finally, what are the conclusions from the case study and what recommendations can be formulated about public–private relations in tourism development?

2. Innovation and Contemporary Heritage Tourism

The key terms for this article are cultural tourism (based on cultural heritage) and innovation. One is justified in saying that the heritage of the area in question would not bring today's outcome if hotel owners had not adopted an innovative approach with the support of NGOs. It seems to follow the rule that the process of tourism innovation refers mostly to the cooperation of autonomous organizations, which covers joint use of resources, the exchange of knowledge and specific experiences, the impact on regional competence and the acquisition of technologies (probably including know-how) of other regional actors (Pechlaner *et al.*, 2005, p. 41). Leadership is another feature of innovation mentioned (Keller, 2006; Zmyślony, 2008; Kozak, 2009).

Innovation is increasingly considered a key factor of success in tourism development and destination management. "Innovation is often seen as one way in which businesses may seek to gain competitive advantage, especially where innovation in the face of competition leads to growth, survival or enhanced profitability" (Page, 2009, p. 400). In particular, in contemporary tourism where services and experiences are performed rather than produced, not separable from consumption, cannot be stored, cannot be owned, are complex and quality is difficult to measure, one may note a shift from materialism to something that can be called "experialism" (Moritz, 2010). Innovation is an inherent part of experience tourism. And still "Innovation" deserved only 10 lines in the Encyclopaedia of Tourism (Hjalager, 2000, p. 310). So what does "innovation in tourism" mean?

We often have a problem of understanding the phenomenon and defining its features, as is the case with innovation in services in general. Most of the studies of innovation in tourism are fundamentally inspired by Schumpeter's work. According to Schumpeter's (1952) proposals, five types of innovation can be identified:

- introduction of new goods,
- introduction of a new method of production,
- opening of a new market,
- conquest of a new source of supply of raw materials of half-manufactured goods,
- creation of a new type of industrial organization.

These innovations are known in short as product, process, market and logistical innovations. A similar approach was taken by Hjalager (2002), who identified product, process, management, logistical and institutional innovations.

Innovation may also be seen from a different point of view, described as technical/administrative innovation, product and process innovation, radical or incremental innovation (Wan *et al.*, 2005). Yet another approach to innovation was presented by Abernathy and Clark (1985) (after Hjalager, 2002), who defined four types of innovation:

- regular,
- niche innovations,
- architectural (change of infrastructure or capacity),
- revolutionary innovations.

Research in the tourism sector led to the conclusion that—first—it is not particularly innovative, and—second—that innovation tends to concentrate on the business level in the form of change of attitude and behaviour towards customers (Hall & Williams, 2008). Some suggest, however, it is the networks that create innovation, although due to dispersion of tourism markets, the networks do not play a significant role because the cost of creation and maintenance is often too high for small and medium-sized enterprises (SMEs; Nordin, 2003; Pechlaner *et al.*, 2005). For obvious reasons, stimulation of networking takes the form of developing the social capital, which is seen as a foundation of any network (Cantner *et al.*, 2010). The complex actions required to innovate the tourism sector explains why most come from either large companies or, more likely, from other economic sectors (Information and communication technologies (ICT), transport, etc.) (OECD, 2006, p. 65). The networking factor (relational approach) seems to offer a useful platform to integrate various other forms of innovation in tourism, as most activities in this sector rely on efforts of many actors.

With all those interesting typologies, one still needs an explanation on how it is born, what are the conditions required to see the innovation and who is an innovator? What role can public intervention (policy) play in creating innovation-oriented tourism? Although some suggest that the success of any destination neither depends on regional planning authority nor destination manager, it seems to be too simplistic to say that only the market decides (OECD, 2006, p. 22). At least through most stages of Butler's (1980) destination, life cycle matters can be influenced by the stakeholders' behaviour, ability to understand the situation and adjust to the demand.

According to the research by Goldenberg *et al.* (2001), successful innovations had some, or all, of the following features:

- they were only moderately new to the market,
- they were based on tried and tested technology,
- they saved money,
- they met customers' needs,
- they supported existing practices.

Against heroic stereotypes, untested innovation brings more chances to go bankrupt than to conquer the market. The most successful innovations researched were those based on the idea of "random events", then "market research", "need spotting" and "solution spotting" (Goldenberg *et al.*, 2001). However, when talking about factors influencing innovation in tourism, one should remember that

- basic innovations come from outside and as such are out of control of tourism sector businesses (transport, ICT, etc.), therefore, they cannot be subject to planning,
- innovations are often marked by the introduction of new enterprises and new services on the market (thematic parks, etc.),
- innovations are often a part of the investment process (new products offered to customers which cumulate and form innovation) (OECD, 2006, pp. 24–25).

One of the increasing major innovations in tourism is the "management of emotions". This is part of the fast developing "experience tourism", where atmosphere created by dramatized (theatralized) places is an element of personal contact, special value services offered to clients (OECD, 2006; Kozak, 2009). This sort of change in service providers' behaviour towards customers does not refer exclusively to large companies. It may be (and often is) easily introduced by SMEs. Even if it is only fake!

In general, innovativeness in tourism can be attributed to three groups of factors:

- supply- or supply-driven determinants (new skills, materials, services and form of organization),
- demand drivers (leisure time, population pyramid and individualization),
- level and pace of competition (influenced by globalization) (OECD, 2006, p. 59).

The form of organization logically also covers well-established networking, propensity of actors to cooperate within the framework or outside of tourism development policies.

Knowing the low propensity of tourism sector to innovate, and the general structure of factors influencing innovativeness, we may ask about the role of tourism development planning. It is one of the factors influencing innovativeness in the tourism sector. Tourist products provide the basis for successful development, but it also needs efficient organizational structures (and let us add: interrelationships) that make it possible to maximize innovation (Stratigea *et al.*, 2006). Bearing in mind the complexity of factors, Janssen and Kiers (1990) developed a triangular model of tourism which takes into account the need to keep balance between efficiency, equity (population distribution) and conservation (of history, culture and nature). From the point of view of further analysis, it is worth noting that in their opinion, there is a growing demand for modern, high quality and diversified tourist activities, which are particularly seen in the cultural (heritage) sector and undergoing significant changes both for demand and supply.

In a contemporary developed world that widely accepts the concept of the sustainable development, a certain level of state intervention is a regular part of tourism sector (Alejziak, 2000; Hall, 2008). To what extent is it successfully used to stimulate innovation? Is public intervention able to explain the development of the Palaces and Gardens Valley Project?

Heritage tourism is understood mostly as a tourist activity realized in areas where material heritage, artefacts and activities tell stories from the past. It is an important, though probably no longer a leading, branch of cultural tourism (Wall & Mathieson, 2006, p. 260; Page & Connell, 2009, p. 46). One of the reasons is on the supply side: the cost of maintenance and adjustment of large and frequently visited historical sites (e.g. Venice) to the needs of mass tourism may lead to compromising the quality of service and living conditions of inhabitants (Russo, 2000). On the demand side, there is a visible change in expectations of tourists towards emotional involvement, feeling of being part of a well-visited historic place, with exceptional service. In a number of places, cultural heritage is the most important tourist asset (Kowalczyk, 2000; Mowforth & Munt, 2009), while in others, it is only one of many assets used to create a complex mega-product (as is the case in metropolises).

In cases of cultural heritage, for obvious reasons, the stress is traditionally put on the authenticity of assets (MacCannell, 1976), but a growing number of researchers see it as a concept which cannot be clearly defined (Selby, 2004; Wall & Mathieson, 2006). Authenticity is understood as objective (traditional authenticity), constructive (projected onto the objects) and existential ("state of Being that is to be activated by tourist activities") (Wang, 1999, p. 351). Furthermore, generally and *en masse*, tourists not only lack the competence to assess the authenticity of a given object, but to a large extent, they are more interested in the impression it makes, the emotions it releases and the memories it creates, than in the often boring "truth" about it. Experience matters.

The attitude towards tourist objects largely depends on psychology and internalized life experience (Urry, 2001; Bagnall, 2003; Selby, 2004). "In other words, its [heritage's] particular meaning and significance are in fact created and then shared by a particular human society at a given time and place in world history" (Hampton, 2005). Poria (2001) stresses the fact that only specific elements of history via certain socio-psychological aspects may become (when filtered by time) a cultural heritage. Poria *et al.* (2004) suggest that visiting the historical sites is—apart from educational or recreational motivation—also a question of emotional involvement, a sense of belonging to the site. In many countries, visiting historical residences belongs to very popular cultural tourism activities. It seems to be much the case in the Palaces and Gardens Valley Project, but can this explain the success?

3. Dolnośląskie Region, Jelenia Góra Valley and the Project

The Jelenia Góra valley (the location of the Palaces and Gardens Valley Project) is located in the Dolnośląskie region, south-western part of Poland. Dolnośląskie belongs to a comparatively well-developed and dynamic part of Poland, with a fast growing capital, Wrocław (700,000 inhabitants) and a number of relatively large towns of 60,000–120,000 inhabitants (Jelenia Góra, Wałbrzych, Legnica and Świdnica) (Figure 1).

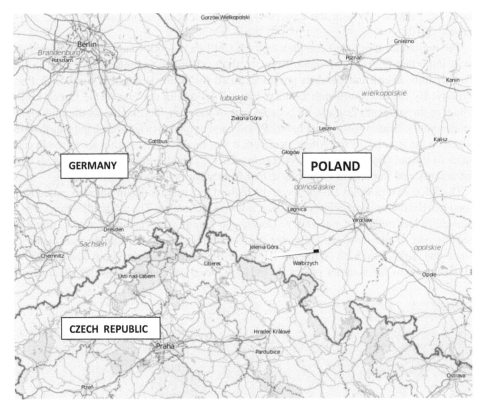

Figure 1. The Dolnośląskie region and Jelenia Góra valley.
Source: Available at http://www.openstreetmap.org/#.
Note: Black arrow shows the location of the Jelenia Góra Valley.

Dolnośląskie borders both Germany and Czech Republic; Jelenia Góra on Czech Republic only. The region is relatively large, both in terms of its population and area, with three million people inhabiting 19,948 km^2. The region is well connected with the large Central European metropolises: Berlin, Prague, Kraków and Warsaw (all within 270–350 km). The central part of the region is formed by the wide River Oder valley and partly covered by large forests. The most densely populated areas are the capital city and highland districts at the foot of the Sudeten, with its regional centres in Wałbrzych and Jelenia Góra. Several resorts (including Lądek Zdrój, one of Europe's oldest, with a mineral water well dating back to the sixteenth century) are located in the Sudeten, a thriving tourist centre serving thousands of visitors. The relatively dense road and rail network (though insufficiently developed towards the Czech Republic) is able to support both local and long distance transport.

Among the strong points of Dolnośląskie is a polycentric network of old historical towns, picturesque villages and mansions in the rural areas, and large parts of this region are protected natural and historical areas. Along with the Wielkopolskie region, Dolnośląskie is one of the most frequently visited and richest parts of Poland in terms of numbers and saturation of rural historical residences (Kozak, 2009). Over 50% of them are palaces, while in the eastern regions, palaces are a minority (Kobidz, 2007; Kozak, 2010).

The region has a rich and complex history. Until the twelfth century, it was one of the most important regions of Poland. Between the twelfth and fourteenth centuries, it was divided into several independent provinces ruled by local members of the Polish Piast dynasty. By the late fourteenth century, they all fell under the rule of the Czech kings, which in the sixteenth century, all became part of the Austrian Empire. In the mid-eighteenth century, Silesia was conquered by Prussia and remained in German hands until 1945, when, on the strength of the Allies' decision, it was finally returned after six to seven centuries to Poland (Davies, 1981, 1984; Zamoyski, 1987) and settled by Poles from all over the country and in particular those resettled from what is today western Ukraine.

The Jelenia Góra valley lies between the highest mountain range in Sudeten called Karkonosze (Krkonose, Herzgebirge) and Kaczawskie mountains. The town of Jelenia Góra is situated in the middle of the valley. Due to the magnificent mountain views, this area became one of the most attractive regions for tourism in the mid-nineteenth century.[1] Since the King Friedrich Wilhelm III of Prussia bought and rebuilt the palace in Mysłakowice as his summer palace in 1831 (Figure 2), the area has attracted numerous

Figure 2. Myslakowice Royal Palace, 2012.
Source: Author's image, 2012.

aristocratic families, not only German, who employed the best architects to redesign their residences. The area was visited by many celebrities of that time: future US President John Quincy Adams, Fryderyk Chopin, Johan Wolfgang Goethe, Alexander von Humboldt, Izabela Czartoryska and many others.

As a result, the area soon represented one of Europe's most dense groupings of palaces incorporating the highest historical and artistic values, built or redeveloped in the past for rich aristocratic families (to name just a few: the Hohenzollerns, Habsburgs, Schaff-gotschs, Radziwills and Czartoryskis) (Foundation, 2012). Interestingly, the area was turned into a unique complex of palaces connected by wide alleys offering views of each other and of the mountains. This carefully planned space lost a lot of its character during and after the Second World War, but its shape is still easily visible on local maps.

After almost 50 years of purposeful neglect by pre-Berlin Wall governments and elites, which has hidden or even erased from common memory the magnificent historical Lower Silesian residences (Kozak, 2008; Korzeń, 2009; Łuczyński, 2010), after 1989, society was faced with the need to cope, tolerate, accept or even internalize the material and immaterial heritage of the western regions of Poland. Three generations of immigrants born there are clearly interested in and proud of the history and heritage of the Dolnośląs-kie region. The Palaces and Gardens Valley Project is one of the finest regional examples of the latter process taking place.

The story started in 2005, when the owners of three local palaces established a Foundation (NGO) whose aim is to protect palaces and parks and other residences in the Jelenia Gora valley, and to promote the (sub)region as an area of outstanding cultural heritage. Through lobbying, they were able to initiate the establishment of the National Culture Park (the first step to be inscribed in the UNESCO World Heritage list).

The Foundation activities are, in fact, an aftermath of developments in the 1990s. This started with the acquisition of the palaces in the area that were in bad physical shape (sometimes in ruins) by new owners and renovated to a high standard (up to four-star hotels). The buyers were Polish businessmen or foundations (under Polish law) established by heirs of the pre-war owners. The first establishments' success (e.g. in Łomnica) initiated further investments. Some suggest that the succession of student workshops, aimed at testifying and promoting the local heritage, had triggered a growth of awareness of the area's values (Korzeń, 2009, p. 161). The activities of Łomnica Palace's owners inspired others to get involved (Korzeń, 2009) (Figure 3).

The history of the intensive cooperation of private owners of local palaces started in the first few years of this century with the outcome of the Foundation of Palaces and Gardens of the Jelenia Góra valley (established in 2005 by the three limited liability companies owning palaces in Wojanów, Paulinum and Karpniki) (Statute, Section 22). All three companies nominate the Foundation Board and are controlled by one person, as the main owner of the aforementioned companies (Krzemińska, 2012). Mr Korzeń, the Foundation CEO, emphasizes that from the very beginning, it was clear that the idea of the Foundation playing a supra-level role of individual hotels in historical residencies would not be appropriate and finally, its main objective was defined as "protection of the palaces with surrounding parkland, manors and other residential buildings in Jelenia Góra valley, and promotion of the region known as the Palaces and Gardens Valley as a special cultural heritage" (Statute, Section 7). This may be fulfilled through spatial development projects of the area, marketing, promoting the protection of the cultural heritage, education, training, pro-ecological activities, research, publishing, etc. (Krzemińska, 2012). The Palaces

Figure 3. Lomnica Palace, 2011.
Source: Author's image, 2011

and Gardens Valley is a 102 km² area where 30 spectacular residences (castles, palaces, manors) are located, as well as outstanding urban complexes, churches and other historical monuments.

Probably, the most outstanding of the Foundation' activities are those aiming to promote the area and which assure its proper ranking among other Polish, European and world cultural heritage sites. In 2008, the Culture Park of the Jelenia Góra valley was established by the Association of Karkonosze Municipalities in the eastern part of the valley, with about 20 historical residences covered (in Bukowiec, Mysłakowice, Łomnica, Wojanów, Wojanów-Bobrów, Karpniki, Miłków, Staniszów (Figures 4 and 5), Kowary and some other locations). This National Park is Poland's largest. In February 2012, 11 centrally located palaces (one in each of Bukowiec, Kowary, Łomnica, Mysłakowice, Staniszów Górny, Wojanów (Figure 6) and Wojanów-Bobrów and two in Jelenia Góra (Figure 7) and Karpniki) were nominated by the President of Poland as registered National Historical Monuments under the name of "Palaces and Landscape Parks of the Jelenia Góra Valley". The next step is planned to register the whole place on the UNESCO World Heritage list.

After less than seven years of operation, there are more than 25 enterprises affiliated with the Foundation, additionally five partner organizations cooperate. At present, some partners have locations outside the Jelenia Góra valley. The process of disseminating best practices and experience to other places and regions has started. One may say that the establishment of a new cultural cluster in the region has been supported.

Figure 4. Staniszów "Water Palace", 2011.
Source: Author's image, 2011.

The Foundation is involved in two major projects or spheres of activities (Foundation, 2012). The first is about revitalizing the 100 ha devastated grange and park in Bukowiec which, after the completion of the renovation process, is going to serve as an Education and Training Centre, possibly teaching parks and gardens conservation (Figure 8). An old barn renovated in 2011 (with co-financing from the Minister of Culture and National Heritage) serves already as a place of education, training, cultural events and exhibitions.

The second project is about promoting the area and takes different forms starting with:

- disseminating information and promoting renovation of historical objects,
- publishing books,
- organizing conferences,
- organizing thematic exhibitions outside the region,
- (aforementioned) lobbying for positioning of the area and its monuments among other monuments and places,
- designating tourist trails throughout the area,
- organizing concerts and theatre performances in local residences (three or four a month in the high season).

In summer 2012, the Festival dell' Arte (2012) took place in Wojanów Palace. All these activities are meant to recreate in the area a spirit of arts and culture, which influenced many top European artists, particularly in the Romantic era in the nineteenth

Figure 5. Staniszów Castle, 2011.
Source: Author's image, 2011.

century. Exhibitions and courses of old handicrafts are being organized in Czarne Manor (on the outskirts of Jelenia Góra subregional capital) (Figure 9). Another recent activity is a "Bajkobus" (meaning: childish fable coach) offering professional puppet theatre performances to children in the area. For more demanding viewers, an opera was offered in Wojanów Castle in August 2012 (Foundation, 2012); probably, just the beginning of a series.

Information about the valley and its heritage is made available both in traditional paper form (books, maps) and a dedicated electronic application for smartphones, which allows easy planning and navigation through the area. It is also possible to book a room in a local hotel, arranging a stay or trip of any length—by foot, car, bike and horse—via the Foundation website (www.dolinapalacow.pl). This is a distinct service from those offered by individual hotels in historical residences. The Foundation and individual hotels cooperate with numerous tourist Polish and global entities, starting from booking.com and hotel reservation system (Korzeń, 2009).

In 2008, the Foundation collected an Elle Style Award for its activities, the best Urban and Cultural Regional Tourist Product of 2008 (by newspaper Gazeta Wrocławska and Regional Tourism Organization) and best Tourist Product of the year 2009 (by Polish Tourism Organization) (Foundation, 2012).

Figure 6. Wojanów Rennaisance Castle, 2011.
Source: Author's image, 2011.

Figure 7. Jelenia Góra Paulinum Palace, 2011.
Source: Author's image, 2011.

Figure 8. Bukowiec Palace, 2011.
Source: Author's image, 2011

4. The Foundation and Innovation

What forms of innovation does the Foundation represent? And is it only the Foundation that is an agent for change? Before answering the questions, let us note that it is not a stand-alone organization: networking is at the core of the philosophy, laying the foundations for their goals and activities. It does not take over any specific management functions of (mostly luxurious) hotels located in historical residences. All partners and affiliates of the Foundation contribute to the Foundation's general objective, i.e. the promotion and conservation of the region's tangible and intangible cultural heritage.

Diverse innovations have been introduced into the area so far. Following the conceptual approaches presented earlier, it has to be emphasized that a number of new projects have been introduced (high quality, experience tourism, luxurious hotel and spa services, heritage-related trips and cultural events). These include new processes through better coordination of stakeholder activities in the area with involvement in wider projects such as the National (Culture) Park establishment, or lobbying for putting several objects on the list of National Historical Monuments. All these, together with wide ICT use, have helped to promote not only hotels, but also—primarily—the area and municipalities with their long and unique history and heritage. There is no local municipality that would not use the Palaces and Gardens Valley Project model to promote itself. Success has many fathers.

Figure 9. Czarne Manor House (Jelenia Góra) Under Renovation, 2012.
Source: Author's image, 2012.

The role of the Foundation is the largest in all the fields where the private sector would find it too expensive or conflicting with its main functions to take the lead. Undoubtedly, it offers a platform to cooperate. Cooperating stakeholders within the Foundation framework are not only hotels, but also museums, education centres, municipalities and their association, owners of historical residences and other entities from the area and—increasingly—from other parts of Dolnośląskie, where there is a high interest in imitating the Jelenia Góra methods.

The Foundation is also seen as successfully promoting the cultural heritage of the valley and of the Dolnośląskie region as a whole, organizing events and exhibitions with the aim of contributing to contemporary cultural life of the region and to familiarize the local population and visitors with the richness of the region's past, influenced by Polish, Czech, Austrian and German and—more generally—European cultural currents. Although there are innovations in several aspects of tourism in the area (product, process, organization, etc.), the real strength of the innovation here seems to lie in its cohesiveness, coordination and persistence in attaining goals clearly defined and attractive for most, if not all key stakeholders in the area. Maybe that is too early to judge, but the Palaces and Gardens project seems to contribute to the creation and strengthening of regional identity.

If one is to gauge the success of area's innovations according to criteria described by Goldenberg *et al.* (2001), they were rather moderate. Instigated from outside by a leader(s) with proven experience in renovation and hotel management in historical residences, they were clearly based on tested technology and able to meet changing needs of the more experienced, affluent and demanding customers. But for the first time in Poland, it has finally brought together such a fruitful and appreciated cooperation of public and NGO sectors; and recently some local administrations as well. From the outset, the networking and cooperation seem to have been the most striking features contributing to the success of the project.

Understanding the history of the Foundation, we now investigate the role of public policy in its development.

5. National, Regional and Local Tourism Development Policy and their Relation to the Jelenia Góra Valley

The issue of the role of innovation in public policy will be analysed used three key policy documents: National Tourism Development Strategy (MSiT, 2008), regional (PART, 2009) and local strategies (Powiat, 2006).

The National Strategy (MSiT, 2008) offers a mix of elements of old and new paradigms. Objectively, it is a modern, product-oriented document. However, when taken on a more operational level (activities attributed to objectives and priorities), it neither concentrates on a few key forms of tourism (everything will be supported), nor clearly defines products (instead most "products" mentioned are tourist trails). It also follows a very traditional approach. For example, in the case of the Dolnośląskie region, the following tourism assets were mentioned:

- forests, mountains, waterfalls, etc.,
- ruins of fortresses, places and history of martyrs, dungeons,
- objects of pilgrimage (Krzeszów Monastery, shrines),
- tourism infrastructure (quantitative analysis only),
- 11 spas (health resorts) out of 43 in Poland,
- hospitals and other health institutions in spas (MSiT, 2008, pp. 18–19).

Neither the Jelenia Góra valley nor the hotels in historical residences (or palaces) are mentioned in the document.

If the National Strategy is not necessarily meant to go into the detailed analysis, one could expect that the regional tourism development strategy (PART, 2009) would give more attention to new, innovative projects. Its analytical section offers assessment of natural and cultural assets, transport accessibility and tourism infrastructure. Analysis is also carried out for tourism subregions (neither NUTS 3,[2] nor NUTS 4 units, borders mostly based on geomorphology)[3]; however, as for the Karkonosze subregion and Izerskie Mountains—bordering the Jeleniogórska valley—the valley is not even mentioned, though it represents an area numerous in historical residences, which have particular meaning in the region's history and culture.

Wider strategic objectives represent an instrumental approach to tourism: socio-economic development of the Dolnośląskie region through tourism development at the regional and subregional levels. Subsequent strategic objectives are as follows:

(1) Creation and development of competitive tourist products of the Dolnośląskie region.
(2) Creation of a modern and efficient marketing system of products, attractions, services and the image of the region and subregions.

(3) Development of regional high-quality tourism infrastructure.

(4) Strengthen human potential of the region for the needs of tourism and preparation of cadres able to serve tourist traffic.

(5) Creation of strong institutional environment supportive to tourism development in the region through activities at the subregional level (PART, 2009, p. 71 and next pages).

Although most of the above-mentioned objectives seem to be reasonably clear and inter-connected, the picture is less optimistic for operational objectives because products and infrastructure are clearly confused. Only two examples—operational objectives—attribu-ted to strategic objective 1 from the list above, are as follows. Objective 1.1 "Development of network products" includes thematic tourist trails[4] (three out of five proposed "network products"). Objective 1.2 "Creation of the qualitative offer of tourist products"—operates only at the level of geographic subregions, not the NUTS level. It appears that only tourist trails are seen as leading regional products (Cistercian, Benedictine, St. James, Piast dynasty castles, industrial heritage, trail of Odra river, of Palaces and Gardens Valley) (PART, 2009, p. 65). And, surprisingly, the authors see trails and subregional product development as a guarantee for an integrated tourism offer and balanced tourist spatial movements (PART, 2009, p. 70).

Furthermore, it is not a product-oriented approach, but an infrastructural one. When the strategy discusses development of the tourism offer around core products, it mentions only two historical residences: the castles of Książ and Bolków (well-kept ruin). Neither is close to Jelenia Góra. Just these two are mentioned even though the region is absolutely the richest in historical residences in Poland, which may serve as a basis for a high-quality competitive European tourism product.

In theory, strategic national and regional documents should be coordinated with the operational programmes of European Cohesion Policy. They should echo the strategic approach. An overview of the projects co-financed in Dolnośląskie by the EU Cohesion Policy under the heading of tourism and culture (or infrastructure for tourism and culture, depending on the region) leads to the conclusion that most of the resources for tourism were used *de facto* for improving the quality of life:

- numerous swimming pools and local sport centres,
- renovation of town halls, theatres and parks,
- renovation of churches and monasteries (only the Krzeszów complex and the Wang church, outside Wrocław city, on the list are real supra-regional attractions),
- turning schools into youth hostels and constructing bicycle trails (MRR, 2010).

The total value received from the EU for the 45 projects analysed reached *ca.* €40 million. The Krzeszów monastic complex alone (two consecutive projects) received one-fifth. The five largest projects (three monastic complexes renovation and construction of two swimming pools) combined received slightly over one-third. Of all 45 tourism and/or culture projects in the Dolnośląskie region supported by EU funding, only 3 were related to the renovation of historical residences: 1 in Legnica (grant of €1.6 million[5]), 1 in the Książ castle complex (grant of *ca.* €0.6 million) and 1 in Żmigród (Gothic tower and palace ruins: grant of *ca.* €0.9 million). Not a single euro was spent on privately owned historical residences, and all the resources were distributed among local public administration units and—to a lesser extent—religious institutions.

The data from the ministerial list of projects suggest that not only historical residences, but tourism, in general, lost the competition with projects related to the quality of life, cultural institutions and administration needs (Kozak, 2010).

At the local level (Jelenia Góra county), where the most valuable, major attractions of the Palaces and Gardens Foundation are located, the authorities do not have a tourism development strategy. The most important strategic document refers to the sustainable development of Jelenia Góra county in the years 2006–2014 (Powiat, 2006). The only sphere where tourism is mentioned relates to "development of tourism—recreational and rehabilitation—medical function" (Powiat, 2006).

6. Conclusions: The Sources of Strength of the Project and the Role of Public Policies

To sum up, the common factor of all three previously analysed strategic documents is a high propensity to prefer a traditional operational paradigm (infrastructure understood as products; natural and cultural assets as key attractors; ignoring administrative units in mapping tourism subregions; and an apparent tendency to reduce tourism to recreational and nature-based forms (plus health tourism)[6]—mass tourism rather than high-quality prestigious products. These typical features at the operational level[7] seem to largely explain why the unique concept developed by those who established Jelenia Góra Palaces and Gardens Valley Foundation was barely noticed in the strategic documents. Of course, an explanation may be provided that when the documents in question were written (2006–2009), the Palaces and Gardens were not yet mature (which started in about 2010). But even at that time, it was widely promoted and presented in the media as a totally new activity and set of products. Most likely, however, the general features of tourism concept and policy at national, regional and local levels meant that many experts and policy-makers were simply unable to notice and properly assess the role played by innovative network projects (initiatives) offering high-quality products based on widely understood cultural heritage and events. The analysed strategies neither identified and supported new innovative projects, nor negatively affected them. They ignored them.

In general, innovation in tourism is recently reduced to new infrastructure development and potentially new products by small businesses (but no clear innovation identification criteria have been developed). Small wonder, then, that financial EU support to "culture and tourism" sector did not go to either any truly new tourism product or anything of innovative character. In practice, the tourism development policy and administration was unable to identify in time and effectively support most new promising and innovative, product-oriented projects. It is just one example of the inability to build tourism development policy on innovation by an administration tied up in an old tourism development paradigm, where assets determine development (Kozak, 2009).

The success factors should be sought somewhere other than public policy. However, the picture is not exclusively black and white. The local and regional administrations are carefully watching the progress and are offering more and more support to the Palaces and Gardens Valley project. The first was definitely the Association of Karkonosze Municipalities and Mysłakowice municipality. Nowadays, with the successful project being promoted all over Poland and abroad, sympathy towards it tends to grow. The most visible example of changing attitudes is the transfer of property rights of 100 ha in Bukowiec to the Foundation, which has developed a revitalization plan of the whole palace, grange and park complex (Koncepcja, 2011) and seeks necessary funding. Public–private partnership in motion, however, outside official structures of administration controlled local tourism organizations and with the leadership coming from the non-public side.

The Palaces and Gardens Valley Project is an example of the initiative developed and organized independently of local or regional tourism organization. Despite all the efforts on organizing the system of (semi)autonomous regional and local tourism organizations, it did not bring spectacular results in the form of stimulation and channelling of local and regional bottom-up initiatives. Similar to the Polish National Tourism Organization which *de facto* is a state organization established as a government agency, they are strongly dependent on the state (Kozak, 2009). As it is well known, life does not tolerate a vacuum. And this is to some extent a story about alternative bottom-up activities that can be defined as a complex tourism innovation.

Innovation in the case analysed here is of multifaceted character. At the product level, its important part lies in the high quality offered both by hotels cooperating with the Foundation, and by the Foundation itself, which specializes in tailor-made services offered to visitors coming with the heritage of the area in mind. A certain amount of know-how and good practices imported from other countries and regions is also obvious, though difficult to assess their role in product development.

The whole idea of the project is based on close interlinkages between hotels and other institutions located in the area, whose mission is historical heritage conservation, culture development and promotion, environment protection or just local development. While in the beginning, innovation of the sort proposed by the Foundation was not met with understanding and support from the public administration, increasing visibility and successes at local, regional and national levels led to significantly tighter links with it. Today, network covering private, public and NGOs has to be seen as a very important organizational tool in the Jelenia Góra valley. Precisely defined aims of the Foundation and division of tasks and roles seen in a wider and long-term perspective made the project more convincing for all stakeholders.

However, probably, the key factor that contributed to such a fast and successful development of the Foundation and its projects (and destination) is not the public tourism policy, but primarily the strong leadership skills shown by the initiator of the Foundation in 2005, president of its Board and successful businessman, owner or co-owner of three palaces in the area. His professional experience and interpersonal skills helped to mobilize a number of people, true stakeholders of local and regional development. Human and social resources mobilized around the idea of protection and the development of the Palaces and Gardens Valley seem to be the strongest asset of the Foundation.

Its value lies in the promotion of truly high quality, precisely defined and innovative goals and products built with the close cooperation of many stakeholders and initiated by a true leader with a vision. This may be a useful example and benchmark for tourism administration. It may also serve as an example on how to use existing assets for tourism and regional development. For instance, a unique chain of Gothic brick-built castles in northern Poland, where only a few offer products of the quality expected (most of them thanks to private sector efforts). The Palaces and Gardens Valley Foundation may also serve as an example how to build a competitive tourism industry under social control and with no harm to local culture or environment, which helps to revitalize the area.

There is little quantitative data about tourism development in the area, as its borders do not conform with administrative NUTS (LAU)[8] units, for which statistical data are being gathered. That is why the conclusions are based first of all on desk research, qualitative data, opinions of stakeholders, *in situ* visits, analysis of offers by hotels and the Foundation and successful promotion of the area at the supra-regional level. It is clear, however, that further studies should be done with more utilization of empirical quantitative data.

As can be seen in the summary, the elements of innovation in the project are multifaceted and relate not only to new product development and marketing (as described by Schumpeter, 1952; Hjalager, 2002); new approach to customers (Hall & Williams, 2008); concentration on import of moderate and elsewhere-tested practices (Goldenberg *et al.*, 2001); and, finally, on effective networking under undisputable leadership (Pechlaner *et al.*, 2005; Zmyślony, 2008). This is an experience that can be of practical value both for public policy-makers and local tourism development leaders. It also shows how profitable the switch from an old to new tourism development paradigm can be. The observation about public bodies is important, which in this case played neither a stimulating nor any other important role. On the contrary, they initially ignored the project and only started to support it after it proved its unique quality. The question arises (for further research): Is the structure of state-controlled tourism organization best prepared to stimulate innovation in tourism? Probably not, at least in the case of highly complex and innovative products. The Dolnośląskie region and Poland are not the only destinations that should analyse the case very carefully. Because it is not about the assets: it is about human and social capital skilfully gathered and mobilized around clearly defined and managed objectives, with a respect for local society and culture. And about the ability to cooperate in attaining long-term goals. Exactly in line with the new development paradigm.

Notes

1. In the KPZK, that is a national spatial development concept (strategic document adopted by the Government in 2011), the Sudeten mountain area, together with the Jelenia Góra valley, is marked as one of the most visually attractive landscapes of Poland (KPZK, 2011, p. 121), though historical heredity is not given much attention.
2. Nomenclature of Territorial Units for Statistics.
3. Which means that they are not planning areas (no authority to develop tourist policy), which makes this territorial division useless for any active tourism development policy.
4. Typical tourist trails marked on the maps, not a service to be bought.
5. Legnica Castle is the seat of the local authorities, while Książ Castle and Żmigród are owned by local governments.
6. This is probably due to the fact that many publicly owned health establishments are still a burden rather than profitable.
7. Visible also in analysis of projects co-financed by the European Cohesion Policy, which suggests that there is a pretty strong connection between operational objectives of strategies and allocation decisions taken within regional operational programmes.
8. LAU means local administrative unit, what in Polish case refers to "powiat" (county) and "gmina" (municipality).

References

Abernathy, W. & Clark, K. (1985) Innovation: Mapping the winds of creative destruction, *Research Policy*, 14(1), pp. 3–22.

Alejziak, W. (2000) *Turystyka w Obliczu Wyzwań XXI Wieku* [Tourism Facing Challenges of the 21st Century], p. 316 (Kraków: ALBIS).

Bagnall, G. (2003) Performance and performativity at heritage sites, *Museum and Society*, 1(3), pp. 87–103.

Boo, E. (1990) *Ecotourism: The Potential and Pitfalls*, Vol. 1 (Washington, DC: World Wildlife Fund for Nature).

Butler, R. W. (1980) The concept of a tourism and cycle of evolution, *Canadian Geographer*, 24(1), pp. 5–12.

Cantner, U., Conti, E. & Meder, A. (2010) Networks and innovation: The role of social assets in explaining firms' innovative capacity, *European Planning Studies*, 18(12), pp. 1937–1956.

Davies, N. (1981) *God's Playground: A History of Poland* (Oxford: Oxford University Press).

Davies, N. (1984) *Heart of Europe. A Short History of Poland* (Oxford: Oxford University Press).

Festival Dell' Arte (2012) Available at http://www.festivaldellarte.eu/pl (accessed 30 March 2012).

Foundation (2012) Foundation of the Palaces and Gardens of the Jelenia Góra Valley. Available at http://www. dolinapalacow.pl (accessed 10 January 2012).

Goldenberg, J., Lehmann, D. R. & Mazursky, D. (2001) The idea itself and the circumstances of its emergence as predictors of new product success, *Management Science*, 47(1), pp. 69–84.

Hall, C. M. (2008) *Tourism Planning. Policies, Processes and Relationships*, p. 302 (Harlow: Pearson Prentice-Hall).

Hall, C. M. & Williams, A. M. (2008) *Tourism and Innovation* (Oxford: Routledge).

Hampton, M. P. (2005) Heritage, local communities and economic development, *Annals of Tourism Research*, 32(3), pp. 735–759.

Hjalager, A. M. (2000) Innovation, in: J. Jafari (Ed.) *Encyclopedia of Tourism*, p. 310 (London: Routledge).

Hjalager, A.-M. (2002) Repairing innovation defectiveness in tourism, *Tourism Management*, 23(5), pp. 465–474.

Janssen, H. & Kiers, M. (1990) *Lesvos ... On its Way to the Future*, ERASMUS Project 1990, Amsterdam and Mytilene: University of Amsterdam and University of the Aegean.

Keller, P. (2006) Towards an innovation-oriented tourism policy: A new agenda? in: B. Walder, K. Weiermair & A. Pérez (Eds) *Innovation and Product Development in Tourism, Creating Sustainable Competitive Advantage*, pp. 55–70 (Berlin: Schmitt).

Kobidz (National Heritage Board of Poland) (2007) *Raport o stanie zachowania zabytków nieruchomych* [Report on Technical State of Heritage Objects]. Available at http://www.kobidz.pl/app/site.php5/Show/337.html (accessed 7 July 2008).

Koncepcja (2011) *Koncepcja Rewitalizacji Założenia Pałacowo – Parkowego w Bukowcu* [Concept of Revitalization of the Palace and Park Complex in Bukowiec]. Available at http://www.dolinapalacow.pl/files/flow/110202_Koncepcja_rewitalizacji.9b797.pdf (accessed 20 June 2012).

Korzeń, K. (2009) Dolina pałaców i ogrodów – nowy produkt turystyczny oparty na dziedzictwie kulturowym Kotliny Jeleniogórskiej [Palaces and gardens valley – new Jelenia Góra valley heredity-based tourist product], in: A. Stasiak (Ed.) *Kultura i Turystyka. Wspólnie Zyskać!*, pp. 159–170 (Łódź: Wyd. WSTH w Łodzi).

Kowalczyk, A. (2000) *Geografia Turyzmu* [Geography of Tourism] (Warszawa: Wyd. Naukowe PWN), p. 287.

Kozak, M. W. (2008) Dwory, pałace i zamki – kosztowne pamiątki czy zasób w rozwoju? [Manors, palaces and castles – costly heritage or development asset?], *Studia Regionalne i Lokalne*, 2(32), pp. 92–110.

Kozak, M. W. (2009) *Turystyka i Polityka Turystyczna a Rozwój: Między Starym a Nowym Paradygmatem* [Tourism and Tourist Policy: Between the Old and New Paradigm], p. 322 (Warszawa: Wyd. Naukowe Scholar).

Kozak, M. W. (2010) Lost Opportunities? Historical Residences in South-Western Poland. Paper presented at 11th Joint World Cultural Tourism Conference, World Cultural Tourism Association, Hangzhou, China, November.

KPZK (*Koncepcja Przestrzennego Zagospodarowania Kraju*) (2011) *National Spatial Development Concept*, p. 240 (Warszawa: Ministerstwo Rozwoju Regionalnego).

Krzemińska, A. (2012) Pan na pałacach [The lord of palaces], *Polityka*, 55(14), pp. 54–56.

Lijewski, T., Mikułowski, B. & Wyrzykowski, J. (2002) *Geografia Turystyki Polski* [Tourist Geography of Poland], p. 289 (Warszawa: PWE).

Łuczyński, R. M. (2010) *Losy Rezydencji Dolnośląskich w Latach 1945–1991* [Fate of the Dolnośląskie Residences in the Years 1945–1991], p. 624 (Wrocław: Oficyna Wydawnicza ATUT).

Maccannell, D. (1976) *The Tourist: A New Theory of the Leisure Class* (New York: Schocken Books).

Moritz, S. (2010) Innovative and Sustainable Products in the Tourism and Hospitality Business. Presentation at Tourism Industry and Education Symposium, March 5–7, 2009, Jyväskylä, Finland. Available at http://www.slideshare.net/st_moritz/innovation-in-tourism-and-hospitality (accessed 25 March 2012).

Mowforth, M. & Munt, I. (2009) *Tourism and Sustainability. Development, Globalisation and New Tourism in the Third World*, p. 424 (Oxford: Routledge).

MRR (Ministry of Regional Development) (2010) *Mapa Dotacji. Województwo Dolnośląskie* [Map of Grants. Dolnośląskie Region]. Available at http://www.mapadotacji.gov.pl (accessed 11 July 2010).

MSiT (Ministry of Sport and Tourism) (2008) *Kierunki Rozwoju Turystyki do 2015 Roku* [Directions for Tourism Development till 2015], p. 128. Available at http://www.dot.org.pl/strategie-i-opracowania-branzowe/archiwum/kierunki-rozwoju-turystyki-do-2015-roku.html (accessed 12 June 2010).

Nordin, S. (2003) *Tourism Clustering and Innovation – Paths to Economic Growth and Development*, p. 90 (Ostersund: ETOUR, Mid-Sweden University).

OECD (2006) *Innovation and Growth in Tourism*, p. 74 (Paris: OECD).

Page, S. J. (2009) *Tourism Management: Managing for Change* (Oxford: Butterworth-Heinemann).

Page, S. J. & Connell, J. (2009) *Tourism: A Modern Synthesis* (London: Cengage Learning).

PART (Polish Agency for Tourism Development) (2009) *Aktualizacja Programu Rozwoju Turystyki dla Wojewodztwa Dolnośląskiego* [Dolnośląskie Region Tourism Development Program: An Update]. Warszawa: PART.

Pechlaner, H., Fischer, E. & Hammann, E.-M. (2005) Leadership and innovation processes: Development of products and services based on core competencies, in: M. Peters & B. Pikkemaat (Eds) *Innovation in Hospitality and Tourism*, pp. 31–58 (Princeton, NJ: The Haworth Hospitality Press).

Poria, Y. (2001) The show must not go on, *Tourism and Hospitality Research*, 3(2), pp. 115–119.

Poria, Y., Butler, R. & Airey, D. (2004) Links Between Tourists, Heritage, and Reasons for Visiting Heritage Sites, *Journal of Travel Research*, 43(19), pp. 19–28.

POWIAT (Jelenia Góra County) (2006) *Strategia Zrównoważonego Rozwoju Powiatu Jeleniogórskiego na Lata 2006–2014* [Strategy of Sustainable Development of Jelenia Góra County]. Jelenia Góra: Powiat Jeleniogórski.

Russo, A. P. (2000) The "Vicious Circle" of Tourism Development in Heritage Destinations. Paper presented at the 40th congress of the Regional Science Association, Barcelona. Available at http://www-sre.wu-wien.ac.at/ersa/ersaconfs/ersa00/pdf-ersa/pdf/34.pdf (accessed 20 March 2012).

Schumpeter, J. (1952) *Can Capitalism Survive?* (New York: Harper and Row).

Selby, M. (2004) *Understanding Urban Tourism. Image, Culture and Experience*, p. 228 (London: I. B. Tauris).

Statute (of the Foundation Palaces and Gardens of the Jelenia Góra Valley) (2005). Available at http://www.dolinapalacow.pl/statut.html (accessed 15 June 2011).

Stratigea, A., Giaoutz, M. & Nijkamp, P. (2006) The potential of virtual organizations in local tourist development, in: M. Giaoutzi & P. Nijkamp (Eds) *Tourism and Regional Development. New Pathways*, pp. 51–70 (Aldershot: Ashgate).

Urry, J. (2001) *The Tourist Gaze*, p. 278 (London: Sage).

Wall, G. & Mathieson, A. (2006) *Tourism: Changes, Impacts and Opportunities*, p. 412 (Harlow: Pearson Education).

Wan, D., Ong, C. & Lee, F. (2005) Determinants of firm innovation in Singapore, *Technovation*, 25(3), pp. 261–268.

Wang, N. (1999) Rethinking authenticity in tourism experience, *Annals of Tourism Research*, 26(2), pp. 349–370.

Zamoyski, A. (1987) *The Polish Way. A Thousand-Year History of the Poles and their Culture*, p. 422 (London: John Murray).

Zaręba, D. (2006) *Ekoturystyka* [Ecotourism], p. 176 (Warszawa: Wyd. Naukowe PWN).

Zmyślony, P. (2008) *Partnerstwo i Przywództwo w Regionie Turystycznym* [Partnership and Leadership in the Tourist Region], p. 155 (Poznań: Wydawnictwo AE w Poznaniu).

World Heritage and Tourism Innovation: Institutional Frameworks and Local Adaptation

SUSANNA HELDT CASSEL & ALBINA PASHKEVICH

School of Technology and Business Studies, Dalarna University, Falun, Sweden

ABSTRACT *The interest in heritage as a tool for destination development has recently been substantial in Sweden, especially when it comes to receiving World Heritage (WH) status. The possibility of using the WH brand in developing tourism products and marketing destinations has great potential for many heritage destinations. The aim of this paper is to discuss innovation processes within heritage tourism. The focus is on the role of WH status as a factor influencing innovative practices at different Swedish WH sites. This study uses qualitative methods, such as interviews and analysis of written material from five selected Swedish WH sites, with in-depth analysis of the Great Copper Mountain in Falun. To what extent does WH status change the preconditions for tourism development at WH destinations? What is the role of institutional frameworks in this process? This paper will show how WH may facilitate tourism innovation mainly through developing new products and marketing strategies, but also by institutional innovations concerning new forms of collaboration and networks.*

1. Introduction

Places that have been declared heritage sites are often considered potential tourism destinations. However, development of tourism at heritage sites involves negotiation of different interests and interpretations regarding the heritage resource and its possible uses (Graham *et al.*, 2000; Heldt Cassel & Pashkevich, 2011). Heritage sites are often built on the memories and remains of previous societies and production processes, but are given new meanings in contemporary contexts. Heritage tourism is a practice where old buildings and cultural assets are reinterpreted and re-imaged within a tourism framework.

Heritage is a multifaceted concept and often describes cultural resources in a region or a specific cultural context. The simple definition of *heritage* as "things worth saving" implies that it necessarily changes over time and that it has economic value (Lowenthal,

1985; Graham *et al.*, 2000; Jones & Shaw, 2007). The concept of heritage has obvious political and rhetorical connotations, given that it consists of a specific selection of memories and histories that are meaningful in a contemporary context (Grundberg, 2002). While this is not to say that heritage has nothing to do with historical facts, the purpose of heritage is to comply with contemporary needs (Lowenthal, 1985; Silvén & Isacson, 1999; Nora, 2001; Timothy & Boyd, 2003).

Lowenthal (1985) and Ashworth (1994) established studies of product innovations connected to re-imagining the past. These became classical examples of using the past to benefit contemporary society. With new contexts of interpretation, the meaning of the sites changes and new potentials for product development appear where old products are reshaped and commoditized (Ashworth, 1994). World Heritage (WH) status provided by the United Nations Educational, Scientific and Cultural Organization's (UNESCO) WH Convention may further complicate the context in which heritage is conceptualized. Heritage sites may also gain new meanings and interpretations useful for developing tourism products. The WH status affects localities and exposes them to a global level of competition with other, similar destinations. Local heritage resources possess an eternal value (Turtinen, 2006). This also means that the heritage has to be preserved and kept in its original state, which might actually conflict with using the heritage resources for tourism purposes (Harrison & Hitchcock, 2005). A WH site also must be managed in a sustainable manner. Certain local institutional arrangements are endorsed by UNESCO to ensure this. Although there is not a clear connection between WH status and successful tourism development, it nevertheless facilitates new forms of institutional arrangements, interpretations and visitors (Heldt Cassel & Pashkevich, 2011).

The WH nomination is already a transformative process for many destinations, since specific rules and regulations regarding management are tied to this status. The promotion of tourism at WH sites is not only a matter of mobilizing support networks and institutions for managing the heritage, but also managing tourism destination development.

The relationship and interdependence between heritage and tourism is well-documented (Graham *et al.*, 2000; Ashworth, 2003). However, there is a fundamental difference in terms of ideological and institutional contexts between heritage tourism and general tourism (Garrod & Fyall, 2000). The most evident difference in policy concerning heritage sites may be illustrated by the classic divide between preservation and exploitation. This divide influences perspectives on what constitutes heritage and for whom it is intended. However, it is not absolute. In practice, tourism and heritage are often intertwined in the development of cultural tourism destinations (Prideaux & Kininmont, 1999; Ho & McKercher, 2004; Manson, 2008). The effects of tourism on heritage are contested, as tourism may provide resources for preservation and development, *yet also* cause deterioration of local traditions and environments. If overdeveloped, heritage tourism may even hamper socio-economic development at the destinations (Hampton, 2005; Gillespie, 2012).

However, tangible heritage resources such as buildings are not the only precondition to developing tourism. They must be conceptualized and packaged as part of creative and dynamic experiences to become successful commercial products (Richards, 2001). The emerging focus on creativity in tourism also implies that consumption is an active experience and the tourism product is based on individualized experiences and innovation. This calls for new angles for utilizing heritage resources within tourism and new interpretations of heritage that may become useful for commercial purposes.

The transformation of heritage meaning in tourism is an innovative process and has been described as a form of "creative destruction" (Hjalager *et al.*, 2008). New uses of old buildings, cultural resources and transformation of meaning are a form of product development when it comes to heritage tourism. One example of this is storytelling, where innovative stories help create new experiences. Storytelling may add value and change the content of tourism experiences in many different ways. It is closely related to the branding of destinations (Mossberg & Johansen, 2006).

According to Hjalager (2010), innovation research in tourism is a young phenomenon. She points at several research gaps considering different aspects of tourism innovation. One of these gaps is concerned with barriers to tourism innovation. Another is driving forces for innovation. This paper addresses these two fields of knowledge by examining preconditions for innovation in heritage tourism at Swedish WH sites. It discusses the role of regulations and institutions connected to WH status and innovation within heritage tourism product development and marketing. The paper also examines the role of local and regional institutional structures for innovative practices brought about by development of a WH tourism destination. Finally, this paper discusses driving forces for innovative product development within heritage tourism. This development occurs by re-imaging and reassessing heritage resources and institutional innovations from local re-organization and new collaborations. This is all driven by the UNESCO requirements for WH sites.

The aim of this paper is to discuss processes of innovation within heritage tourism. The focus is on the role of the WH status as a factor influencing innovative practices at different Swedish WH sites. Special attention is given to the case of the Great Copper Mountain in Falun. To what extent does the WH status change the preconditions for tourism development at WH destinations? What is the role of institutional frameworks at the local level?

Heritage tourism is actively developed in many peripheral or former industrial regions. This is a new potential for economic development and regeneration. Efforts to develop heritage tourism are often part of strategies to revalue the local culture and find new uses for old buildings and industrial landscapes (Ray, 1998). The symbolic transformation of landscapes and buildings from production to consumption and experiences is not always easy. This transformation is perhaps most evident in industrial heritage, since it involves reassessing former production landscapes and industrial objects (Silvén & Isacson, 1999). Restructuring the local economy from primary production or heavy industry towards service industries such as tourism highly depends on local resources and institutions, which may either support or hinder this development (Heldt Cassel & Pashkevich, 2011).

From the perspective of economic geography, industrial districts and innovation systems (Saxenian, 1994; Amin & Thrift, 1994; Storper, 1995), these restructuring processes seem to depend on the ability of stakeholders and networks to adapt and reorganize to meet the challenges of new economic activities (Bathelt & Boggs, 2003) such as heritage tourism (Heldt Cassel & Pashkevich, 2011).

2. Analytical Framework for the Study of WH Sites in Sweden

In recent years, debates about WH status as a driver of tourism growth have become more nuanced, and tourism is considered as not necessarily always leading to the sustainable use of the heritage (Smith, 2002; Garden, 2006; Landorf, 2009; Jimura, 2011). Several studies concluded that multiple stakeholder participation is an important element for sustainable, heritage tourism development (Aas *et al.*, 2005; Landorf, 2009). Heldt Cassel and

Pashkevich (2011) analyzed the role of stakeholder collaboration and institutional structures supporting tourism development at heritage sites. A recent study by Camison and Monfort-Mir (2012) suggested that organizational structures based on interaction and co-creation among several actors is, in fact, a type of institutional innovation. These structures are also able to facilitate diffusion in product development, if supported by necessary policies (Camison and Monfort-Mir, 2012, p. 787).

The current study utilizes qualitative methods in order to collect in-depth information concerning stakeholder participation and collaboration processes behind heritage management and also tourism product development at the WH sites in Sweden. The insights regarding the process of product development and innovations could be understood and evaluated based on information collected from the five Swedish WH sites. The secondary data concerning these sites consisted of marketing material found in various media sources, such as electronic media, newspapers and magazines. The five sites studied were the Church Town of Gammelstad in Luleå, the Great Copper Mountain in Falun, the Royal Domain of Drottningholm in Stockholm, the Hanseatic Town of Visby and the Naval Port of Karlskrona. These sites all represent part of Sweden's cultural heritage. Apart from the general overview of these WH sites, we also used a case study approach to obtain specific insights into the development processes at the WH site of the Great Copper Mountain of Falun, Sweden.

In-depth interviews with the main actors/stakeholders connected to the nomination and development process of the Great Copper Mountain in Falun served as a main method of investigation. The nomination process and further development of the Great Copper Mountain in Falun formed the basis for discussions regarding innovation processes taking place at the site. Fifteen interviews were conducted. The subjects were representatives from local and national bodies responsible for various aspects of handling site development. Representatives came from the following key organizations: the National Heritage Board, the County Administration Board, Falun Municipality, the Great Copper Mountain Trust, the regional museum of Dalarna and the destination management organization Södra Dalarna AB.

Interviews were conducted in 2007, with some follow-up interviews in 2012.The semi-structured interviews lasted between 40 and 80 min. The facilitators used a guide that included some principle questions, but allowed for respondents' own input and discussion. The interviews were digitally recorded with permission from the informants, who were guaranteed confidentiality.

Validation and support for the analysis of the situation at the Swedish WH sites came from relevant secondary data from published official documents, research papers and articles along with information from all 14 Swedish WH sites. Texts in English and Swedish were collected concerning the scenery presentation, exhibitions, consumption activities and additional information. Approximately 700 pages of written material were analyzed. The texts were organized into groups related to themes and topics, and a content analysis was then applied for structuring and interpreting the empirical material.

3. WH Status and Strategies of Marketing and Product Development

Recently, there has been substantial Swedish interest in heritage as a tool for destination development, especially when it comes to receiving WH status. The prime role of the UNESCO's WH Convention, adopted in 1972 and supported by 189 states as of March

2012, was preservation of the world's natural and cultural heritages that have universal value to humankind. In 1985, Sweden signed the UNESCO's convention concerning the Protection of the World Cultural and Natural Heritage. By doing so, Sweden agreed "to adopt a general policy that gave the cultural and natural heritage a function in the life of community and integrate the protection of that heritage into comprehensive planning programs" (UNESCO, Article 5, 1972). Sweden has since developed a well-functioning structure of heritage protection through the implementation of a new Heritage Conservation Act in 1998 (National Heritage Board, 2012). UNESCO's WH status has become increasingly used to raising international awareness, prestige and possible spin-offs based on the re-use of heritage for tourism development and local employment (Herbert, 1995; Ashworth & Tunbridge, 2000; Leask & Fyall, 2006; Turtinen, 2006). Getting added to the WH list is the most prestigious marker that a heritage destination can achieve, but this status must also be interpreted and filled with meaning at each of the heritage sites. The uses and impacts of the WH status and its importance for the economic development at various levels have been discussed in several studies (Leask & Fyall, 2006; Rakik & Chambers, 2008; Jimura, 2011).

For a very short time in the 1990s and early 2000s, 14 Swedish WH sites were added to the UNESCO's WH list. Table 1 lists these sites in chronological order of their inscription. Figure 1 locates all sites on the territory of Sweden following the same chronological order.

Table 1. Details of Swedish WH sites

WH site (year of WH inclusion in parentheses)

---

(1)   *The Royal Domain of Drottningholm* (two royal castles, theatre and park) (1991)

(2)   *Birka and Hovgården* (Viking trading sites from years 700 to 900AD) (1993)

(3)   *Engelsberg Ironworks* (ironworks with buildings and industrial equipment from eighteenth to nineteenth centuries) (1993)

(4)   *The Rock Carvings in Tanum* (prehistoric carvings dating to Bronze Age) (1994)

(5)   *The Woodland Cemetery/Skogskyrkogården in Stockholm* (cemetery combining buildings and landscapes created by two well-known architects, Asplund and Lewerentz, between 1914 and 1940) (1994)

(6)   *The Hanseatic Town of Visby* (remains of the middle ages Hanseatic town, with well-preserved parts, town wall and other architecture) (1995)

(7)   *The Church Town of Gammelstad* (traditional church town in northern Sweden) (1996)

(8)   *The Lapponia Area* (last big wilderness, nomadic area and representing a mixed WH sites) (1996)

(9)   *The Naval Port of Karlskrona* (naval base founded in 1680) (1998)

(10) *The Agricultural Landscape of Southern Öland* (agrarian landscape, including villages, pastures, etc.) (2000)

(11) *The High Coast* (natural WH sites, mountain formation with iso-static uplift as a result of deglaciation that exceeds other known examples) (2000)

(12) *Great Copper Mountain and Falun* (copper mountain with surrounding landscape from sixteenth to seventeenth centuries) (2001)

(13) *Grimeton Radio Station in Varberg* (wireless telecommunication centre from the period following First World War) (2004)

(14) *Struves Geodetic Arc* (a chain of survey triangulations carried out by the German astronomer Struve to establish the exact size and shape of the Earth) (2005)

Source: author's compilation.

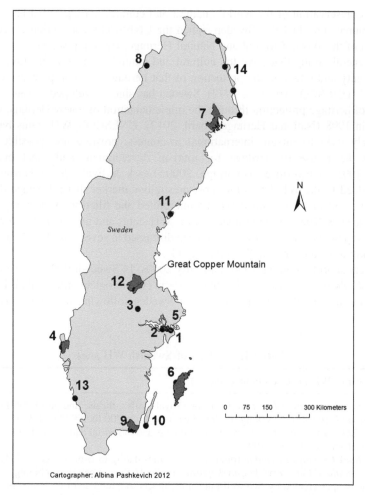

Figure 1. Sweden's 14 WH sites and the site of the Great Copper Mountain.
Source: Albina Pashkevich (2012).

By the end of the 1990s, when Sweden added nine nominations to the WH list, some researchers expressed concern that adding even more sites to this list would undermine the WH brand (Runesson, 2000). Despite the expressed concerns, by the mid-2000s, five more sites received the same status. Turtinen (2006) noted that negotiations to achieve a nomination to the WH list depended on controversies, networking with the experts and "diplomacy of the corridor talks and cocktail party discussions" (p. 107). WH status was generally granted to those places already receiving a considerable number of domestic and international visitors. In most cases, it was suggested that gaining the status of a WH site would be a quality stamp of a world-class destination (Magnusson & Karlsson, 2002, p. 36). The development of new or refined heritage tourism products at the Swedish WH sites is closely tied to the very fact that these sites transformed from places of local or national interest to an international arena.

Previous studies examined the tourism management and planning issues connected to nominating heritage sites and gaining WH status. Ronström (2008) highlighted the re-interpretation of heritage and the consequences for development of heritage tourism, with examples from the Hanseatic Town of Visby (see also Cedergren, 2009). Magnusson (2002) looked at the Church Town of Gammelstaden in Luleå (see also Magnusson & Karlsson, 2002). Alzén (2006) and Cedergren (2009) examined the Naval Port of Karlskrona. Several studies have also pointed out that the use of heritage is highly contested (Alzén, 2006; Ronström, 2008; Cedergren, 2009), and close cooperation among all involved may resolve many of the disputes concerning the ways these destinations develop.

3.1 *Appearance and Marketing of WH Sites as Unique and Valuable*

The way in which WH sites advertise themselves could be interpreted as local adaptations to destination development after the inscription to the WH list. The WH sites used in this study distinguished themselves from other tourist destination by using phrases such as "unique" or "a-one-of-a-kind-encounter". Moreover, texts presenting the heritage site often use phrases such as "exciting", "exotic", "extraordinary" or "impressive". Such promotion attempts to captivate potential visitors.

In this respect, information around the Church Town of Gammelstad is a very typical example, stressing that it is a "world-class attraction", "the biggest of its kind" and "outstanding and the best preserved" (Gammelstad, 2012). Many of the other studied sites use similar slogans and formulations in marketing texts. One of the reasons for using the superlatives and stressing these extraordinary qualities could be that the Swedish WH sites are remote in relation to other parts of Europe. Visitors to these remote locations need to be highly motivated and experienced in consuming these types of attractions.

The information and marketing materials' focus on the unique character and the intrinsic value of the WH sites is also connected to specific periods in time. This drawing on historical relevance and importance for the society at the time was one of the reasons for these sites to appear on the WH list, and they are presented as outstanding examples typical for a certain period in time (Turtinen, 2006, p. 60). Two of the sites specifically depict Swedish national identity and pride as a formerly strong military and industrial nation: the Naval Port of Karlskrona and the Great Copper Mountain in Falun.

These sites are also part of urban regeneration programmes, initiated by the Swedish state to compensate for the industrial decline hitting these areas. These revitalization campaigns, based on cultural or industrial heritage, took place during the 1980s and 1990s. They were supported by regional and local governments facilitating the utilization of cultural heritage for commercial purposes (Grundberg, 2000, 2002; Westin & Paju, 2003, Molin *et al.*, 2007). The WH status of the town of Karlskrona not only contributed to potential value creation within destination development, but also towards re-imaging the declining town and industrial area (Turtinen, 2006, p. 64). Large parts of historical buildings and the environment within the WH site are devoted to contemporary uses. The main goal with the WH destination of Karlskrona was to utilize the old character of the town in a functional way, rather than turning the site into an open-air museum.

The image of the Hanseatic Town of Visby is depicted in a similar way, especially emphasizing its "alive and attractive" character to its visitors. The concept of Visby as a "non-stop party town" adds further to this dimension (Ronström, 2008, p. 8). The marketing material yet again communicates the message that there is a value in everyday use of the heritage (Gotlandnet AB, 2012).

An important part of destination and product marketing at WH sites is developing ways to increase visitors' secondary spending. The focus is mostly on dining and shopping. All of the sites studied advertise a variety of choices. There is everything from the small pleasant café to the first-class restaurant serving "outstanding cuisine, top quality food", in the Old Town of Luleå and the Great Copper Mountain in Falun (see also Pashkevich & Boluk, 2010). Everything concerning the consumption of a meal supports the exclusive appeal of the WH site. After all, it is not necessary to visit the actual WH site to experience the genuine atmosphere of the attraction. All that is needed is to book a table at one of the restaurants with "excellent menus" "performing" "genuine food" and "crafting" (Gammelstad, 2012).

Shopping is another popular activity at WH sites. Visitors can buy "exclusive and original works of art" and "beautiful old objects" (Royal Palace of Drottningholm, 2012). The history of the heritage site becomes interconnected to the pieces of traditional craft made either by indigenous people (Sami), in the case of Old Town in Luleå, or professionals who have their workshops at the WH site (Gammelstad, 2012). The intention is to show that history and traditions are still alive. Phrases such as "extremely great values", "well-preserved remains of human activities" and "living tradition" act as markers for an outstanding quality of products created at these sites.

3.2 New Stories and Activities in Falun

As shown above, stories that help strengthen the idea of historical significance and international connection are an important part of destination marketing for the five WH sites. This is particularly apparent for the WH in Falun. According to the WH coordinator in Falun (interview March 2012), the WH status added a new dimension in tourism development activities; namely a new type of storytelling used to market and sell this site to visitors. The stories show historical representations of Falun and the people that used to live there, and add to the notion of Falun as historically valuable both nationally and internationally. The WH status has boosted the process of storytelling and helped broaden an audience and further facilitated reconnection of Falun's history to international and global economic and cultural processes. Interviewees gave other examples of storytelling in order to refine old guided tours. One example was how the guided tours at the mine and the surrounding residential neighbourhoods developed via engagement of non-profit organizations such as the local history society. One of these is a popular "ghost tour", which is not recommended for young children (Interviews with representatives from regional tourism board and regional museum of Dalarna).

One of the largest events during the summer months is "Falun then (Falun Då)", with direct connection to the history of the development of Falun as a mining town. There are guided tours, including drama, street theatres, music and exhibitions. These history days were organized by the regional museum of Dalarna, together with the non-profit organization "Friends of Falun". This storytelling through cultural events was very much in line with UNESCO's requirements for implementing information and educational services for the wider public, as well as informing visitors about other similar places around the world (interview with representative from Mining Museum). In the early 2000s, educational campaigns targeting school teachers were also set up by the regional museum of Dalarna to raise the awareness about the values supported by UNESCO's WH Convention. Schoolchildren at high schools, gymnasiums and primary schools were also targeted. Visits to the mine and the Great Copper Mountain became parts of courses on local history in schools. Children can experiment and test their knowledge on everything from mining to engineering at the Technical Workshop (Figure 2).

Another development that added yet another dimension towards further product development was commodification of Gamla Staberg, one of the three parts of Falun WH. It is a master miner's estate located 10 km east of Falun. The baroque gardens of Gamla Staberg were restored in 1999, and it changed owners several times since then. Nowadays, it has become a popular place for visitors to the well-known restaurant, summer café and beautiful old gardens (Gamla Staberg, 2012). Visitors get something extra as part of the meal experience at the café. They do not necessarily know that the café is actually a part of the WH site, but when they find out, it adds extra value to their visit. As the WH coordinator of Falun stated:

> Suddenly they [the visitors] are a part of something bigger, a context that was not known for them prior their visit. All of a sudden it is not only a cup of coffee with a cake that they enjoy while spending their time, they also become visitors at one of the best preserved historical environments of Sweden.

The managers at Gamla Staberg developed new products that were not only connected to the historical context of the site or the baroque garden, but also targeted other interest groups, such as owners of the vintage British cars (Goodoldengland, 2012). This opened up the WH site to completely new markets and audiences.

Figure 2. Buildings at the Great Copper Mountain visiting area.
Source: author's image (2012).

Product development based on the WH site in Falun from the beginning mostly focused on the mine as an entry point for visitors. Efforts were made to raise public awareness about the WH value. In 2002, a visitors' centre was built at the mine where the connections between all parts of the heritage in Falun are explained and exemplified and general information concerning the UNESCO's WH sites is made available. Recently, major development efforts and new tourism products are now focused on tightening and unifying the different parts of the heritage to make it more salable.

However, the WH status also called for restrictions on certain activities. A WH site has rules and regulations regarding preservation of the heritage resources for future generations. Preservation of the mining landscape and the mine itself is extremely costly. The management organization (the Trust) is mainly focused on preserving the heritage, not developing tourism products (Heldt Cassel & Pashkevich, 2011). According to the managers from the Trust, some of the ideas put forth regarding event and adventure activity development were stopped due to risk of accidents and the site being damaged and destroyed by visitors. Instead, the site has focused on activities targeting corporate businesses, including conferencing and, dining, as well as appreciation of the historical buildings around the site (Figure 3).

The five studied Swedish WH sites represent a broad spectrum of different ways to make use of the heritage. Apart from focusing on the core product, almost all the sites are also actively promoting visitors' secondary spending. They use a variety of strategies to maximize their profits from tourism. These activities could have an exotic (Medieval Week in Visby) or even exclusive (Church Town and Great Copper Mountain) touch.

Figure 3. Part of the mining area with one of the highest shaft head buildings to the left.
Source: author's image (2012).

However, they quite often are confined to activities that do not allow visitors their own interpretation of the heritage at the site (guided tours at the Great Copper Mountain and Naval port of Karlskrona) or to construct their own experiences (Alzén, 2006; Heldt Cassel & Mörner, 2011). Handcraft shops and shopping for other exclusive items are also part of this development, as well as tailor-made corporate programmes and study visits confined to the sites. Exclusive dining and coffee shops add yet another dimension towards further product development at the sites.

All sites strongly rely on their WH status for their marketing strategies. The status is used for branding and innovative marketing within destination development. Their main ambition is to create year-round destinations with a variety of activities for visitors, while also broadening visitor profiles. However, a successful development of heritage tourism destination is not just a matter of marketing and product development. A substantial part of the process is about organizational arrangements. The next section of the paper will focus on institutional innovations concerning cooperation among groups at the site.

4. Organizational Structure and Institutional Innovation at the WH Site of Great Copper Mountain in Falun

The Great Copper Mountain in Falun was added to the UNESCO WH list in 2001. This came about as a result of interest, negotiations and global politics, as well as mobilization of local resources and the formation of new organizational arrangements. A few requests from UNESCO had to be fulfilled for the site to achieve WH status (Turtinen, 2006). The institutions previously engaged in site preservation and management provided the necessary knowledge and capacity to make all of the necessary arrangements for Falun to become a WH site. These were well-established national and regional bodies such as the National Heritage Board, the County Antiquarian, representing the County Administrative Board and the regional museum of Dalarna. In addition, local competencies tied to the Mining Museum located on the mine in Falun ensured sustainable heritage preservation at UNESCO's request.

The institutions involved in the early process of planning and management for Falun's WH nomination provided and coordinated knowledge concerning protecting and safeguarding the mining heritage's material values. Organizations, including the Great Copper Mountain Trust (hereafter the Trust), the municipality of Falun (led by the mayor of Falun), and senior managers from the regional destination management organization handled other parts of heritage management. This included maintenance, tourism planning and information. More detailed descriptions of the specific functions of each actor in this process can be found in Heldt Cassel and Pashkevich (2011, pp. 62–64). All these institutions and stakeholders formed a collaborative network to pursue WH status and ensure sustainable management of the site. This new form of collaboration and resource and competency mobilization resulted in the Falun receiving WH status in 2001. One of the representatives from the Heritage Board in Falun further explains:

Somehow, everyone knew that we were going to succeed with this (nomination). Those who worked with the nomination had put all of their personal beliefs into this process. Swedes are especially well-suited in complying with rules set up by the UNESCO's WH Committee while applying for the nomination due to their ability to present things in a correct matter, the way others want us to do. We are good at obeying the rules and it fits that part of the Swedish mentality.

It should be noted that not all nomination procedures go as smoothly as the one in Falun. One of the 2005 Swedish nominations to the WH list, the "Farms of Hälsingland" had a delayed nomination process due to the absence of well-established organizational structure and weak local support networks, with no prominent actor leading tourism development (Westlund, 2011). Although playing by the rules of a specific code adopted behind the scenes at UNESCO's meetings could speed up the nomination process (as in the Swedish High Coast nomination, discussed in Turtinen, 2006, p. 96), it is vital to present a functioning organizational structure and solid planning for how the potential site would be administered.

One of the study interviewees described the role of all the actors trying to facilitate the WH site in Falun:

We have managed to tear down lots of barriers and old-fashion thinking among these actors. It is very important to have all of them sitting together in order to combine the sometimes contradicting notions of preserving the heritage, and at the same time being able to create new products for our visitors.

When the nomination to the WH list became a reality, one of the representatives from this organizational network group admitted that it was difficult to realize the full extent of the success with the nomination.

We became a part of something much bigger than we could imagine, we had a model that could be interesting for other World Heritage sites to follow. Actors in Falun had much better organisation and understanding on what should be done. But at the same time, one could say that nobody fully realised the whole range of obligations connected to the management of a World Heritage. Everyone only looked at the possibilities and maybe they were blinded by them.

Nomination work even influenced the involvement of other local representatives from the tourism industry (hotel and restaurants owners, etc.). The common efforts to create an organization that could meet UNESCO's requirements resulted in a direct growth within the Falun tourism industry. The tourism industry had grown by 20% in 2002, in comparison to 2001 (when the Great Copper Mountain appeared on the list of WH sites). The executive director of the major destination management organization in Dalarna evaluated the results of this success:

One should be humble for success, but at the same time we should feel proud... We started the whole range of activities connected directly to the World Heritage in Falun. This will become a factor for the sustained growth for us. (Falu Kommun, 2003)

Nowadays there are some 900–1000 persons visiting the mine in Falun every day during the summer season, which is also the busiest time of the year for the business (communication with WH coordinator, June 2012). The mine experienced a considerable growth in the number of visitors taking part in the various events and activities since the year 2007, when visitors to the mine numbered 219,000 people. This has grown by 30% in the year 2011 with some 285,000 visitors visiting the site annually (communication with WH coordinator, July 2012).

Representatives from the Falun WH site organization concluded that their cooperation and mobilization of knowledge and resources was one of the key factors leading to nomination. The network also allowed them to continue to work together while utilizing the promise of the WH brand. From the practitioners' point of view, tourism development depended on continually upgrading and re-inventing the tourist product for different categories of visitors. However, tourism industry representatives expressed their concerns that this process became more complex, as those involved in preservation issues were sometimes reluctant to changes involving commercialization and increasing visitor numbers.

The institutional structure created to successfully nominate Falun to the WH list has been slightly modified since then. The municipality of Falun, realizing the potential of tourism development in the area, created a WH coordinator position in 2002, right after the nomination. The coordinator's main tasks are to facilitate marketing efforts of the regional tourist organization that is partly owned by the municipality (nowadays called Södra Dalarna AB). Furthermore, the coordinator must approve all visitor information regarding the WH in Falun. This person is also responsible for managing contacts with the National Heritage Board, other Swedish WH sites and the Nordic WH Foundation, as well as handling regular contact with UNESCO's Heritage Committee when it makes periodic inspections concerning the preservation of the site.

It became obvious that the nomination process was only a first step towards realizing WH tourism destination potential. Many people with different interests complicated the destination development of the WH site, where no particular person took full responsibility for reaching specific goals (Interview with representative from the regional museum of Dalarna). There are varying views on how to manage heritage tourism (Heldt Cassel & Pashkevich, 2011). At the same time, many tourism developers noted that it is vital to reach a balance between a correct interpretation of the past and what visitors and customers require, in order to properly commodify the history of the mine and its surroundings.

It is clear that the joint efforts of several large organizations made it possible for Falun to become a WH site. According to the WH coordinator, the institutional setting around the site in Falun became a model of organizational arrangements and cooperation for the rest of the Swedish WH sites. The organizational network set up to meet UNESCO's requests can be seen as an institutional innovation driven by WH site regulation and policies. Once given WH status, the same organizational arrangement continued to work, not only for preservation of heritage, but also for managing tourism development.

Still, in this respect it is important to point at the role of the Trust and its managers at the WH site. The historically close relationship between the Trust and the company Stora Enso makes it difficult to influence the image of being financially well-off, which is not really the case as the maintenance of the site is indeed a costly process. The real estate manager at the mine highlights the fact that "We are a private actor that takes care of the site of the universal importance and one would expect an investment plan from other large players, such as the municipality of Falun". However, up until today the delivery of the financial support has not been organized on a regular basis. Moreover, over time, the mine became a public space that could be used by the local inhabitants, and is looked upon as a service provider in the same way as any public organization is in Sweden.

Yet, another downside of having many actors involved in the decision-making process is that "one cannot take decisions without thinking of the consequences concerning all of the involved parties and this gets frustrating sometimes" (Personal communication with the real estate manager at the mine, September 2010). This means that the actors need to continue working together on developing the brand of the WH site in Falun, as the destination development process faces new challenges every day.

5. Concluding Discussion

This paper has shown how WH status may facilitate tourism innovation through developing new products and marketing strategies, but also how new collaboration and networks can develop and manage WH tourism destination. The role of the WH status is mainly related to national and international importance, and values ascribed to the WH sites through UNESCO policies and regulations.

However, a great amount of work should be done to inform visitors of these specific values. It is obvious that the Swedish WH sites have put a great deal of effort into doing just this. As the WH status lifted, these heritage sites to a level of national and international attention, the advertisement and marketing effort had to be adjusted. This important and valued discourse indirectly influences marketing efforts and the type of products offered at the sites. Becoming a WH site is often thought of as something that will automatically increase the number of visitors, mainly those interested in exclusive (and more expensive) consumption experiences. This vision can be seen in the WH site marketing and information material. The targeted market segments in all the sites studied seem to be the more affluent groups in society. Visitor centres with souvenir shops, exclusive handicrafts, cafés and fine dining are all common at the WH sites.

The WH status awarded to the Great Copper Mountain of Falun was a result of cooperation. It is possible to conclude that Falun's cultural heritage helped develop a more complete tourism destination after its nomination as a WH site. The tourism products have been refined and value has been added through the cooperation of commercial and non-commercial entities and their common efforts of storytelling in different forms. These include: guided tours for many different audiences; stories through films; signboards at the visitor's centre and storytelling connected to different parts of the heritage sites, including restaurants and open gardens.

However, tourism activities at the mine are being restricted by regulations imposed by the national heritage institutions focused on preservation. These restrictions are particularly important, since they are also supported by UNESCO's WH Convention. The balance between preservation and commercialization is an ongoing issue where stakeholders have different opinions on how to best manage the site. However, the fact that Falun is a WH site is not its main challenge regarding further development of tourism products. It is possible to conclude that it is not always easy to combine tourism and heritage preservation, as in the case of the Great Copper Mountain in Falun.

The WH status is used for branding and promotes innovative thinking within destination development. This is most evident in Falun, with new forms of collaboration to manage the WH site and meet UNESCO's requirements. These new organizations were created as a direct consequence of the WH nomination. This has led to development and practice changes within the destination management organization in Falun. More stakeholders than before are now engaged in managing heritage tourism, and WH status has raised the interest for tourism activities among businesses and public administration in Falun.

References

Aas, C., Ladkin, A. & Fletcher, J. (2005) Stakeholder collaboration and heritage management, *Annals of Tourism Research*, 32(1), pp. 28–48.

Alzén, A. (2006) Demokrati och kultur-varv, in: A. Alzén & P. Aronsson (Eds) *Demokratiskt Kulturarv: Nationella Institutioner, Universella Värden, Lokala Praktiker*, pp. 139–163 (Lindköping: Linköping University, Electronic Press).

Amin, A. & Thrift, N. (Eds) (1994) *Globalization, Institutions, and Regional Development in Europe* (Oxford: Oxford University Press).

Ashworth, G. J. (1994) From history to heritage: From heritage to identity: in search of concepts and models, in: O. Svidén, G. Ashworth & P. Larkham (Eds) *Building a New Heritage: Tourism, Culture, and Identity in the New Europe*, pp. 13–30 (London: Routledge).

Ashworth, G. J. (2003) Heritage, identity and place: For tourists and host communities, in: S. Singh, D. J. Timothy & R. K. Dowling (Eds) *Tourism in Destination Communities*, pp. 79–98 (Wallingford: CABI).

Ashworth, G. J. & Tunbridge, J. E. (2000) *The Tourist-Historic City: Retrospect and Prospect of Managing the Heritage City*, 2nd ed. (Amsterdam: Pergamon).

Bathelt, H. & Boggs, J. (2003) Towards a reconceptualization of development paths: Is Leipzig's creative industries cluster continuation of or a rupture with the past? *Economic Geography*, 79(3), pp. 265–293.

Camison, C. & Monfort-Mir, V. (2012) Measuring innovation in tourism from the Schumpeterian and the dynamic-capabilities perspectives, *Tourism Management*, 33(4), pp. 776–789.

Cedergren, P. (2009) Fysisk Planering I Världsarv – Exemplen Falun, Karlskrona och Visby. Thesis: Blekinge Tekniska Högskola.

Falu Kommun (2003) Succéår för Besöksnäringen i Falun. Available at http://www.falun.se/NäringslivsAktuellt (accessed 20 January 2012).

Gamla Staberg (2012) Om Gamla Staberg. Available at http://www.stabergrestaurang.se/om-gamla-staberg/ (accessed 9 March 2012).

Gammelstad (2012) Mer om Kyrkstaden. Available at http://www.lulea.se/gammelstad (accessed 20 January 2012).

Garden, M. (2006) The heritagescape: Looking at landscapes of the past, *International Journal of Heritage Studies*, 12(5), pp. 394–411.

Garrod, B. & Fyall, A. (2000) Managing heritage tourism, *Annals of Tourism Research*, 27(3), pp. 682–708.

Gillespie, J. (2012) Buffering for conservation at Angkor: Questioning the spatial regulation of a World Heritage property, *International Journal of Heritage Studies*, 18(2), pp. 194–208.

Goodoldengland (2012) Good Old England. Welcome. Available at http://www.goodoldengland.se (accessed 20 April 2012).

Gotlandnet AB (2012) Besöksmål Visby Innerstad. Available at http://www.gotland.net/sv/att-gora/besoksmal-gotland (accessed 20 April 2012).

Graham, B., Ashworth, J. G. & Turnbridge, J. E. (2000) *A Geography of Heritage. Power, Culture and Economy* (London: Arnold).

Grundberg, J. (2000) *Kulturarvsförvaltningens Samhällsuppdrag: En Introduktion till Kulturarvsförvaltningens Teori och Praktik*, 33, Department of Archaeology, Gothenburg: Gothenburg University.

Grundberg, J. (2002) *Kulturarv, Turism and Regional Utveckling* Report 2002:9, Östersund: European Tourism Research Institute.

Hampton, P. (2005) Heritage, local communities and economic development, *Annals of Tourism Research*, 32(3), pp. 735–759.

Harrison, D. & Hitchcock, M. (Eds) (2005) *The Politics of World Heritage: Negotiating Tourism and Conservation* (Clevedon: Channel View Publications).

Heldt Cassel, S. & Mörner, C. (2011) A legacy of mining: Visual representations and narrative constructions of a Swedish heritage tourist destination, *Tourism, Culture & Communication*, 11(1), pp. 1–15.

Heldt Cassel, S. & Pashkevich, A. (2011) Heritage tourism and inherited institutional structures: The case of Falun Great Copper mountain, *Scandinavian Journal of Hospitality and Tourism*, 11(1), pp. 54–75.

Herbert, D. (Ed.) (1995) *Heritage, Tourism and Society* (London: Mansell).

Hjalager, A-M. (2010) A review of innovation research in tourism, *Tourism Management*, 31(1), pp. 1–12.

Hjalager, A-M., Huijubens, E., Nordin, S., Flagestad, A. & Knutsson, Ö. (2008) *Innovation Systems in Nordic Tourism* (Oslo: Nordic Innovation Centre).

Ho, P. S.Y. & McKercher, B. (2004) Managing heritage resources as tourism products, *Asia Pacific Journal of Tourism Research*, 9(3), pp. 255–266.

Jimura, T. (2011) The impact of world heritage site destination on local communities: A case study of Ogimachi, *Shirakawa-mura, Japan, Tourism Management*, 32(2), pp. 288–296.

Jones, R. & Shaw, B. (Eds) (2007) *Geographies of Australian Heritages: Loving a Sunburnt Country?* (Aldershot, England: Ashgate).

Landorf, C. (2009) Managing for sustainable tourism: A review of six cultural World Heritage Sites, *Journal of Sustainable Tourism*, 17(1), pp. 53–70.

Leask, A. & Fyall, A. (Eds) (2006) *Managing World Heritage Sites* (London: Elsevier/Butterworth-Heinemann).

Lowenthal, D. (1985) *The Past is a Foreign Country* (Cambridge: Cambridge University Press).

Magnusson, T. (2002) *Världsarv och Turism: de Svenska Världsarven ur ett Turistiskt Perspektiv* (Östersund: European Tourism Research Institute).

Magnusson, T. & Karlsson, E. (2002) *Gammelstads Kyrkstad: en Undersökning av Besökarna i ett Världsarv* (Östersund: European Tourism Research Institute).

Manson, R. (2008) Be interested and beware: Joining economic valuation and heritage conservation, *International Journal of Heritage Studies*, 14(4), pp. 303–318.

Molin, T., Müller, D., Paju, M., and Pettersson, R. (2007) *Kulturarvet och Cntreprenören – om Nyskapat Kulturarv i Västerbottens Guldrike (Cultural Heritage and Entrepreneur – Newly Created Heritage in Västerbotten's Gold of Lappland), Riksantikvarieämbetet*, Report No. 2007:5, Stockholm.

Mossberg, L. & Johansen, E. N. (2006) *Storytelling - Marknadsföring i Upplevelseindustrin* (Lund: Studentlitteratur).

National Heritage Board (2012) Riksantikvarieämbetes Historia. Available at http://www.raa.se/cms/extern/vart_uppdrag/var_historia.html (accessed 15 April 2012).

Nora, P. (2001) Mellan minne och historia, in: S. Sörlin (Ed.) *Nationen Röst: Texter om Nationalismens Teori och Praktik*, pp. 365–394 (Stockholm: SNS Förlag).

Pashkevich, A. & Boluk, K. (2010) Projecting Images: Marketing in the Case of two World Heritage Sites in Sweden. Paper presented at ATLAS conference, Limassol, Cyprus, November 3–5.

Prideaux, B. & Kininmont, L-J. (1999) Tourism and heritage are not strangers: A study of opportunities for rural heritage museums to maximize tourist visitation, *Journal of Travel Research*, 37(3), pp. 299–303.

Rakik, T. & Chambers, D. (2008) World heritage: Exploring the tension between the national and the 'universal', *Journal of Heritage Tourism*, 2(3), pp. 97–110.

Ray, C. (1998) Culture intellectual property and territorial rural development, *Sociologia Ruralis*, 38(1), pp. 3–20.

Richards, G. (Ed) (2001) *Cultural Attractions and European Tourism* (Wallingford: CABI).

Ronström, O. (2008) A different land: Heritage production in the Island of Gotland, *The International Journal of Research into Island Cultures*, 2(2), pp. 1–18.

Royal Palace of Drottningholm (2012) Drottningholm Palace. Available at http://www.kungahuset.se (accessed 4 March 2012).

Runesson, L. (2000) Kulturarvets Symboliska Kraft. Available at http://mainweb.hgo.se/Forskning/kulturarv2001.nsf (accessed 15 April).

Saxenian, A. (1994) *Regional Advantage: Culture and Competition in Silicon Valley and Route 128* (Cambridge, MA: Harvard University Press).

Silvén, E. & Isacson, M. (Eds) (1999) *Industriarvet i Samtiden* (Stockholm: Nordiska Museets Förlag).

Smith, M. (2002) A critical evaluation of the global accolade: The significance of World Heritage site status for Maritime Greenwich, *International Journal of Heritage Studies*, 8(2), pp. 137–151.

Storper, M. (1995) The resurgence of regional economies, ten years later: The region as a nexus of untraded interdependencies, *European Urban and Regional Studies*, 2(3), pp. 191–221.

Timothy, D. & Boyd, S. (2003) *Heritage Tourism* (New York: Pearson Education).

Turtinen, J. (2006) *Världsarvets Villkor: Intressen, Förhandlingar och Bruk i Internationell Politik* (Stockholm: Stockholm University). Available at http://urn.kb.se/resolve?urn=urn:nbn:se:su:diva-1248 (accessed 1 January 2012).

UNESCO (1972) Convention Concerning the Protection of the World Cultural and Natural Heritage Article 5. Available at http://whc.unesco.org/en/conventiontext (accessed 15 February 2012).

Westin, L. & Paju, M. (2003) Bidrar det svenska kulturarvet till regionernas attraktivitet? *PLAN*, 4(2003), pp. 17–21.

Westlund, J. (2011) Hård Kritik mot det Stora Hälsingegårdsprojektet. Hälsingland/Söderhamns-Kuriren, 4 June. Available at http://helahalsingland.se/halsingland/1.3672319 (accessed 15 April 2012).

Beyond the Transfer of Capital? Second-Home Owners as Competence Brokers for Rural Entrepreneurship and Innovation

INGEBORG NORDBØ

Department of Business Administration and Computer Sciences, Faculty of Arts and Science, Telemark University College, Bø, Norway

ABSTRACT *The current paper addresses the possible role of second-home owners as competence brokers in terms of rural entrepreneurship and innovation. Empirically, the paper draws on a case study of second-home owners from two municipalities in Telemark, one of the regions with the highest densities of second homes in Norway. Data were collected using a semi-structured questionnaire on 2200 second-home owners and with a response rate of 43% and 47%, respectively. The study results show that the second-home owners demonstrate in different ways a genuine interest in their second-home community, and also a willingness to use their knowledge and competence to contribute to the development of the local economy. Furthermore, we have also seen that an impressive number of second-home owners are educated to a higher level, within a variety of industrial fields and sectors, and have extensive managerial and hands-on experience from establishing and developing companies: in other words, they have both the interest and willingness and the required skills and experiences to become important competence brokers for local entrepreneurship and innovation.*

1. Introduction

The branding of tourism and second homes as an opportunity for rural development and revitalization is deeply embedded in Norwegian discourses on regional and rural policies. Langdalen (1980) argues that second homes, as a means of spurring rural economic development, dates back to the beginning of the 1960s when the proposal for Norwegian membership in the European Economic Community (EEC) raised a debate over the consequences of land ownership that had been opened to people from other EEC member countries. A comprehensive study was initiated which resulted in three main objectives for second-home planning in Norway, where one of those objectives was for second homes to stimulate the local economy in the remote rural districts (Langdalen, 1980, p. 139). Second homes have primarily become a strategy for economic development, business opportunities and diversification of traditional sectors such as farming and fishing (Farstad, 2008; Hidle *et al.*, 2010; Overvåg & Berg, 2011). The focus of second-home tourism as a catalyst for rural economic development is also highly reflected in the Norwegian research literature on second homes. To a great extent, this literature has focused on empirical analyses of how the "construction" and "use" of second homes (including maintenance and local consumption) might strengthen the local rural economy (Velvin *et al.*, 2000; Ericsson & Grefsrud, 2005; Farstad, 2008). Theoretically, this approach is often referred to as the "capital-transfer perspective" as it focuses on the transfer of capital from the place of residence to the second-home community (Ericsson *et al.*, 2005).

Labrianidis (2004) argues that two highly interrelated elements are characteristic for the economic picture of rural areas in Europe; namely, the dominance of small and microscaled businesses and the entrepreneurial capacity of the local population as the primary motivators for economic growth. However, limited job opportunities and economic decline have led to falling populations and the out-migration of the most educated in many locations and thus a growing concern about how to build a critical mass of rural entrepreneurship (Butler & Clark, 1992; OECD, 1994; Long & Lane, 2000; Labrianidis, 2004).

Recently, therefore, some researchers have been debating if second-home owners can be seen as a type of semi-immigrant that could be part of, or help to build, the critical mass of rural entrepreneurship and innovation. It is assumed that second-home owners might have a sort of loyalty and attachment to the destination other than as ordinary tourists, since they return to the same location, often spending long periods of time there. Furthermore, apart from capital, second-home owners may possess resources such as professional (expert and financial) networks.

The debate has been further fuelled by the increased standard of second homes, the introduction of six weeks' holiday, and improved technology and greater flexibility at work that have allowed for more extensive and frequent use of the recreational homes (Kaltenborg, 1998; Taugbøl *et al.*, 2001; Arnesen, 2003; Ericsson *et al.*, 2005). However, from a European perspective, the claim that second homes are major drivers of economic and social change in rural areas is highly contested (Gallent *et al.*, 2005). On the contrary, the few empirical studies that have been undertaken in other European countries tend to illustrate that second-home owners are reluctant to undertake tasks or become involved in the second-home community that disturbs the "recreational modus" or remind them about obligations and work situation in their ordinary everyday life (e.g. Hiltunen, 2004). Ericsson *et al.* (2005) also admit that systematic knowledge about what they label the "transfer of competence" perspective (as opposed to the "capital-transfer" perspective) is missing.

The above controversies form the backdrop for this paper, which addresses the role of second-home owners as competence brokers in terms of rural entrepreneurship and innovation. The paper's literature review identifies and discusses key properties and elements related to the concept of competence, its close relationship with the concept of knowledge, and elements of, and requirements for, competence and knowledge transfer. The paper then presents the result of an empirical investigation of 2200 second-home owners in Telemark, one of the counties with the highest density of second homes in Norway.

The study maps relevant competences of the second-home owners such as education, managerial and entrepreneurial experiences and also their willingness to participate in processes and forums of knowledge transfer in their second-home community, e.g. their willingness to be mentors for local entrepreneurs or sit in on local companies' boards. A main hypothesis is that the second-home owners might possess the necessary competences in order to contribute to local development in their second-home community, but if they are not willing to take on a more active role in terms of knowledge transfer, the debate regarding second-home owners as competence brokers for rural entrepreneurship and innovations is rather futile. The paper, thus, also links the relationship between the competences of the second-home owners and their willingness to participate to local community development both more generally and within a number of specific areas. Finally, the paper frames and discusses the "capital-transfer" perspective and the "competence-transfer" perspective within the wider context of contemporary changes within policies and theories for rural development.

2. Competence and Knowledge Transfer

A search within international and national journals and books revealed no paper or study that empirically or theoretically addresses the role of second-home owners as competence brokers specifically, nor the "transfer of competence" perspective as labelled by Ericsson *et al.* (2005) more generally. In general, research on aspects of competence and knowledge has been notably less marked in tourism than in other sectors of the economy (Stamboulis & Skayannis, 2003; Cooper, 2006; Xiao, 2006; Shaw & Williams, 2009). In terms of emerging areas of research on competence and knowledge in tourism, unsurprisingly most to date is found within the field of business and management (Yang & Wan, 2004; Cooper, 2006; Hallin & Marnburg, 2008; Shaw & Williams, 2009; Thomas, 2011), innovation and networks (Hjalager, 2002, 2010; Novelli *et al.*, 2006) and recently also within the field of rural tourism (Hernández-Maestro *et al.*, 2009; Brandth *et al.*, 2010). Most of the papers within the business and management-oriented research deal with issues of knowledge management and transfer, and most of the empirical studies embodied, according to Shaw and Williams (2009), are from the hospitality sector and larger firms, mainly hotels. This, however, contrasts with Thomas's observations (2011, p. 2), who in terms of knowledge transfer in tourism argues that: "Much of what has been undertaken to date has been concerned with smaller enterprises, destination development or both ... Little, if any, research has involved larger tourism enterprises".

Within the field of rural tourism research, we see a tendency to focus more on personal characteristics. This can be seen in the study of Hernández-Maestro *et al.* (2009), which highlights the knowledge of the entrepreneurs as a source of competitive advantage; or the study by Brandth *et al.* (2010), which focuses on farm-tourist hosts and who they are in terms of education and competence.

According to Jacobson (2007), a framework is a representation of key theoretical concepts and their underlying structures, and is often designed to facilitate the practical application of theoretical ideas. In this respect Cooper's (2006) model for knowledge management for tourism highlights, some important aspects of which two overreaching lines of thoughts were used to structure the point of reference for the empirical research undertaken. First of all, he pinpoints the need to map and capture the relevant knowledge, filtering out the irrelevant aspects. Second, he points to the flows of knowledge and the necessity of models for knowledge transfer. In terms of the first point, the management literature has given considerable emphasis to the types of knowledge available to organizations (Shaw & Williams, 2009). Some of the findings/research from the management literature was found fruitful in so far as mapping and capturing the relevant knowledge of second-home owners in the present study, and also in terms of identifying how knowledge relates to the concept of competence. Awad and Ghaziri (2004, p. 33) argue that knowledge is "understanding gained through experience or study". Cooper extends this understanding and adds an active element to the concept, arguing that broadly speaking knowledge can be defined as "the *use* of skills and experience, to add intelligence to information in order to make decisions or provide reliable grounds for action" (Cooper, 2006, p. 52).

Conceição and Heitor (1999) distinguish explicitly between knowledge and competence and argue that competence is a "higher order of skills" including higher levels of education, but also more generic capacities such as creativity, risk taking and initiative. Furthermore, in the management literature and adopted by a number of tourism researchers (Hjalager, 2002; Nordbø, 2009; Brandth *et al.*, 2010) much attention has been given to Polyani's (1958, 1966) distinction between tacit and codified knowledge, of which both are considered important to capture. Codified knowledge refers to knowledge that is transmittable in formal, symbolic language (know-that, as per formal education identified above), while tacit knowledge (know-how) is intuitive, hard to articulate and acquired through experience (Polyani, 1966; Edmondson *et al.*, 2003), or passed from master to apprentice (Cooper, 2006). Tacit knowledge is, therefore, considered more difficult to interpret and transfer from one individual to another, and since it is difficult to imitate it is also considered a key source of competitive advantage for many enterprises (Shaw & Williams, 2009). Cavusqil *et al.* (2003, p. 9) highlight that tacit knowledge can be found both at the individual level in particular skills, as well as within abstract forms and collectively which thus "typically resides in top management".

The second line of thought that relates to Cooper's (2006) model for knowledge management is the emphasis placed on models for knowledge transfer, or what Shaw and Williams (2009) refer to as the "vehicles of knowledge transfer". O'Hagan and Green (2004, p. 128) highlight that academics have revealed that the transfer of knowledge is dependent on the quality and quantity of social interaction between individuals. According to Bouwen (1998), relational knowledge refers to the construction of meaning that appears among social actors involved in generating and using knowledge. Social capital is closely connected to social networks and refers more precisely to a complex account of people's relationships and the ways in which social ties can be activated to produce particular types of benefits (Field, 2003, p. 136). Social capital can facilitate knowledge transfer, and it is the strength of individual relationships rather than the proximity which determines the effect outcome (Shaw & Williams, 2009).

In the undertaken research, it was, therefore, considered not only useful to map the competences of the second-home owners, but also to identify different models or vehicles of knowledge transfer and to map the willingness of the second-home owners to take part in such settings. Shaw and Williams (2009) highlight that the vehicles of knowledge transfer most relevant to tourism are those dealing with human mobility and networks. Conceição and Heitor (2002) have their departure in the concept of the learning economy as opposed to the knowledge economy. They argue that to enhance the processes of producing and exchanging knowledge through the build-up of learning and knowledge networks, these networks must follow local specific conditions to adapt, engage and mobilize local actors and agents.

Similarly, Shaw and Williams (2009, p. 329) point to three types of networks that they consider particularly relevant in terms of tourism: foreign direct investment (including interlocking directorships); cluster/learning regions; and communities of practice. Although their perspective is directed at the inter-organizational level, two of their networks were considered interesting in terms of identifying vehicles for knowledge transfer with relevance to the current study. This relates first and foremost to the "interlocking directorships" which, according to Mizruchi (1996, p. 271), occur when "a person affiliated with one organization sits on the board of directors of another organization". Interlocking directories are thus increasingly seen as an instrument of the transferral of tacit knowledge and the idea that directors can provide collective tacit knowledge that is critical to firm performance (Boyd, 1990). Mizruchi (1996, p. 284) and O'Hagan and Green (2004, p. 129) argue that the value of interlocks has changed from being a mechanism of control to becoming a mechanism of communication.

The second type of network, which was found to have some type of relevance in terms of the present research, is the concept of "communities of practice", again a concept that according to Shaw and Williams (2009) has been neglected within the tourism literature. Communities of practice, they argue, may take the form of a business community informally organized or more formal organizations.

3. Research Area

The empirical research underlying this paper was conducted among recreational home-owners in the mountainous regions of Telemark, an area located in south-east Norway. The municipalities of Tinn and Vinje were picked for case studies. According to Taugbøl et al. (2001), approximately one-third of the second homes in Norway are located in the counties of Hedemark, Oppland, Buskerud and Telemark, and about 40% of the increment in new second homes, most of which are in the mountains or inland, takes place in these regional counties.

In general, both Vinje and Tinn have a long and interesting history in terms of tourism development including second homes, and Rjukan, the municipality centre of Tinn, is often described as the cradle of tourism in Norway (Dahl, 2000). Vinje is a famous destination for cross-country skiing and The Rjukanfossen waterfalls in Maristujuvet Gorge were a famous tourist attraction until they were tamed at the beginning of the twentieth century to produce power for Norsk Hydro's new industry. However, as for many other rural mountain villages in Europe and Norway, Tinn and Vinje have witnessed a sharp decline in population since the 1960s mainly due to the decline in primary and industrial production. According to Overvåg and Berg (2011, p. 430), primary production employment in the mountain areas of eastern Norway has decreased by 28% since 1995. In Vinje, and Tinn especially, the restructuring and outsourcing of several of Hydro's core production lines, further accelerated the trend, and forced the municipalities to look for alternative sources of economic development.

During the last decades, attention has thus increasingly turned toward tourism, mainly the development of ski resorts, including the construction of a number of cabin plots and purpose-built holiday residents. As of 1998, the total number of second homes in Tinn was 1879; by January 2008, the number had increased to 2803. In Vinje, the number was 2873 in 1998 and 4165 in 2011 (Statistics Norway, 2011). The increasing size and standard of the second homes and external second-home ownership are characteristic of the development. Both the municipalities of Tinn and Vinje have also invested extensively in telecommunications and other infrastructural developments during the last years to facilitate more frequent and extended use of the second homes.

Overvåg and Berg (2011, pp. 430–433) argue that all in all, the rough picture is that large parts of the mountain municipalities in eastern Norway are experiencing simultaneous decline and ageing of the permanent population, combined with a decrease in primary industries, on the one hand, and a considerable increase in temporary in-migration of rather wealthy, middle-aged second-home owners, on the other. In these places they argue, and especially in those having a considerable tourist industry, second homes and recreation seem to expedite rural change.

The research underlying this paper was conducted in relation to the "Hyttefolk" project. This was a three-year (2007–2009) cooperation between the municipalities of Vinje and Tinn and Telemark County Council, within the framework of the cooperation among Telemark's mountain regions. The aim of the project was to look into second-home owners' contribution to local development both within and beyond the transfer of capital. All second-home plots in the municipality of Tinn were included in the study, while in Vinje, the study was concentrated on one cabin plot: that of the community of Øyfjell. Today, both Tinn and Vinje municipalities have many types of second homes. Øyfjell is one of the most remote communities in Vinje and the village have initiated several projects, among them Øyfjell City, to reverse the negative out-migration and to attract settlers and businesses to the village. The community has an extensive number of second homes and has recently started working with second-home owners to include them in the future economic development plans for the village.

4. Operationalization and Methodological Considerations

A semi-structured questionnaire, containing both quantitative and qualitative data facilitating a triangulation of methods, was used within the case areas (Walle, 1997). As discussed in Section 1, one of the main aims of the study was to map and capture the relevant competences of second-home owners in terms of their possible role as catalysts for rural entrepreneurship and innovation. In this respect, a synopsis of the literature review shows that emphasis is placed on capabilities related to formal education, managerial and business experiences and more generic capacities such as creativity, risk taking and initiative.

However, the more generic capacities of the competence concept were omitted from this study as they were considered to be rather difficult to measure empirically. To look into issues such as creativity and risk taking would imply a more qualitative and in-depth approach which would have been too expensive and time consuming, and also not consistent with the aim of a sample size of 2200 second-home owners. The codified knowledge of the respondents was thus mainly mapped through the formal education. This was divided into predefined categories related to the level of education (primary, secondary and tertiary, where tertiary refers to education at university and/or university college level); and through a mapping of the education related to position and industry sector. It was considered most relevant to map aspects of the more tacit knowledge of the owner/managers' current job titles and positions (predefined categories related to employed, top and middle management expertise) and their experiences with entrepreneurial activity (e.g. business start-ups/acquisition).

The second main aim of the study was, as formerly argued, to map the willingness of second-home owners to take on more active roles as competence brokers in terms of entrepreneurship and innovation in their second-home community. First, a specific question aimed at shedding light on the place attachment and the alleged willingness of the second-home owners to contribute to developing their recreational community was developed. Second, a specific question was introduced that related to a number of predefined vehicles of knowledge transfer, in accordance with the discussion of interlocking directories and communities of practice, as identified in the literature review.

The questionnaire provided both closed answers to facilitate quantitative comparison as well as an open field for qualitative comments and inputs. The qualitative comments provided important additional information and often clarified, specified and concretized the quantitative data. The recreational homeowners were contacted at their permanent addresses through a recreation home register maintained by the local municipalities' authorities. Second-home owners with residence in Tinn and Vinje were excluded. Correspondingly, 43% and 47% of all second-home owners in Øyfjell and Tinn with permanent addresses outside the municipalities returned the questionnaires at the first request. No further reminder was sent as we were only interested in getting in touch with those second-home owners who clearly demonstrated an interest and willingness to participate.

5. Tracing the Competence of Second-Home Owners

As argued above, one of the main aims of this study was to map and capture the relevant competences of second-home owners in terms of their possible role as catalysts for rural entrepreneurship and innovation. The following presents the main results related to the first part of the empirical study.

5.1 Age

Age was included in the analysis since it is natural to assume that different age groups have different motivations, competence and time/resources to assume responsibilities in terms of acting as competence brokers in the recreational community. Tacit knowledge is, as argued by Polyani (1966), acquired through experience where, in most situations, there is a correlation between experience and age. Furthermore, age might also be related to access to established networks and available time. The age distribution of the respondents is thus presented in Table 1.

We see that age distributes quite evenly between the two locations and that in both case areas more than one-third of the respondents are between 41 and 50 years old. Furthermore, in both locations the vast majority (88% in Tinn and 79% in Øyfjell) are between the ages of 41 and 69. This corresponds to other investigations in Norway which draw a picture of second-home owners as wealthy and middle-aged citizens (Overvåg & Berg, 2011). In tourism research, "empty nesters" are defined as couples where the children have left home (Swarbrooke & Horner, 2007), and are often described as an interesting segment since they possess less tight finances and more time at their disposal than, for example,

Table 1. Age distribution

	Tinn	Øyfjell
Age	%	%
<30	1	1
31–40	7	6
41–50	34	34
51–60	23	23
61–69	10	13
>70	1	2
Unanswered	1	2

Note: $N = 848$ in Tinn and $N = 182$ in Øyfjell.

families with younger children. We may thus highlight the fact that in the case of Tinn, 74% of the second-home owners who, as we will see later in Table 5, confirm that they are interested in contributing actively to development in their recreational community are within this age group. Moreover, among those >61, there will be a number of retired people who often spend longer periods of time in their recreational community, and who might have had long professional careers, including managerial or entrepreneurial experience, which potentially could be interesting in terms of knowledge transfer – we will return to this later.

5.2 *Gender*

It was also considered relevant to take into account the gender distribution of second-home owners in Tinn and Øyfjell as illustrated in Table 2.

We observe that the majority of the respondents are men (61% in Tinn and 57% in Øyfjell). There are probably various reasons for this, one being that the questionnaires were addressed according to who is registered in the municipal records as the owner of the property. Another reason might be that many of the questions directly focus on managerial and entrepreneurial experiences, which might have appealed more to the male of the household, given the fact that the majority of business leaders and board members in Norway still are men. In 2006, women constituted 47% of the work force in Norway, but only 29% of all managerial positions were held by women and among top management, the figure was only 23% (Statistics Norway, 2006a).We can, therefore, see that with reference to the vehicles of knowledge transfer the number of second-home owners who in Table 5 indicate that they would like to sit in on the board of a local company 80% are men.

Table 2. Gender distribution

	Tinn	Øyfjell
Gender	%	%
Male	61	57
Female	36	40
Unanswered	3	3

Table 3. Educational level

Educational level	Tinn	Øyfjell
	%	%
Primary	7	8
Secondary	27	32
Tertiary (University/university college)	64	56
Unanswered	2	4

5.3 Educational Level

The results for Tinn and Øyfjell with reference to the educational level according to the predefined categories as identified are shown separately in Table 3.

The chart illustrates that 64% of the respondents in Tinn and 56% of the respondents in Øyfjell have an educational level equivalent to university college or university. These numbers are interesting when compared to the general level of education in Norway where the equivalent is 28.3% (Statistics Norway, 2006b). For Tinn and Vinje for the same age group "only" 17% and 22%, respectively, hold a university or university college degree (Statistics Norway, 2008b). While other research has primarily demonstrated that second-home owners have higher incomes than the average population (Flogenfeldt, 2006; Vågane, 2006), this study demonstrates that it also relates to education.

5.4 Managerial and Entrepreneurial Experience

With reference to the findings related to managerial and entrepreneurial experience, the results are presented in Table 4.

The table illustrates that 48% of the second-home owners in Tinn have a managerial position in their current job, 15% of these as top management and 33% as middle managers. Furthermore, 22% of the second-home owners currently run their own company. In Øyfjell, we see that 50% of the second-home owners hold some kind of managerial position, but compared to Tinn, the percentage of top managers is lower. Furthermore, substantially fewer second-home owners in Øyfjell run their own company. The findings

Table 4. Managerial and entrepreneurial experiences

Managerial and entrepreneurial experiences	Tinn	Øyfjell
	%	%
Top manager	15	11
Manager	33	39
Own company	22	14
Employed	38	45
Other	10	13
Unanswered	6	8

Notes: Note that the figures in Table 4, 8 and 9 do not add up to 100% since it was possible to tick more than one box. For example, some of the second-home owners run their own company part time.

Table 5. Willingness to contribute to community development

	Tinn	Øyfjell
Willingness to contribute to local community development	%	%
Yes	17	14
No	39	41
Do not know	36	36
Unanswered	8	9

are interesting as they indicate that the second-home owners in both Øyfjell and Tinn have tacit knowledge in terms of managerial and entrepreneurial experiences, which could potentially benefit local businesses and entrepreneurs.

6. Second-Home Owners and Knowledge Transfer

6.1 *Willingness to Contribute to Local Community Development*

One of the central questions of the investigation was aimed at mapping whether the second-home owners were "at all" willing to take on an active role in the development of their second-home community. To increase the question's validity, we emphasized that the role should be "active", focusing on the municipality level and not the local cabin plots. We also emphasized the fact that it was not only development in terms of attractiveness as a second-home community, but also as in terms of a good place to live. Table 5 reveals the responses.

We can see that in Tinn 17% of the respondents confirm that they would like to become actively involved in community development, while 36% express that they are unsure and 39% do not want to participate. Although one could argue that at first glance 17% does not seem a lot, one has to remember that 17%, for example, equates to 141 respondents who would like to play an "active" role as agents for change in Tinn.

The second-home owners were, however, also asked to elaborate on why they wanted or did not want to take on an active role, and a total of more than 200 second-home owners completed this information, which allowed for the grouping of the qualitative feedback according to the answers "yes", "no" and "don't know". With reference to those who confirmed an interest in participating, the answers can be grouped according to five sub-categories.

(1) "A sense of belonging" includes a number of answers that express the strong attachment many second-home owners feel to the recreational community, as the following examples illustrate: "Because I want that people shall be able to see and 'know' about Øyfjell and how nice and good it is here".

(2) "Unexplored potentiality" indicating that some second-home owners feel that their recreation community has unexplored potential for development, for instance within tourism as this statement illustrate: "I think Tinn including Møsvann has great tourism and travel potential. Currently this is pretty badly exploited".

(3) "Second-home owners as a resource" referring to second-home owners who express that they long for the local inhabitants and municipality to see them as a resource

and not just as a nuisance: "We like both the people and the area, and we would like to be regarded as a resource, not just as 'second-home immigrants'".

(4) "Specific areas" includes a number of statements about specific areas in which the second-home owners want to participate: "Am very interested in food and culinary traditions. Can contribute quite a lot on the commercial side of things", or "Develop the Gvepseborg area to increase the traffic on Krossobanen".

(5) "Miscellaneous" embraced those arguments and comments which did not fit into the other four mentioned categories.

Clearly, these findings illustrate that a number of second-home owners have an interest in taking on a more active role as competence brokers in the recreational community, perceiving that they have the necessary knowledge and competence, or what they themselves in most cases label "resources". Furthermore, if we look into the qualitative comments related to the "do not" and "do not know" categories, we find a quite nuanced picture, where a number of the respondents indicate that they would like to contribute to development in or near the area of their cabin plot, but not in the municipality as such: "As second-home owners at Gvepseborg we would like to help develop the specific area".

6.2 *Vehicles for Knowledge Transfer*

The second main question related to competence transfer was, as stated, to try to grasp in which types of networking activities and what sort of cooperation the second-home owners were willing to participate. The respondents were asked to tick off their response according to a number of predefined vehicles of knowledge transfer in terms of rural entrepreneurship and innovation. Both the included categories and the second-home owners' responses are revealed in Table 6. In this respect, therefore, it is interesting to observe that quite a few of the respondents who answered "no" or "don't know" to the more general question in the former section (Table 5), have nevertheless ticked a number of the specific alternatives in Table 6.

From Table 6, we see that the second-home owners are indeed interested in becoming involved in different types of local networks and cooperation activities. On a more general basis, we see that 66 second-home owners in Tinn confirm that they would like to "make an effort to develop the local business life", 61 respondents are interested in "being a mentor to a local company" and 108 second-home owners would like to "be part of the board of a local company". According to Statistics Norway (2008a), there are a total of 137 companies in Tinn with more than 4 employees and we could thus argue that there are in fact enough interested second-home owners to sit in on most of these boards. On a more general basis, we see that the second-home owners are interested in contributing to establish new "local meeting arenas" (39 respondents in Tinn, four in Øyfjell).

Another category which was considered important in terms of knowledge transfer and local entrepreneurship and innovation was that of "moving or establishing your own company" with one respondent saying: "[I] have considered looking at the possibility of transferring parts of our business to Tinn". Thus, in Tinn, 26 second-home owners actually confirm such an interest, while in Øyfjell only one respondent ticked this category. For a small rural community such as Tinn, these numbers present an interesting possibility for business development, diversification and construction of the critical rural entrepreneurial

Table 6. Vehicles for knowledge transfer

Vehicles for knowledge transfer/areas of participation	Tinn		Øyfjell	
	Number	%	Number	%
Be a mentor for a local company	61	7	7	4
Be part of the board of a local company	108	13	9	5
Sit on a committee for local development	73	9	5	3
Make an effort to develop local business life	66	8	5	3
Move or establish your own company	26	3	1	1
Get involved in local political work	12	1.5	0	0
Participate in establishing local meeting arenas	39	5	4	2
Participate inlocal neighbourhood activities and collective work	92	11	27	15

Notes: $N = 848$ in Tinn and $N = 182$ in Øyfjell. It should be noted that in analysing the responses related to Table 6, it was considered more interesting to look at the total number of respondents within each category, than to look at the percentages in terms of the total respondents. When percentages are included, this is done in to allow a comparison between the two case areas. Indicated percentages are in relation to the total number of respondents.

mass. Speaking of which, a couple of second-home owners have actually taken the step and moved their company to Tinn.

It was also considered relevant for this study to look into the willingness and interest of second-home owners with respect to participating in local political networks, not the least since local political incentives and regulations lay important assumptions for the development of local businesses and entrepreneurs. On the more general basis, the second-home owners were asked about their willingness to "get involved in local politics", and more specifically their willingness to "sit in on committees for local development". From Table 6, therefore, we can see that 12 second-home owners have expressed a more general interest in getting involved in local political work in Tinn, against none in Øyfjell. Furthermore, 73 respondents in Tinn showed an interest in getting involved in "committees for local development", while in Øyfjell the number was 5. Apart from the category of "local neighbourhood activities and collective work" (92 respondents in Tinn, 27 in Øyfjell), we observe interestingly enough that for all the other categories the interest or will to participate is higher in Tinn than in Øyfjell.

6.3 Competences, Willingness and Participation Combined

As stated Section 1, the paper also sets out to link the relationship between the competences of the second-home owners and their willingness to participate in local community development. A number of cross-analyses were conducted to test these relationships. First of all, we mapped the level of education among the second-home owners who gave a positive response in Table 5. The results from this cross-analysis are presented in Table 7.

While there is no clear cut answers from Øyfjell, in Tinn we see that of the second-home owners willing to contribute to local community development, 78% has a university or university college degree. Bearing in mind that the general educational level among the second-home owners in this study was found to be very high compared to the national average, we see that this tendency seems to be even more accentuated in the cross-analysis.

Table 7. Relationship between education and participation willingness

Willingness combined with education	Tinn		Øyfjell	
	Sample (%)	Average in study (%)	Sample (%)	Average in study (%)
Primary	2	7	4	8
Secondary	19	27	32	32
Tertiary	78	64	56	56
Unanswered	1	2	8	4

Note: N = 169.

The managerial and entrepreneurial experiences of the second-home owners in the sample are summarized in Table 8.

The most notable finding from Table 8 is that the number of second-home owners that are "employed" decrease significantly compared to the average among the second-home owners in the two case areas (from 38% to 24% in Tinn and from 45% to 12% in Øyfjell). Correspondingly, the number of second-home owners who are either top managers, managers or run their own company increases. With reference to "top manager", we see an increase from 15% to 18% in Tinn and from 11% to 25% in Øyfjell. Among the second-home owners who run their own company there is an increase from 22% to 25% in Tinn and from 14% to 17% in Øyfjell. The percentage of second-home owners having a managerial position in Øyfjell also rose significantly (from 39% to 46%), while there is a decrease in Tinn (from 33% to 29%). Again, it seems that there is a clear correlation between willingness to participate to local community development and the second-home owners' competences, as expressed here through a managerial/entrepreneurial respondent's experiences: "It's always interesting to get involved in developments where we are. We have many ideas, thoughts and opinions, not to mention resources, which we could contribute".

To further test the relationship between the competences of the second-home owners and their willingness to participate, we also decided to map the managerial and entrepreneurial experience among the second-home owners in Tinn and Øyfjell, who in Table 5 ticked a number of the predefined vehicles for knowledge transfer. The vehicles picked for cross-analyses were "be part of the board of a local company", "be a mentor for a local company", "sit on a committee for local development", "make an effort to

Table 8. Relationship between managerial experiences and participation willingness

Managerial and entrepreneurial experiences	Tinn		Øyfjell	
	Sample (%)	Average in study (%)	Sample (%)	Average in study (%)
Top manager	18	15	25	11
Manager	29	33	46	39
Own company	25	22	17	14
Employed	24	38	12	45
Other	2	10	0	13
Unanswered	0	6	0	8

develop local business life" and "participate in establishing local meeting arenas". The findings are presented in Table 9.

Table 9 is thus highly interesting as it demonstrates a clear correlation between the managerial and entrepreneurial experiences of the second-home owners and their specific areas of interest(s) in terms of participation. In this respect, we see for instance that a strikingly high number of second-home owners, who are willing to be a part of the board of a local company or to be a mentor for a local company, are top managers (respectively, 35% and 38%), while only 17% and 16%, respectively, are "employed". Furthermore, we also see that among those second-home owners who want to make an effort to develop local business life, 44% run their own company. Furthermore, company owners are well represented (35%) among those who want to sit on a committee for local development.

With reference to the more general question of participation in establishing local meeting arenas, we see that the number of employed is quite a bit higher than for the other vehicles presented (65%). Analysing the qualitative comments related to this alternative, reveals that there are basically two reasons for this: first, to "participate in establishing local meeting arenas" does not require any specific competence; second, the more general character of the question also appeals to second-home owners who are not necessarily interested in meeting places for business purposes, but rather meeting places for cultural activities and the like. However, a number of the qualitative comments still illustrate that several respondents have indicated competence transfer as a main motivation for wanting to participate in establishing local meeting arenas: "Possibility to come into contact with business life in order to exchange ideas and do networking."

7. Conclusion

The recent focus on second-home owners as competence brokers in terms of rural entrepreneurship and innovation only can be understood when placed within an overreaching frame of recent changes in theories and policies for economic growth and rural and

Table 9. Relationship between second-home owners' experiences and participation willingness

Vehicles for knowledge transfer/areas of participation	Managerial and entrepreneurial experience (Tinn and Øyfjell)				
	Top manager (%)	Manager (%)	Own company (%)	Employed (%)	Other (%)
Be part of the board of a local company	35	32	32	17	7
Be a mentor for a local company	38	32	32	16	4
Sit on a committee for local development	27	27	35	23	9
Make an effort to develop local business life	24	30	44	17	9
Participate in establishing local meeting arenas	14	35	30	65	5

regional development. While economic growth traditionally has been explained as a result of increases in the labour and capital forces or technological change, over the last decades, we have witnessed an increased attention towards human and intellectual capital (see, e.g. Conceição and Heitor, 2002). In this respect, Lundvall and Johnson (1994) claim that capitalism has entered a new stage in which knowledge is the most important source, and learning the most important process in terms of economic growth.

Theories and policies for rural development have undergone sharp transformations since the 1990s. The most notorious are thus seen through the shift in ideology from the idea of rural areas as rather passive recipients of regulations, information and subsidies into empowering local agents (as rural entrepreneurs, farmers, administrators, etc.) by knowledge generation and transfer as the prime drivers for entrepreneurship, innovation and competitive advantages (Cannarella & Piccioni, 2006). The use of new knowledge and competence to stimulate innovation and development is considered essential for destinations, industries and individual enterprises (Hjalager, 2002; Cooper, 2006; Hallin & Marnburg, 2008).

The theoretical thinking underpinning what is labelled the "knowledge/learning economy" is also visible in Norwegian rural and regional development policies; for instance, through the change in policies for value creation with an increased focus on competence innovation and increased knowledge and processing (Hidle *et al.*, 2010, p. 146); or through the alignment of the system- and network-oriented means that the three national government agencies (Innovation Norway, SIVA and the Research Council) possess to stimulate innovation and entrepreneurship in companies and in rural and regional projects. During the last decade, there has been an increasing focus on clusters, networks, R&D, cooperation, and knowledge exchange and transfer initiatives.

Purpose-built second-home tourism has increased substantially in rural parts of Norway during the last decades and has raised a number of contested space issues (Overvåg & Berg, 2011) and challenges in terms of environmental impacts, retirement and nursing homes, taxation issues, etc. In the Norwegian media, discourse about second-home owners in descriptions such as "trouble makers" and "invaders" occur quite frequently, and we are often faced with heated conflicts between second-home owners and landowners or second-home owners who complain about charges for rubbish collection or local property taxes.

We have, however, encountered surprisingly few of this kind of second-home owner in the study underlying this paper. On the contrary, we have "met" a group or segment of second-home owners who, in different ways, demonstrate a genuine interest in the recreational community, and a willingness to use their knowledge and competence for its betterment. Furthermore, we have also seen that an impressive number of second-home owners possess higher education qualifications within a number of industrial fields and sectors, and extensive managerial and hands-on experience from establishing and developing companies: in other words, they have both the interest and willingness *and* the required skills and experiences to become important competence brokers for local entrepreneurship and innovation.

Clearly, second-home owners in the eastern part of Norway are a powerful group having many resources with which to make their voices heard (Overvåg & Berg, 2011), but also a potential powerful group in terms of their contribution to local entrepreneurship and innovation. However, neither the competence of the second-home owners nor their willingness to contribute to development in the recreation community lead to entrepreneurship and innovation per se, unless there also exist a willingness and favourable absorption capacity for new ideas in the receiving milieu, and policies that facilitate competence transfer. A legitimate question in this respect, as succinctly forwarded by one of the second-home owners in Tinn: "What does the local population want of us second-home owners? Are we welcomed?"

How the local population, including politicians, authorities and the supportive environment act in terms of facilitating and following up the demonstrated willingness of the respondents, will be incremental in terms second-home owners as competence brokers for rural entrepreneurship and innovation. Hidle *et al.* (2010) argue that the policies for rural development in Norway are still, by and large, based on the rural-urban divide as a platonic categorization, but that the increased second-home mobility challenges this categorization; for instance with reference to taxes, the national register as well as the administrative borders between municipalities in general. However, given the large proportion of the "population" that second-home owners make up in a number of outlying municipalities in Norway today, the role of second-home owners' in terms of rural entrepreneurship and innovation needs to be properly addressed both in rural and regional debates and policies, and in research.

References

Arnesen, T. (2003) Blir Hyttefolk Fastbuande? Conference paper, 'Framtidsretta Hyttebygging', Høiland Farm, Årdal, Ryfylke, Norway.

Awad, E. & Ghaziri, H. (2004) *Knowledge Management* (New Jersey: Pearson Education).

Bouwen, R. (1998) Relational construction of meaning in emerging organization context, *European Journal of Work and Organizational Psychology*, 7(3), pp. 299–319.

Boyd, B. (1990) Corporate linkages and organizational environment: A test of the resource dependency model, *Strategic Management Journal*, 12(2), pp. 317–355.

Brandth, B., Haugen, M. S. & Kroken, A. (2010) *Farm tourism: A question of gender and competence?* Paper no 1/10, Bygdeforskning, Trondheim.

Butler, R. & Clark, G. (1992) Tourism in rural areas: Canada and the United Kingdom, in: I. R. Bowler, C. R. Bryant & M. D. Nellis (Eds) *Contemporary Rural Systems in Transition, Vol. 2: Economy and Society*, pp. 166–186 (Wallingford, Oxon: CABI).

Cannarella, C. & Piccioni, V. (2006) Dysfunctions and sub-optimal behaviours of rural development networks, *International Journal of Rural Management*, 2(1), pp. 29–56.

Cavusgil, S. T., Calantone, R. J. & Zhao, Y. (2003) Tacit knowledge transfer and firm innovation capability, *Journal of Business and Industrial Marketing*, 18(1), pp. 6–21.

Conceição, P. & Heitor, M. V. (1999) On the role of the university in the knowledge economy. *Science and Public Policy*, 26(1), pp. 37–51.

Conceição, P. & Heitor, M. V. (2002) Knowledge interaction towards inclusive learning: Promoting systems of innovation and competence building, *Technological Forecasting and Social Change*, 69(7), pp. 641–651.

Cooper, C. (2006) Knowledge management and tourism, *Annals of Tourism Research*, 33(1), pp. 47–64.

Dahl, H. (2000) *Rjukan Bind I, II, III* (Kragerø: PDC Tangen).

Edmondson, A. C., Winslow, A. B., Bohmer, R. M. J. & Pisano, G. J. (2003) Learning how and learning what: Effects of tacit and codified knowledge on performance improvement following technology adoptions, *Decision Sciences*, 34(2), pp. 197–223.

Ericsson, B. & Grefsrud, R. (2005) *Fritidshus i Innlandet: Bruk og Lokaløkonomiske Effekter*, rapport nr. 06/2005, Lillehammer: Østlandsforskning.

Ericsson, B., Arnesen, T. & Overvåg, K. (2005) *Fra Hyttefolk til Sekundærbosatte. Et Forprosjekt*, rapport nr. 04/2005, Lillehammer: Østlandsforskning.

Farstad, M. (2008) *Med Bygda i Bytte: Forholdet Mellom Urbane Andrehjemsiere og Fastboende i rurale Områder, Belyst ved Hjelp av Sosial Bytteteori*, Notat 10/08, Trondheim: Senter for bygdeforskning.

Field, J. (2003) *Social Capital* (London: Routledge).

Flogenfeldt, T. (2006) Second homes, work commuting and amenity migrants in Norway's mountain areas, in: L. A. G. Moss (Ed.) *The Amenity Migrants: Seeking and Sustaining Mountains and Their Cultures*, pp. 232–244 (Wallingford: CABI).

Gallent, N., Mace, A. & Tewdwr-Jones, M. (2005) *Second Homes: European Perspectives and UK Policies* (Aldershot: Ashgate).

Hallin, C. A. & Marnburg, E. (2008) Knowledge management in the hospitality industry: A review of empirical research, *Tourism Management*, 29(2), pp. 366–381.

Hernández-Maestro, R. M., Muños-Gallego, P. A. & Santos-Requejo, L. (2009) Small-business' owners' knowledge and rural tourism establishment performance in Spain, *Journal of Travel Research*, 48(1), pp. 58–77.

Hidle, K., Ellingsen, W. & Crickshank, J. (2010) Political conceptions of second home mobility, *Sociologia Ruralis*, 50(2), pp. 139–155.

Hiltunen, M. J. (2004) Second Housing in Finland – Perspective of Mobility. Paper presented at the 13th Nordic Symposium in Tourism and Hospitality, Aalborg, Denmark, November 4–7.

Hjalager, A. M. (2002) A review of innovation research in tourism, *Tourism Management*, 31(1), pp. 1–12.

Hjalager, A. M. (2010) Repairing innovation defectiveness in tourism, *Tourism Management*, 23(5), pp. 465–474.

Jacobson, N. (2007) Social epistemology. Theory for the 'Fourth Wave' of knowledge transfer and exchange research, *Science Communication*, 29(1), pp. 116–127.

Kaltenborg, B. P. (1998) The alternate home – Motives for recreation home use, *Norsk Geografisk Tidsskrift*, 52(3), pp. 121–134.

Labrianidis, L. (2004) Introduction, in: L. Labrianidis (Ed.) *The Future of Europe's Rural Peripheries*, pp. 1–27 (Aldershot: Ashgate).

Langdalen, E. (1980) Second homes in Norway – A controversial planning problem, *Norsk Geografisk Tidsskrift*, 34(3), pp. 139–144.

Long, P. & Lane, B. (2000) Rural tourism development, in: W. Gartner (Ed.) *Trends in Outdoor Recreation, Leisure and Tourism*, pp. 299–308 (Cambridge: CABI).

Lundvall, B. Å. & Johnson, B. (1994) The learning economy, *Journal of Industry Studies*, 1(2), pp. 23–42.

Mizruchi, M. S. (1996) What do interlocks do? An analysis, critique and assessment on interlocking directories, *Annual Review of Sociology*, 22, pp. 271–298. Available at http://www.jstor.org/discover/10.2307/2083432?uid=3738344&uid=2&uid=4&sid=21101875696393 (accessed 14 September 2012).

Nordbø, I. (2009) Living with tourism: The challenges and constraints of small scale rural tourism businesses in Norway and Chile, PhD dissertation, Aalborg University, Aalborg.

Novelli, M., Schmidt, B. & Spencer, T. (2006) Networks, clusters and innovation in tourism: A UK experience, *Tourism Management*, 27(6), pp. 1141–1152.

OECD (1994) *Tourism Strategies and Rural Development* (Paris: OECD).

O'Hagan, S. B. & Green, M. B. (2004) Corporate knowledge transfer via interlocking directories: A network analysis approach, *Geoforum*, 35(1), pp. 127–139.

Overvåg, K. & Berg, G. N. (2011) Second homes, rurality and contested space in Eastern Europe, *Tourism Geographies*, 13(3), pp. 417–442.

Polyani, M. (1958) *Personal Knowledge* (London: Routledge and Kegan Paul).

Polyani, M. (1966) *The Tacit Dimension* (London: Routledge and Kegan Paul).

Stamboulis, Y. & Skayannis, P. (2003) Innovation strategies and technology for experience-based tourism, *Tourism Management*, 24(1), pp. 35–43.

Shaw, G. & Williams, A. (2009) Knowledge transfer and management in tourism organisations: An emerging research area, *Tourism Management*, 30(3), pp. 325–335.

Statistics Norway (2006a) Utdanningsnivå i Befolkningen. Available at http://www.ssb.no/emner/04/01/utniv/tab-2007-08-27-03.html (accessed 25 August 2007).

Statistics Norway (2006b) Mot Maktens Tinder?. Available at http://www.ssb.no/vis/emner/00/02/10/ola_kari/makt/main.html (accessed 6 June 2006).

Statistics Norway (2008a) Tabell 03109: Bedrifter, Etter Næring og Antall Ansatte (K). Available at http://statbank.ssb.no/statistikkbanken/Default_FR.asp?PXSid=0&nvl=true&PLanguage=0&tilside=selectvarval/define.asp&Tabellid=03109 (accessed 10 April 2008).

Statistics Norway (2008b) Educational level among inhabitants in Tinn and Vinje, e-mail from B.C. GRAVAAS, Avdeling for personstatistikk/Seksjon for utdanningsstatistikk.

Statistics Norway (2011) Tabell 05467. Eksisterende Bygningsmasse. Antall Fritidsbygninger og Fritidsbygninger per Kvadratkilometer (K). Available at http://statbank.ssb.no/statistikkbanken/Default_FR.asp?PXSid=

0&nvl=true&PLanguage=0&tilside=selecttable/hovedtabellHjem.asp&KortnavnWeb=bygningsmasse (accessed 25 September 2011).

Swarbrooke, J. & Horner, S. (2007) *Consumer Behaviour in Tourism* (Oxford: Butterworth-Heinemann/Elsevier).

Taugbøl, T., Vistad, O. I., Nellemann, C., Kaltenborn, B. P., Flyen, A. C., Swensen, G., Nybakken, A., Horgen, B. C., Grefsrud, R., Lein, K., Sivertsen, J. B., & Gurigard, K. (2001) Hyttebygging i Norge. En Oppsummering og Vurdering av Ulike Miljø-og Samfunnsmessige Effekter av Hyttebygging i Fjell-og Skogtraktene i Sør-Norge, Oppdragsmelding 709, Trondheim: Norsk Institutt for Naturforskning (NINA), pp. 1–65.

Thomas, R. (2011) Business elites, universities and knowledge transfer in tourism, *Tourism Management*, 33(3), pp. 553–561.

Vågane, L. (2006) Daglige Fritidsaktiviteter, Hytte-og Båtliv og Svenskehandel, Oslo, Transportøkonomisk Institutt (TØI).

Velvin, J., Drag, E., & Soltvedt, L. P. (2000) *En Kartlegging av Hytteturisme som Ledd i Utvikling av Bærekraftige Bygdesamfunn*, Rapport nr. 17, Kongsberg: Høgskolen i Buskerud.

Walle, A. H. (1997) Quantitative vis a vis qualitative tourism research, *Annals of Tourism Research*, 24(3), pp. 524–536.

Xiao, H. (2006) Towards a research agenda for knowledge management in tourism, *Tourism and Hospitality Planning and Development*, 3(2), pp. 143–157.

Yang, J. T. & Wan, C. S. (2004) Advancing organizational effectiveness and knowledge management implementation, *Tourism Management*, 25(5), pp. 593–601.

Innovation and Destination Governance in Denmark: Tourism, Policy Networks and Spatial Development

HENRIK HALKIER

Department of Culture and Global Studies, Aalborg University, Aalborg East, Kroghstræde, Denmark

ABSTRACT *For more than a decade, tourist destinations in Denmark have experienced decreasing market shares and numbers of international visitors in comparison with the early 1990s. Despite this stagnation, destination development initiatives and national tourism policies have continued largely unaltered, relying on traditional efforts like collective marketing and local visitor information services, while giving limited priority to innovation-oriented measures that could improve the international attractiveness of Danish destinations by renewing the tourist experiences available. The article argues (1) that important reasons for the slow adoption of new destination development strategies can be found in the domination of tourism-related policy networks by short-term sectoral and localist interests, and (2) that recent reforms of subnational and sectoral governance have only improved the prospects of introduction of more innovation-oriented destination development policies to a limited extent.*

1. Introduction

For more than a decade, tourist destinations in Denmark have experienced difficulties as the market share of international visitors has decreased in comparison to what can be nostalgically viewed as "the good old days" of the early 1990s (Danmarks Statistik, 2012). The national tourist organization VisitDenmark (VisitDenmark, 2010) and subnational destination management organizations (DMOs) like *VisitNordjylland* (VisitNordjylland.dk, 2007) have of course been acutely aware of this. However, the response of public and private actors has not resulted in strategic initiatives that have managed to counter increasing competition in the European and global markets for tourist experiences, by renewing the experiences available to visitors. In an age where the access to new and exotic tourist destinations has increased dramatically due to the combined rise of internet-based booking and budget air-travel (Boniface & Cooper, 2005; Weaver & Lawton, 2002), traditional efforts, such as collective marketing combined with local information services for visitors, have clearly not been able to maintain the international attractiveness of Denmark and Danish destinations.

This article seeks to establish (1) that an important reason for the slow adoption of more innovation-oriented destination development strategies can be found in the domination of destination development and Danish tourism policy by short-term sectoral and localist interests; and (2) that recent reforms of subnational and sectoral governance have only improved the prospects for introduction of more innovation-oriented policies for destination development to a limited extent.

The text falls into three parts. First, an institutionalist conceptual framework for the analysis is outlined on the basis of a brief review of key contributions to the literature on destination development. There then follows an analysis of national and regional destination development policies, which focuses in particular on the changing institutional context for tourism policy, including the role of stakeholders in policy-making, and the relatively stable objectives and policy instruments involved. On this basis, the prospects for future change in the direction of more innovation-oriented destination governance in Denmark are assessed, and finally some general implications of the Danish case are discussed.

2. Conceptualizing Tourism Destination Development

In the literature on destination development much attention has traditionally been given to, on the one hand, the marketing and promotion used to attract visitors to a particular area (Morgan, 2004; Pike, 2004; Therkelsen, 2007; Therkelsen & Halkier, 2008; Wang & Xiang, 2007); and, on the other hand, the aggregate outcome in terms of touristic activities and economic growth (Butler, 1980; Hall, 2008, Chapter 8; Kauppila et al., 2009). In recent years, more consideration has been given to governance and policy-making in tourism destinations (Dredge et al., 2011; Hall, 2008), focusing especially on DMOs (Elbe et al., 2009; Presenza et al., 2005), network and stakeholder relations (Dredge, 2006; Haugland et al., 2008; Henriksen & Halkier, 2009; Jamal & Getz, 1995; Presenza & Cipollina, 2010; Sautter & Leisen, 1999; Wray, 2009) and to a lesser extent on policy instruments (Halkier, 2008; Haugland et al., 2008).

Specifically, a good deal of attention has been devoted to two areas, namely (a) the difficulties for destinations in promoting innovation, and (b) the role of stakeholders in policy-making. With regard to innovation, a recurring theme has been that there are relatively limited levels of innovation because of the lack of financial and human resources among the small and micro firms that dominate many tourist destinations. This makes coordination and public sector initiatives important factors in bringing about change and renewal in many tourist destinations (Halkier, 2010; Hall & Williams, 2008; Henriksen, 2012; Hjalager, 2010).

This, in turn, leads to the second point, i.e. importance of stakeholder involvement, where the literature has focused in particular on the exclusion of local community groups and environmental interests, and the predominance of actors with a strong economic interest in tourism, either directly as private investors or indirectly through tax income and job creation (Dredge et al., 2011; Hall, 2008, Chapter 8; Jamal & Getz, 1995).

When viewed together, these bodies of literature show that it is obvious that conservatism with regard to destination development (or no-development) can be pursued by any group of stakeholders for a variety of reasons. Hence, the question of the origins of policy innovation and innovation policies remains an empirical one, although the existing literature would clearly seem to suggest that changes are likely to be small and incremental.

Much of the literature cited above draw on various forms of network theory, and to enable a comprehensive analysis of destination development policies and their associated governance structures, this article places individual interactions between tourism-related sectors in a wider context by taking its point of departure in an institutionalist approach to the study of politics and policy (Halkier, 2006, Chapter 3). For the purpose of this study, a simplified version has been employed, focusing on the three core relations that are involved in the policy process—the destination and its external context, the DMO and its political sponsors, and the DMO and its policy targets—as illustrated in Figure 1.

Understanding the socio-economic context of tourist destinations is crucial, given that tourism involves the mobility of visitors, who may decide to travel elsewhere according to their preferences for touristic experiences, and the offers of competing destinations (Weaver & Lawton, 2002). From a policy perspective, the political context of the destination is, however, also important, as the ability of actors to engage in destination development activities will be affected by the powers and other resources at the disposal of, e.g. local authorities or inter/national regulations of DMO activities. Thus, the political context involves both local preferences and national regulation of what local government and tourist bodies can do to promote the visitor economy in their area (Halkier, 2008; Hall, 2008, Chapter 8).

The relationship between the destination DMO and its political sponsors is important because strategies and resources to pursue these are likely to be influenced by those who supported the setting up of an agency dedicated to tourism development (Nilsson, 2007; Presenza & Cipollina, 2010; Sautter &Leisen, 1999).

Finally, the relationship between the DMO and its policy targets is important because strategies can only influence tourism development if they are translated into concrete aims and instruments on the basis of knowledge about what drives key actors in the destination. Then, of course, these policy targets may still decide not to support a particular initiative because it collides with other concerns perceived to be more important (Halkier, 2006, pp. 121–124; Hall, 2008, Chapter 8).

All in all, the application of these institutionalist conceptualizations in the analysis of the development of destination development initiatives and tourism policies, before and after the most recent reform of subnational governance in Denmark, should be able to illuminate reasons for the surprising degree of stability in public policy in the face of disappointing results for the Danish visitor economy.

Figure 1. An institutionalist perspective on destination development.
Source: Inspired by Halkier (2006, Figure 3.1).

3. Destination Governance: Continuity in Flux

Speaking of "Danish tourism" is inaccurate in the sense that several types of inter/national visitor flows combine to make up the aggregate headline of tourist movements within the territory. In economic terms, two main types of activities remain important generators of income, namely

- leisure holidays, mostly involving accommodation in rented second homes in coastal areas
- business tourism based on conference and meeting facilities, especially in Copenhagen.

As illustrated in Figure 2, leisure tourism accounts for around two-thirds of tourist expenditure in Denmark, with international visitors contributing more than domestic travellers, while the significant business tourism market is dominated by domestic activities. This generates an overall picture of at least two distinct types of tourist destinations (see Boniface & Cooper, 2005), namely, on the one hand, the coastal leisure destinations set in rural and often peripheral areas relying on natural resources such as empty sandy beaches, and on the other hand, the urban destinations with their emphasis on cultural and other man-made attractions.

While this makes it fairly straight-forward for regional and local destinations to present a clear profile to potential visitors, heterogeneity is of course a challenge for national attempts to create a unified brand for Denmark as a tourist destination (Gyimóthy & Ren, 2011; Therkelsen & Halkier, 2008). But perhaps even more important, especially in times with stagnation in overnight stays and a significant decrease in international visitors as illustrated in Figure 3, this dualism would also seem to complicate tourism governance and destination development strategies.

Until the end of the 1980s, the development of tourism in Denmark was organized in two tiers: (a) the Danish Tourist Board, *Danmarks Turistråd*, was primarily engaged to promote international markets sponsored by central government, and (b) local efforts, often organized through cooperation between local authorities and voluntary tourist associations, concentrated on servicing tourists already in the local area, as well as engaging in some promotional efforts (Lyck, 2003; Schultz, 1988). In other words, tourism policy was not something that central government monopolized. Yet, as the degree of

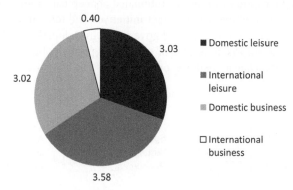

Figure 2. Tourist expenditure in Denmark by origin and purpose.
Source: Elaborated on the basis of VisitDenmark (2010, p. 10, in billion euro, 2010).

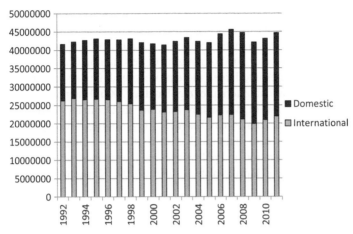

Figure 3. Tourist overnight stays in Denmark by origin.
Source: Elaborated on the basis of Danmarks Statistik (2012).

direct interaction between the local and the national levels appears to have been limited, the situation can best be described as a coexistence of centralized national promotional efforts and a host of competing local actors in the parts of Denmark where tourism was a major activity.

From the late 1980s onwards, the void between the local and the national levels has gradually been filled by organizations and policies; a change driven both from below and from above, but only to a limited extent by the regions themselves (Halkier, 2008; Kvistgaard, 2006; Lyck, 2003). In some cases, private tourist enterprises formed networks focusing on the marketing of particular areas. But in most destinations, partnerships with a wider policy focus—not just promotional activities, but also quality improvement of firms and services for tourist—were initiated by local authorities and tourist associations, and later financially supported from the national level. Eventually in the mid-1990s, a nation-wide system of regional tourism boards was initiated by central government, with respon-sibility not just for promotion of their region to prospective tourists, but also for more innovation-oriented activities. These boards were co-funded by regional and local govern-ment as well as (for particular projects) private sectors within tourism (Feerup, 2001). The regional boards were subsequently refashioned in the wake of a major reform of subna-tional government in 2007, so that each of the six new so-called *Regional Growth Fora*, partnership bodies responsible for regional economic development, would sponsor a regional level sectoral destination development organization (Halkier, 2011). In parallel with the extension of the role for intermediate geographical tiers, other forms of meso-level governance have also been introduced through the setting up of public–private "alliances" with responsibility for particular areas of tourism activity, e.g. "active leisure holidays" and "conference tourism" (Halkier *et al.*, 2008; Hansen *et al.*, 2004).

From the late 1980s onwards, the governance in Denmark of tourism in general and des-tinations in particular have clearly been subject to a series of attempts to introduce new ways of promoting development, and three important consequences of this would seem to have materialized.

First, the introduction of new levels of tourism development policy between the local and the national level meant that the geography of governance became an issue in its own right, with localities traditionally competing for tourists being increasingly prompted to work together for the greater good of a region or destination. Overcoming past rivalries and merging local structures into larger, more professional, units is a challenging situation well-known in the international literature (e.g. Dredge, 2006; Haugland *et al.*, 2008; Jamal & Getz, 1995). In the case of destination building in Denmark, local tourism bodies, especially in coastal and rural areas, have a long tradition for involvement of not just local businesses but also individual citizens through membership subscriptions; and hence issues of organization and policy become intertwined with issues of local identity and place attachment (Henriksen & Halkier, 2009; Kvistgaard, 2006; Therkelsen, 2009).

Second, the new governance structures invariably resulted in an increasing involvement of industry representatives at all levels—from the local via the meso to the national. This is because emphasis was given to the creation of partnership-type arrangements between public and private sectors, which recognized the need for both to be involved for successful development, something that is also reflected in the international literature (Bjørk & Virtanen, 2005; Bramwell & Lane, 2000; Hall, 1999). Given the long-standing involvement of local tourism sectors and civil society representatives (Andersen *et al.*, 2000; Kvistgaard, 2006; Schultz, 1988) and, indeed, the importance generally attached to participation of social partners in the context of a Scandinavian welfare state (Christensen & Christiansen, 1992; Thuesen, 2011) this is hardly surprising, and the outcome has been the creation of a dense but loosely coupled sectoral policy network in which industry representatives played a prominent role. At the same time, however, it is also noticeable that most of the funding continued to come from public sources, thereby giving government the possibility to shape strategies and policies. Therefore, the governance of tourism development in Denmark would seem to resemble a text-book type partnership where asymmetrical resource interdependencies (public funding and private business knowledge) form the basis for joint development activities (Bjørk & Virtanen, 2005; Halkier & Flockhart, 2002; Jamal & Getz, 1995; Östhol *et al.*, 2002).

Third, from a process perspective, more than two decades of organizational flux seem to have created doubts about the long-term authority and the role of individual organizations; especially because unclear divisions of labour with regard to policy tasks continue to create a fertile breeding ground for inter-organizational bickering and distrust. The long-term outcome of this would seem to have been a bolstering of rather conservative attitudes regarding development strategies and policy instruments, in order to secure short-term stability, rather than venture into long-term development commitments with partner organizations, which may have been discontinued before efforts come to fruition at some point in the future.

In other words, changes in the governance of Danish tourist destinations would seem to have resulted in a situation where geographic localism and short-term interests were likely to be prominent features in policy-making. The following section will take a closer look at how these governance changes may have influenced the strategies for destination development and, in particular, the extent to which innovation in products and services became part of destination development in Denmark.

4. Destination Development: Edging beyond Marketing

Destination development in Denmark, as elsewhere in Europe and beyond (Hall, 2008), has had two constant elements in recent decades. In the 1970s and 1980s, tourism policy was a one-dimensional affair in terms of policy instruments because the main activity was promotion of Denmark, or parts thereof, to prospective tourists through advertising, press coverage and leaflets, produced and distributed by national and local tourism bodies (Lyck, 2003; Schultz, 1988). In short, the existing product was taken for granted and efforts concentrated instead on making it visible to prospective or existing visitors through market communication. Both these activities persist, with the role of VisitDenmark being exclusively devoted to international promotion since 2010 (Økonomi-og Erhvervsministeriet, 2010), and a host of subnational DMOs and tourist information offices continuing to provide guidance about local visitor attractions and experiences (Danske Destinationer, 2012).

Originally this the-more-the-merrier "boosterist" (Fayos-Sola, 1996) promotional approach to tourism development was based on the assumption that Denmark received too few visitors, and that increasing their numbers would improve the state of the national economy in general, and the balance of payment in particular (Schultz, 1988). But from the early 1990s, the perception of the challenges facing Danish destinations began to change, with tourism being seen as a sector in which growth should be stimulated not just by marketing existing experience offers, but also through the development of new products and improved level of services (Danmarks Turistråd, 1992; Erhvervsfremmestyrelsen, 1993; Ministeriet for Kommunikation og Turisme, 1994). Ten years later, these were still seen as the major challenges. For example, the 2006 tourism policy white paper still focused on growth through renewal of experience products, improved competences and continued international marketing (Økonomi-og Erhvervsministeriet, 2006). With the new perception of the nature of the "tourism challenge", new strategies of change came on the political agenda to supplement the traditional emphasis on national marketing and local visitor services. Organizational and informational resources became crucial in the attempts to bring public and private partners together in joint projects aimed at developing new experiences capable of attracting more or possibly, new types of visitors, often the so-called "best-agers", couples travelling without children outside the main summer season in order to enjoy culture, food, etc. (see, e.g. VisitDenmark, 2009; VisitNordjylland.dk, 2010). It is, however, also interesting to note that the new policy activities were unevenly distributed in the Danish system of public sector tourism governance. The marketing of existing experience offers, to improve the use of existing capacity in accommodation and attractions, was still an important policy activity. Innovation projects and competence (quality) development tasks were primarily undertaken at the intermediate regional level, while the national level focused on international marketing (Halkier, 2011)—and after 2010 exclusively so (Økonomi-og Erhvervsministeriet, 2010). In short, there was a shift towards a more innovation-oriented policy paradigm in terms of destination development; but also one that placed the main responsibility for this important task close to where tourism takes place, i.e. in the localities visited by tourists.

Compared to other areas of spatial economic policy, the aims and methods of tourism destination development have been relatively conservative in the sense that improving the use of existing capacity through collective international marketing—of the country, region or locality—remains an important priority within the tourism policy network, especially for private but also among public stakeholders. This largely makes sense from a macro-economic perspective: bed-nights are perishable goods that cannot be stored for later use, and the many small firms and attractions with limited financial resources have not been used to (or perhaps will not be capable of) taking care of effective and efficient international promotion through joint efforts (Wanhill, 2001; Weaver & Lawton, 2002).

Until now this specific tourism market failure has, however, been addressed through what could be argued to resemble the ongoing state aid to, e.g. shipyards that the EU has committed itself to reducing dramatically (Wishlade, 2008). International promotion is being subsidized by public funds with no demands being made of tourism firms (e.g. in terms of quality or product development) other than that they themselves have to co-fund marketing activities. Even if individual firms decide not to contribute, they still benefit from place promotion efforts—making the problem of free-riding all too real.

This form of ongoing subsidies for marketing is unknown in most other areas of economic activity (with the possible exception of agriculture), and hence it is hardly surprising that the choice of policy instruments has become a political issue in its own right; not least after the (partial) integration of tourism into the mainstream governance structures for business development at the regional level, the Regional Growth Fora. At least one of these, the Central Denmark Region (*Region Midtjylland*), has decided not to co-fund marketing of tourism destinations (Midtjysk Turisme, 2011). Conversely, private sectors argue that contrary to more speculative innovations in new experiences a significant increase in marketing would have immediate benefits, not just for existing private tourism business, but also for the public sector. These benefits would take the form of increased tax revenues, which would cover significant parts of the initial subsidies or, possibly, generate a surplus (Copenhagen Economics, 2008, 2010).

All in all, a change has taken place in destination development policy in recent decades, with more emphasis being put on efforts aiming to stimulate innovation in the experiences offered by tourist destinations, through individual private and public sectors and, not least, their joint efforts in networks and partnerships. At the same time, there are clearly limits to the extent of change in that marketing remains, by some distance, the single most important policy measure employed to promote growth in destinations throughout Denmark.

5. Conclusion: Innovation, Governance and Development in Tourist Destinations

The inquiry into the relationship between innovation and governance in tourist destinations has demonstrated that recent decades have seen a string of initiatives aimed at stimulating innovation in individual enterprises and destinations to address prolonged stagnation in the Danish visitor economy. Notwithstanding, political attention and financial resources would still seem to concentrate on maintaining and extending the promotion of existing experience offers, mostly in the form of destination marketing where the virtues of individual localities are promoted to potential visitors to ensure the better use of existing capacity in terms of accommodation and attractions, and hence improve the financial position of private firms and public sector tax incomes.

An important reason for this seems to be an extensive involvement of industry partners in the policy networks around tourism and destination development, in combination with a relatively weak political direction given to these networks by public sectors. The first factor is in a sense unsurprising, given that leisure tourism in particular—and by implication coastal tourist destinations around the country—remains dominated by a large number of small sectors with limited financial and organizational resources. Including these in the policy process through membership of associations or DMOs makes a lot of sense, because without their active participation, new initiatives would find it difficult to come to fruition. At the same time, the political lead provided by public tourism development bodies would seem, despite occasional protestations to the contrary, to have been relatively weak, and thus the preference of small private sectors for short-term effectiveness of public intervention has continued to dominate. While innovation has increasingly been on the agenda, its translation to policy activities has been uneven and remained secondary compared to the resources' allocation to marketing and place promotion.

The change of governance set up in the wake of the 2007 local government reform could potentially have an important impact on the aims and methods of tourism destination development in Denmark, because tourism was incorporated into the mainstream business development system. Here, it is interesting to note that although public funding for regional tourism policy has, of course, been routed through the new Regional Growth Fora business development partnerships, in practice, responsibility for both strategy development, and (less surprisingly) implementation, has in effect been delegated to regional tourism boards which tended to be modified successors to the organizations operating since the mid-1990s. Meanwhile, the new regional tourist boards have become increasingly integrated in a vertical tourism policy network, running from the local/destination level to VisitDenmark at the national level, through mutual representation on governing boards as well as joint development and marketing projects.

Although the new regional tourism boards have, therefore, come under increasing pressure to stress innovation as part of their development strategies, in practice their strategies will be more inspired by the sectoral network of like-minded specialists—and indeed their private-sector partners in the tourism industry—than the general requirements of their new regional sponsors. In short, the relationship between the two existing policy networks would, at the moment, seem to entail a kind of co-habitation rather than outright integration. A co-habitation where tourism-specific aims and methods—expanding the activities of existing firms through subsidized destination marketing—are being sheltered by being pursued through a sector-specific organization, which is concurrently part of a parallel vertical tourism policy network.

Perhaps a way out of this policy conundrum could be to place much more emphasis on the integration of different policy instruments, i.e. tying innovation and marketing much more closely together in ways that have been tried out in connection with a major—but now somehow defunct—national attempt to strengthen all-year tourism in selected coastal destinations across Denmark (Toppen af Danmark, 2009; VisitDenmark, 2007). This could create an incentives' structure that combines short-term and long-term economic benefits for private sectors; but, of course, these still need to be willing and able to, for example, engage themselves in development networks and to undertake innovative investments with uncertain returns. An important precondition for such a strategy to work would, therefore, be to create motivation and boost risk-willingness by producing and distributing new knowledge about trends in tourism demands, and development activities in competing destinations—and to create a governance structure that allows for involvement of key stakeholders without giving them the power to veto innovative measures.

Although the current article has been set in a Danish context, many of the issues addressed are also known in the literature on destination development policies in

Europe and beyond: localism and short-termism of private and public stakeholders, making it difficult to change the development trajectory of destinations through innovation of services and experiences in the light of changing demand patterns. The future challenge, both from an analytical and a policy perspective, is therefore not so much to document these difficulties further, but rather to seek to understand examples where significant progress has been made towards a more innovative approach to destination development.

References

Andersen, J., Kvistgaard, P. & Therkelsen, A. (2000) *Turistforeningens Rolle i Fremtidens Turisme i Nordjyllands Amt* (Aalborg: TRU, AAU).

Bjørk, P. & Virtanen, H. (2005) What tourism project managers need to know about co-operation, *Scandinavian Journal of Hospitality and Tourism*, 5(3), pp. 212–230.

Boniface, B. & Cooper, C. (2005) *Wolrdwide Destinations. The Geography of Travel and Tourism*, 4th ed. (Amsterdam: Elsevier).

Bramwell, B. & Lane, B. (Eds) (2000) *Tourism Collaboration and Partnerships. Politics, Practice and Sustainability* (Clevedon: Channel View).

Butler, R. W. (1980) The concept of a tourist area cycle of evolution: Implications for management of resources, *Canadian Geographer*, 24(1), pp. 5–12.

Christensen, J. G. & Christiansen, P. M. (1992) *Forvaltning og Omgivelser* (Herning: Systime).

Copenhagen Economics (2008) *Vækst i Turisterhvervet – Rapport til Turisterhvervets Samarbejdsforum* (Copenhagen: Copenhagen Economics).

Copenhagen Economics (2010) *Problemet i Dansk Turisme. Konsekvenser for Danmark* (Copenhagen: Copenhagen Economics).

Danmarks Statistik (2012) *Overnatningstal*. Available at www.visitdenmark.dk (accessed 28 July 2012).

Danmarks Turistråd (1992) *Fælles Fodslaw: Turisme, Miljø, Planlægning* (København: Danmarks Turistråd).

Danske Destinationer (2012) *Danske Destinationer* (Randers: Danske Destinationer).

Dredge, D. (2006) Policy networks and the local organisation of tourism, *Tourism Management*, 27(2), pp. 269–280.

Dredge, D., Jenkins, J. & Whitford, M. (2011) Tourism planning and policy: Historical development and contemporary challenges, in: D. Dredge & J. Jenkins (Eds) *Stories of Practice: Tourism Policy and Planning*, pp. 13–36 (Farnham: Ashgate).

Elbe, J., Hallen, L. & Axelsson, B. (2009) The destination-management organisation and the integrative destination-marketing process, *International Journal of Tourism Research*, 11(3), pp. 283–296.

Erhvervsfremmestyrelsen (1993) *Ressourceområdet Turisme/fritid: En Erhvervsøkonomisk Analyse* (København: Erhvervsfremmestyrelsen).

Fayos-Sola, E. (1996) Tourism policy: A midsummer night's dream? *Tourism Management*, 17(6), pp. 405–512.

Feerup, N. (2001) *Bredt Samarbejde i Dansk Turisme: En Præsentation of de Regionale Turismeselskaber* (Rønne: Destination Bornholm).

Gyimóthy, S. & Ren, C. B. (2011) Dansk nation branding: Praksis i forandring? *Økonomi & Politik*, 84(4), pp. 56–68.

Halkier, H. (2006) *Institutions, Discourse and Regional Development. The Scottish Development Agency and the Politics of Regional Policy* (Brussels: PIE Peter Lang).

Halkier, H. (2008) Regional development policies and structural reform in Denmark. From policy segmentation towards strategic synergy? in: O. Bukve, H. Halkier & P. D. Souza (Eds) *Towards New Nordic Regionalism. Politics, Administration and Regional Development*, pp. 201–225 (Aalborg: Aalborg University Press).

Halkier, H. (2010) Tourism knowledge dynamics, in: P. Cooke, C. D. Laurentis, C. Collinge & S. Macneill (Eds) *Platforms of Innovation: Dynamics of New Industrial Knowledge Flows*, pp. 233–250 (London: Edward Elgar).

Halkier, H. (2011) Erhvervspolitik mellem det lokale og det globale? Dansk turismepolitik under forandringspres, *Økonomi & Politik*, 84(4), pp. 11–24.

Halkier, H. & Flockhart, J. E. (2002) The Danish cases: Bottom-up initiatives between regional and national environments, in: A. Östhol & B. Svensson (Eds) *Partnership Responses – Regional Governance in the Nordic States*, pp. 41–84 (Stockholm: Nordregio).

Halkier, H., Therkelsen, A. & Berg Schmidt, P. (2008) Turisme i nordjylland: Status og fremtidsmuligheder, in: J. L. Christensen (Ed.) *Hvad Skal Nordjylland Leve Af?* pp. 194–203 (Aalborg: CRU, Aalborg Universitet).

Hall, C. M. (1999) Rethinking collaboration and partnership: A public policy perspective, *Journal of Sustainable Tourism*, 7(3–4), pp. 274–289.

Hall, C. M. (2008) *Tourism Planning: Policies, Processes and Relationships*, 2nd ed. (Harlow: Pearson Prentice Hall).

Hall, C. M. & Williams, A. (2008) *Tourism and Innovation* (Abingdon: Routledge).

Hansen, E., Kvistgaard, P. & Smed, K. (2004) *Midtvejsevaluering af Turismealliancer og Apydspidsprojekter* (København: Erhvervs-og Byggestyrelsen).

Haugland, S. A., Ness, H., Grønseth, B.-O. & Aarstad, J. (2008) Development of tourism destinations: An integrated multilevel perspective, *Annals of Tourism Research*, 38(1), pp. 268–290.

Henriksen, P. F. (2012) Small tourism firms' inter-organisational relations and knowledge processes: The role of social embeddedness in networks: The case of the municipality of Viborg, Denmark, PhD Thesis, Culture and Global Studies, Aalborg University.

Henriksen, P. F. & Halkier, H. (2009) From local promotion towards regional tourism policies: Knowledge processes and actor networks in North Jutland, *Denmark, European Planning Studies*, 17(10), pp. 1445–1462.

Hjalager, A.-M. (2010) A review of innovation research in tourism, *Tourism Management*, 30(1), pp. 1–12.

Jamal, T. B. & Getz, D. (1995) Collaboration theory and community tourism planning, *Annals of Tourism Research*, 22(1), pp. 186–204.

Kauppila, P., Saarinen, J. & Leinonen, R. (2009) Sustainable tourism planning and regional development in peripheries: A Nordic view, *Scandinavian Journal of Hospitality and Tourism*, 9(4), pp. 424–435.

Kvistgaard, P. (2006) *Problemer og Magt i Regional Turismepolicy* (Aalborg: Aalborg Universitetsforlag).

Lyck, L. (2003) *Turismeudvikling og Attraktioner i et Strategisk Perspektiv* (København: Nyt fra Samfundsvidenskaberne).

Midtjysk Turisme (2011) *Ny VÆKST i Turismen – En Strategi for en Mere Fokuseret og Professionel Turisme i Region Midtjylland Frem Mod 2020 (udkast)* (Silkeborg: Midtjysk Turisme).

Ministeriet for Kommunikation og Turisme (1994) *Turistpolitisk Redegørelse 1994* (København: Ministeriet for Kommunikation og Turisme).

Morgan, N. E. A. (2004) *Destination Branding. Creating the Unique Destination Proposition*, 2nd ed. (Amsterdam: Elsevier).

Nilsson, P. Å. (2007) Stakeholder theory: The need for a convenor. The case of Billund, *Scandinavian Journal of Hospitality and Tourism*, 7(2), pp. 171–184.

Økonomi-og Erhvervsministeriet (2006) *Redegørelse af 25 Januar 2006 om Dansk Turisme* (København: Økonomi-og Erhvervsministeriet).

Økonomi-og Erhvervsministeriet (2010) Lov om visitdenmark (L 159), *Folketingstidende C*.

Östhol, A., Svensson, B. & Halkier, H. (2002) Analytical framework, in: A. Östhol & B. Svensson (Eds) *Partnership Responses – Regional Governance in the Nordic States*, pp. 23–39 (Stockholm: Nordregio).

Pike, S. (2004) *Destination Marketing Organisations* (Amsterdam: Elsevier).

Presenza, A. & Cipollina, M. (2010) Analysing tourism stakeholders networks, *Tourism Review*, 65(4), pp. 17–30.

Presenza, A., Sheehan, L. & Ritchie, J. R. B. (2005) Towards a model of the roles and activities of DMOs, *Journal of Hospitality, Tourism and Leisure Science*, 3(1), pp. 1–16.

Sautter, E. T. & Leisen, B. (1999) Managing stakeholders: A tourism planning model, *Annals of Tourism Research*, 26(2), pp. 312–328.

Schultz, H. J. (1988) *Dansk Turisme i 100 År, 1888–1988* (København: Danmarks Turistråd).

Therkelsen, A. (2007) Branding af turismedestinationer: Muligheder og problemer, in: A. Sørensen (Ed.) *Grundbog i Turisme*, pp. 215–225 (København: Frydenlund).

Therkelsen, A. (2009) *All-year tourism: A knowledge event at destination Mariagerfjord, North Jutland, Denmark, TRU progress*, Department of History and International Studies, Aalborg University.

Therkelsen, A. & Halkier, H. (2008) Contemplating place branding umbrellas. The case of coordinated national tourism and business promotion, *Scandinavian Journal of Hospitality and Tourism*, 8(2), pp. 159–175.

Thuesen, A. A. (2011) Partnerships as associations: Input and output legitimacy of LEADER partnerships in Denmark, *Finland and Sweden, European Planning Studies*, 19(4), pp. 575–594.

Toppen af Danmark (2009) *Naturen+ i Lysets Land. Handlingsplan for Udvikling af Helårsturisme i Toppen af Danmark 2009–2011* (Frederikshavn: Toppen af Danmark).

VisitDenmark (2007) *Kystferiestrategi i Retning Mod Helårsturisme* (København: VisitDenmark).
VisitDenmark (2009) *Vores Rejse. En Fælles Strategi For Dansk Turisme* (København: VisitDenmark).
VisitDenmark (2010) *Denmark's Tourism Performance in Europe 2000–2009* (København: VisitDenmark).
Visitnordjylland.dk (2007) *Vision 2020. Visions-og Strategiprocess for Nordjysk Turisme. Tilstandsrapport* (Åbybro: VisitNordjylland.dk).
Visitnordjylland.dk (2010) *Fyrtårn Nordjylland. Nordjysk Turismestrategi 2011–2013* (Åbybro: VisitNordjylland.dk).
Wang, Y. & Xiang, Z. (2007) Toward a theoretical framework of collaborative destination marketing, *Journal of Travel Research*, 46(1), pp. 75–85.
Wanhill, S. (2001) Issues in public sector involvement, in: B. Faulkner, E. Laws, G. Moscardo & H. W. Faulkner (Eds) *Tourism in the Twenty-First Century*, pp. 222–242 (London: Continuum).
Weaver, D. & Lawton, L. (2002) *Tourism Management*, 2nd ed. (Milton: Wiley).
Wishlade, F. G. (2008) Competition and cohesion – coherence or conflict? European Union regional state aid reform post-2006, *Regional Studies*, 42(5), pp. 753–765.
Wray, M. (2009) Policy communities, networks and issue cycles in tourism destination systems, *Journal of Sustainable Tourism*, 17(6), pp. 673–690.

Tourism Lobbying in Bavaria: Between Ignorance, Parochialism and Opportunism

MARKUS PILLMAYER & NICOLAI SCHERLE

Department of Cultural Geography, Catholic University of Eichstätt-Ingolstadt, Eichstätt, Germany

ABSTRACT   *The subject of lobbying in the context of destinations is still a largely unstudied research field both in relation to specific destinations and from the perspective of planning. This is all the more remarkable when we consider that—despite its ambivalent public perception—successful lobbying is a crucial success factor in the positioning of destinations on a highly globalized tourism market with its rapidly changing supply and demand structures. In this article, we analyze the current lobbying structures in Bavaria, one of the leading European destinations. Bavarian tourism finds itself in an exceedingly complex situation today caught between diminishing competitiveness, especially considering the persistent investment backlog, and exceedingly ambitious tourism policies. Using semi-structured interviews we investigated how key policy-makers and representatives of the tourism business currently appraise tourism lobbying in Bavaria. From their assessments, we derive recommendations that should help to optimize lobbying structures and processes.*

1. Introduction

Wolf-Dieter Zumpfort, a member of the board of Touristik Union International, the largest travel business in the world, and until 2003 chairman of *Collegium*, the prestigious association of lobbyists, is one of the few high-ranking tourism players who has admitted to being a lobbyist. During an interview he commented on the image of lobbying:

> In the hierarchy of the professions professors and parsons are at the top and politicians, journalists and lobbyists at the very bottom. But that doesn't bother me. Wherever a bias is expressed, I try to straighten things out. And through my own example I try to make it clear that being a lobbyist is a serious business and a normal part of politics. (as cited in Leif & Speth, 2003, p. 95)

Political decisions have a long-term effect on the scope of economic agents' actions. Interest groups have always tried, therefore, to influence the political agenda (Andersen & Woyke, 2009). When we examine both the public and the scientific discussion on the representation of interests, we see that in our contemporary society the individual is increasingly being eclipsed by organizations of the most varied types. It is quite natural for groups or their representatives to try to help shape, implement and influence political decisions, for rational reasons and/or power politics (Boessen & Maarse, 2009). They have all of them assumed an extraordinarily complex task, for they are mouthpiece for individuals or small groups who are not able to take part in political affairs or cannot do so sufficiently.

As the quote by Zumpfort at the beginning showed, the image of lobbying is still ambivalent and often downright negative. For instance, in Germany, which is considered the most important tourist source market in the world (DRV, 2010), only the website of the German Hotel and Restaurant Federation has a link of its own to lobbying activities. None of the other relevant pressure groups make explicit reference to the topic. In fitting with this image is the slightly exaggerated quote by Scheff and Gutschelhofer (1998, p. vii), who point out: "Lobbying—everything happens in secret, behind closed doors. Society is already completely at the mercy of these lobbyists. These people operate so furtively that many dictionaries [...] do not even know the term 'Lobbying'." Lobbyists, so it at least appears, dread the public eye. In many cases, the public does not become aware of lobbying activities until confidential information is leaked or the interests of the represented groups are not sufficiently respected (Leif & Speth, 2003).

Because lobbying is so often mystified, not only among the public, but also at times in the scientific community (Homan, 2007, p. 412), we would like to take a problem-centred approach to the phenomenon of lobbying in tourism and the implications for the tourism industry and the makers of tourism policies. We will use the example of Bavaria. Though in the past years more attention has been paid to the topic of lobbying in general (Coen & Richardson, 2009; Michalowitz, 2007), research dealing specifically with lobbying in tourism is still mostly in its infancy, apart from some rather implicit references within the context of issues of power and governance (Hall, 2003; Timothy, 2007). The few exceptions include works by Pillmayer (2005) and Zaugg (2004), which deal particularly with lobbying from the perspective of specific destinations and with questions relating to intensified professionalization of the same. Lobbying can indeed be a meaningful instrument for bringing together the tourism industry and makers of tourism policies, if the protagonists succeed in articulating their projects in the right place. It can be the crucial factor that determines whether a project is ultimately successful or not—in terms of its own goals.

In consideration of the complexity of the subject, we would like to examine primarily the following issues:

(1) What role does tourism lobbying currently play in reconciling the conflicting interests of the makers of tourism policies and the tourism business? The background for this will be the current challenges to tourism destinations and the adoption of the new concept on tourism by the Bavarian state government.
(2) Can lobbying in Bavarian tourism act as a suitable link between the tourism industry and the makers of tourism policies?

(3) What factors characterize successful tourism lobbying?

The starting point for the paper is an empirical survey of important decision-makers in both politics and the tourism industry. Bavaria was chosen as study area primarily for the following two reasons: first, the study area is the leading German tourism destination in terms of both business volume and number of overnight stays (FUR, 2010). Likewise, it is one of the most important European tourism areas (Bayerisches Staatsministerium für Wirtschaft, Infrastruktur, Verkehr und Technologie, 2010). Second, in 2008, the Bavarian state government officially recognized tourism as one of its leading economic sectors and tourism is to be expanded greatly in the coming years by means of political measures at the state, federal and European Union levels (Bayerische Staatsregierung, 2008, p. 26).

To facilitate the contextualization of the phenomenon, we will begin in the following section with a concise review of the development of lobbying. In connection with this, we will look into the processes that influence lobbying and the theoretical academic approaches to lobbying. For a better understanding of our study area, the subsequent section will introduce the current Bavarian tourism structures and the chief challenges facing the Bavarian makers of tourism policies. The focus will be on the guidelines for tourism adopted in 2010. After that we will introduce the methodological procedure employed in the empirical survey. Finally, the empirical section will present and discuss selected results of the empirical survey. This, we hope, will provide insights into the problems facing lobbyists in consideration of the conflicting interests of the tourism industry and the makers of tourism policy in Bavaria. The focus will deliberately lie on the point of view of the persons involved, because only this will give us a nuanced depiction of the current situation. In the last section, we will hazard a final assessment of the findings and offer a forecast as to which measures could be successfully taken for tourism lobbying in tourist destinations.

2. The Art of Taking Influence: Conceptual Approach to the Phenomenon of Lobbying and the Role of Tourism Interest Groups

2.1 Lobbying, the Scientific Context

With only a few exceptions (the United Business Institute and the European Centre for Public Affairs in Brussels; the Brunel University West London; the University of Loughborough and the Deutsche Universität für Weiterbildung [Berlin University for Professional Studies]), it is not possible in Europe to study lobbying as an independent degree programme, in contrast to the US.

This circumstance is surprising, especially in the context of political science, in which intensive research has been done on organized interests since the end of the Second World War, so that a comparatively extensive pool of monographs, case studies, textbooks and theoretical volumes exists (Berry & Wilcox, 2006). In spite of the relatively intensive analysis of associations and their interest groups, the social sciences have paid only scant attention to the complex of lobbying as a whole (e.g. lobbying by companies, lobbying by non governmental organizations (NGOs), etc.), as, for instance, Coen and Richardson (2009) and Graziano (2001) lament. Not until the beginning of the 1990s did the term lobbying, or lobbyism, gradually take hold in the scientific literature. An important stimulus for the intensified research interest is considered to have been the adoption of the

Treaty of Maastricht, whose complex transnational bargaining process was continuously accompanied by lobbyists and accordingly aroused the interest of the scientific community (Michalowitz, 2007). Most studies on the representation and protection of interests concentrate on organized interests in the form of various (trade) associations or NGOs (Berry & Wilcox, 2006). Lobbying by companies or by freelance or public affairs consultants has only moved into the focus of attention little by little.

This section will present some selected theoretical references for a more detailed scholarly understanding of lobbying. That the "art of influencing" is still judged critically, at least on an explicit level, especially in the non-English-speaking countries (Haller, 2008), is reflected not only in rather unflattering descriptions, such as "lobbyism follows the logic of conspiratory backdoor bargaining" (Palazzo & Scherer, 2008, p. 581) or "lobbyism is more worse [sic] than corruption" (Lambsdorff, 2007, p. 48). It is also not easy to integrate into a theory (Sedlenieks, 2004, p. 125). Thus, Lambsdorff (2007) emphasizes that even today there is, unfortunately, no theory available that allows the various approaches to reform to be put into a comparative perspective. Hence, a theoretical basis for lobbying must be viewed as a composite of several theories. Lobbying can be explained up to a certain degree by several theoretical approaches, e.g. Aglietta's structuration theory (2000, p. 17ff.) or Boyer's regulation theory (1990, p. 7ff.). As the following remarks will show, however, another approach appears ultimately more productive.

According to Bramwell (2006) and Eising (2004), the development of the various theoretical approaches is a process of pluralism from neo-corporatist political patterns to complex pluralistic political networks. Each of the perspectives varies, depending on the role played by the political level or the interest groups in the decision-making process, on what type of interaction there is and who are the dominant actors. The corresponding approaches have in common that they all endeavour to understand the relationship between social self-organization, state sovereignty (with the ideal of appropriate legal regulation of public welfare) and the democratic legitimation of political processes or the control of the same. The approaches follow the insight that organized interests should no longer be seen only as pressure groups, but as agents who increasingly assume a conciliatory function. Pressure groups are no longer potential challengers of state sovereignty. Along with a number of other groups they are indispensable helpers in the formulation and enforcement of policies (Dredge & Jenkins, 2003; Tyler & Dinan, 2001a).

Corporatism describes forms of involvement of social groups in political decision-making processes (Feltenius, 2002). The term is derived from the Latin word *corporativus* and signifies "to form a body". In this context, Rommetvedt (2000, p. 112) describes, "administrative corporatism and lobbyism as types of relations between public authorities and organized interests".

Neo-corporatism is based on the voluntary involvement of social organizations. The aim of neo-corporatist participation is to commit diverse groups to joint agreements and to integrate—also referred to as "incorporate"—organized interests into politics and allow them to participate in the formulation and implementation of political decisions (Michael, 2001). According to Andersen and Woyke (2009, p. 425), they have a conciliatory, intermediary function. Neo-corporatism abandons the concepts of influence theory (pluralism and neo-pluralism), which point in only one direction, without merely assuming the opposite position, and describes the political development of pressure groups and the state. In comparison to pluralism, neo-corporatism is characterized by voluntary involvement in the pressure group, cooperation and coordination with the state and the formulation and implementation of decisions that are binding for society as a whole. Neo-corporatism assumes from the outset, as Andersen and Woyke (2009, p. 426ff.) show, that the state has a direct or indirect influence on the formation of interest groups and the organization of collective interests.

A possible approach that can be applied in this context is the "Public Choice Theory", also known as "New Political Economy" (Downs, 1998). Along the lines of the study by Zaugg (2004) and in accordance with the insights of the New Political Economy, we based our work on general economic assumptions of rational action, methodological individualism and the axiom of self-interest. Thus, lobbying is seen as being a social exchange on the "marketplace" of political rents. A political rent is, as Svaleryd and Vlachos (2009) show, income that is granted by the state or by bureaucratic institutions that, as a rule, requires a direct service in return. It is a matter of attaining special advantages for groups. The attempt to acquire additional rents is referred to as rent-seeking (Svendsen & Svendsen, 2010). Information is gathered, processed and passed on, exchanged, so to speak (Woolcock, 2005); we will go into the latter aspect in more detail in the course of this paper. Schematically this "marketplace" can be visualized according to Müller and Zaugg (2005, p. 31) as follows:

The involved actors and/or exchange partners are NGOs and/or organizations or even individual persons that can be interpreted as so-called rent maximizers (Figure 1) and, to ensure their own existence, as maximizers of their level of organization.

Those who are able to award rents include political and bureaucratic agents who pursue self-serving goals such as re-election, status, esteem, a large staff, high income, etc., and therefore attempt to maximize their own value by gaining voters. These actors can thus be interpreted as vote or budget maximizers.

On the other side are, for example, NGOs, who offer politicians and officials services in return, quite according to the exchange principle of "do ut des"[1] (Pies, 1996, p. 23). These services are the chief objects of lobbying and are thus referred to as exchange goods. The availability of goods for exchange is the actual precondition for exercising influence.

Ultimately, the crucial factor is the credibility of the lobbyist with which he attempts to offer exchange goods. Conceivable instruments or potential exchange goods can be information, refraining from exercising economic power (= market power), monetary benefits (= finances), votes, legitimacy or help in decision-making (Bennett, 2002). Unfortunately, as Lessing remarks in this context (2006, p. 323), "to crack through lobbyism, you need a way to get the attention of members of Congress. But until the system is changed, the only way to get their attention is money". Parliamentarians and officials, on the other hand, have such exchange goods as political rents (e.g. the creation of favourable conditions, state-run programmes, laws conducive to tourism, etc.), information on the political feasibility of individual proposals or on the political agenda as well as finances for compensating for help in decision-making.

In this context, the Public Choice Theory, with its basic element of exchange or exchange goods, seems the most plausible for describing the situation in a specific destination (in our case Bavarian tourism). As Edgell et al. (2008) and Zaugg (2004) point out, tourism lobbying takes place in the marketplace of political rents. The makers of tourism policy play the crucial role, for it is they who determine the legal environment and the structures (Hall & Jenkins, 2004). It is, therefore, quite natural for people to try to influence the relevant decision-makers because as O'Brien (2010, p. 565) points out, Public

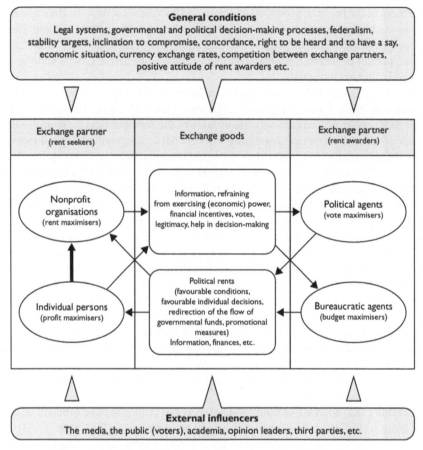

Figure 1. Model of lobbying structure and political district borders.
Source: draft by the authors.

Choice Theory proposes that political decisions are made not in the public interest, but rather in the interests of those making these decisions.

Here, the criteria or rules according to which various exchange partners coordinate measures remain of crucial importance. In fact, as Hall and Jenkins (2004) point out, the question of coordination poses great challenges for all involved, because the biggest problem in successful lobbying is always the lack of coordination between the involved persons. Often projects are doomed to failure from the outset because interest groups are not able or willing to coordinate their steps within the group or to consider the possibility of joining forces with other interest groups that may have a similar or identical goal.

The large number of (exchange) processes cannot be reduced to only a few at the micro and macro levels but must be viewed from a holistic perspective. In point of fact, the exchange processes are so complex that a more nuanced view of them must be taken. Organizations and associations are not simply a cluster of socio-political actors with shared goals engaged in loose interaction. As soon as they appear in public as a formal institution they make use of a number of communication channels and this again requires coordination between various levels and actors (Hula, 1999). The wide variety of interests, or rather demands, includes more than just an economic component; they likewise comprise at least a political and cultural dimension. It becomes apparent that an interest group not only acts as a group of individuals pursuing a common goal; to successfully realize its goal, it disregards asymmetrical divisions of labour and power issues in the spirit of a "corporate actor" (Schneider *et al.*, 2006). In this situation, the measures that require coordination include preparation and planning, procuring information and taking a glimpse behind the scenes. Nevertheless, as Hall (1999) points out, coordination is a political measure in the broadest sense of the word. This proves to be exceedingly complex, because when it comes to the tourism industry, and to tourism policy, the decision-making process involves a great number of groups. Only successful coordination ultimately leads to successful lobbying (Kollman, 1998).

As we will show in the course of the paper, this is the order of the day in Bavaria as well. For a better understanding of the subject matter, the following section will present the basic features of the tourism business and of tourism policies in Bavaria and the challenges they are facing.

2.2 Tourism Interest Groups and Their Role in the Conflicting Priorities of the Bavarian Tourism Business and the Makers of Tourism Policy

All over the world, the influence of interest groups is increasing. Political decisions influence the scope of action of all economic actors. Consequently, interest groups have always tried to influence policy-makers. When we examine the public and the academic discussion on the representation of interests, we see that in our contemporary society the individual is increasingly being eclipsed by organizations of the most varied types (Binderkrantz, 2005; Dredge & Jenkins, 2003). It is quite natural for groups or their representatives to try to help shape, implement and influence political decisions for rational reasons and/or power politics. According to Hall (2007, p. 122), "many stakeholders can be categorised as being 'interest groups'. The term "interest group" tends to be used interchangeably with the terms "pressure group", "lobby group", "special interest group" or "organized interests". An interest group can best be defined as "any association or organisation that makes a claim, either directly or indirectly, on government so as to influence policy without itself being willing to exercise the formal powers of government".

A first important contribution to our understanding of the subject was made by Tyler and Dinan (2001b, p. 460). They identify six types of interest groups in the tourism context, all of which influence decisions on tourism policy: umbrella groups, professional groups, government agencies, representatives of tourism intermediaries, pressure groups and trade groups/associations. These interest groups exert influence in order to obtain appropriate resources (financial resources, time, regulations, information, etc.). Hall and Jenkins (2004) point out that interest groups always shape political decision-making processes proactively. This also includes financial support for measures of all types. For their part, interest groups use their own resources or join forces with other interest groups to use their resources to attract the attention of politicians.

Interest groups refer to any groups that, on the basis of one or more shared attitudes, make certain claims upon other groups in society for the establishment, maintenance or enhancement of forms of behaviour that are implied by the shared attitudes. The shared attitudes, moreover, constitute the interests. Some of these attitudes are represented by interest groups asserting that the behaviour implied by the attitudes should be encouraged, discouraged or altered.

It is an incontrovertible fact that these groups, even though they are not mentioned at all in the constitutions of democratic states, play an important role in the political process as intermediaries between voters and parties or politicians (Kavanagh, 2006). The relationship between interest groups and political decision-makers is thus a reciprocal affair with fluid boundaries. Power plays an important role in this context (Coles & Church, 2007), because power is the dependent resource; it is not static and varies depending on the resources that interest groups and political decision-makers are willing to introduce into a decision-making process on a given issue. Ultimately, the interest groups that have the most power in the decision-making process are those who have the most resources and also know how to use them in the most prudent manner. With regard to tourism policy, power is the dominant factor, as Hall (2003) demonstrates. Power influences the interaction between individuals, organizations and third parties and has a direct influence on the formation of tourism policies and the manner in which decisions on tourism policy are implemented.

3. Tourism Structures and Current Challenges for the Makers of Bavarian Tourism Policy

Tourism is one of the most important branches of the economy in Bavaria and its economic significance has grown tremendously in the past two decades. With over 26 million arrivals and over 75 million overnight stays in 2009, Bavaria remained undisputedly the most frequently visited destination in Germany, as in the last 5 years, despite high growth rates in competing German states.

According to data from the Bavarian Ministry of Economic Affairs, Infrastructure, Transportation and Technology (Bayerisches Staatsministerium für Wirtschaft, Infrastruktur, Verkehr und Technologie, 2010) tourists spend more than €25 billion per year in Bavaria. Around 310,000 employees work in hotels and restaurants. These employment figures are higher than in Bavaria's two other key sectors, the automobile industry (225,785 employed persons) and the machine-building industry (198,109 employed persons). Traditionally the most important pillar of Bavarian tourism is its hospitality industry, which is comprised primarily of small- and medium-sized enterprises, of which there are 42,000. Of the approximately 576,000 beds, 34.7% are in hotels, 15.4% in bed and breakfasts, 14.5% in inns, 13.6% in holiday homes and holiday flats, 6.9% in pensions, 6.6% in leisure centres, holiday centres and training centres and 8.6% in other types of accommodation.

The immense economic significance of the Bavarian tourism structures should not obscure the fact that for a number of years Bavaria has struggled with exceedingly complex problems that, in the eyes of the makers of tourism policy, represent a stumbling block to the further development of tourism. These include a repeatedly deplored investment backlog especially for small- and medium-sized businesses. The causes of this backlog can be traced primarily to two factors. On the one hand, credit terms are tighter as a result of Basel II.[2] On the other hand, in many cases, it is unclear who will continue to operate the business in the future, because the economic situation in Bavaria is so good that more and more young people are deciding to go into other fields in which they consider the wage structures and working hours more attractive (Weiermair & Kronen-berg, 2004).

The situation is aggravated by the fact that owing to the strained budget situation in the past years, the public sector has made hardly any investments at the local level. This fact has only been partially compensated for by public–private partnership projects, particu-larly in comparison with important competing destinations such as Tyrol or Switzerland (Pechlaner & Sauerwein, 2002). A further competitive disadvantage vis-à-vis competing destinations is the still comparatively low degree of professionalization of the training pro-grammes for tourism. Only in the past few years have college level degree programmes gradually been developed (Dewhurst *et al.*, 2006). For many years training for work in tourism was limited almost exclusively to vocational schools.

Fortunately, the makers of tourism policy seem meanwhile to have recognized the immense challenges facing tourism in Bavaria if it is to continue to develop, a fact that is at least partially reflected in the main foci of the guidelines for tourism policy adopted in 2010, as also given in Table 1.

The Bayern Tourismus Marketing GmbH (BayTM: Bavarian Tourism Marketing Ltd) serves as the umbrella organization. Its activities are managed by the six large interest groups, or rather the six main partners (the tourism boards of Allgäu/Bavarian Suabia, Franconia, Munich-Upper Bavaria and Eastern Bavaria; the Bavarian Hotel and Restau-rant Federation and the Bavarian Spa Association).

The four tourist boards for their part are composed of smaller regional tourist boards, advertising initiatives (co-operations between individual towns and/or small regional tourist boards) and individual towns. The Bavarian Hotel and Restaurant Federation rep-resents hotels, gastronomic establishments and selected closely associated strategic part-ners. The Bavarian Spa Association represents all spas and health resorts.

Other smaller interest groups are also partners in the BayTM and have considerable influence on the large interest groups either because of their geographical location in Bavaria, their membership in committees, cooperation agreements, or associate or direct memberships. Here, it is evident that there is considerable potential for conflict, because the other interest groups have to act and decide in the interest of the large interest groups on the one hand, and in the interest of BayTM on the other. This structure is embedded in the political system, or rather the economic and social system, of the Federal Republic of Germany and the Free State of Bavaria.

With this diverse, interlinked structure, as illustrated in Figure 2, it was hoped that all interests could be combined under one umbrella and could act in concert. Tourism

Table 1. Main foci of the new guidelines for tourism policy adopted by the Bavarian state government

---

- Increased support for small- and medium-sized tourism enterprises
- Intensified upgrading of the local tourism infrastructure
- A quality initiative for basic and advanced training in tourism
- Increased professionalization and economic orientation of tourism marketing
- Heightened tourism orientation in other political spheres

Source: Bayerisches Staatsministerium für Wirtschaft, Infrastruktur, Verkehr und Technologie (2010, p. 33ff).

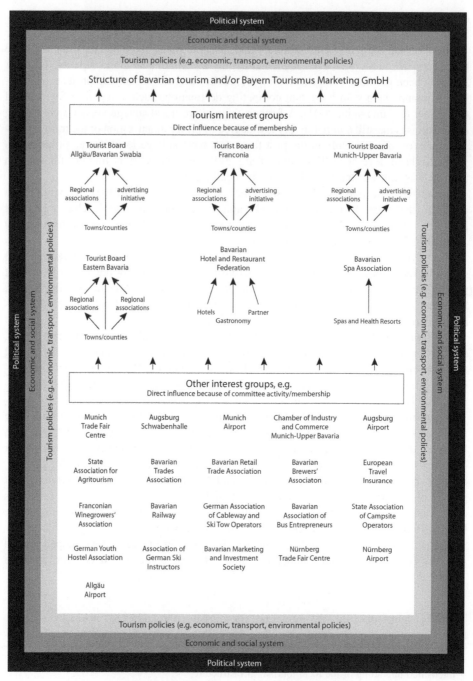

Figure 2. The structure of Bavarian tourism.
Source: draft by the authors based on www.bayern.by.

expertise and political competence were to be pooled, supported by representatives from the Bavarian business world. Since tourism is also an enabling industry, this integrated structure seemed the ideal condition to be optimally prepared for future challenges. This hope soon proved to be a fallacy, however, because the individual special interests rapidly surfaced and alleged professional discussions ended up in verbal infighting. Furthermore, the political representatives proved to be a great burden to the expert committees. Lacking expertise, decisions were made that had nothing to do with reality, some involving enormous financial costs. The result was soon a high degree of disillusionment, because those who were responsible had to recognize that the original goals could not be reached with the existing structures. Even today, 10 years after it was founded, it has not been possible to restructure the BayTM appropriately and to solve the known issues actively and lastingly (Figure 3).

The key problem with regard to tourism policy in Bavaria lies precisely in the outlined structures and also in the scope of BayTM. For one thing it soon became obvious that because of the differing functions, memberships and involvement of individuals or

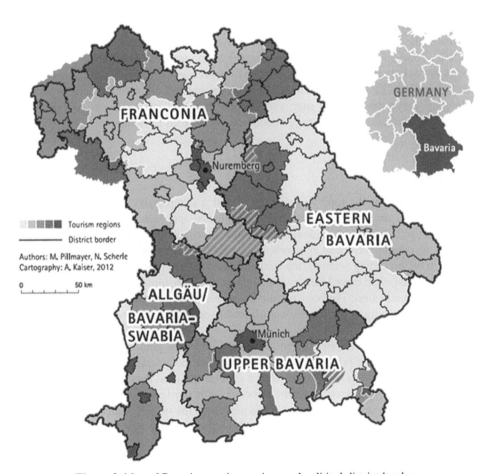

Figure 3. Map of Bavarian tourism regions and political district borders.
Source: Draft by the authors.

entire interest groups, conflicts of interest were inevitable or that differing views would collide. Especially, the fact that the Bavarian Minister of Economic Affairs is simultaneously the chairman of the supervisory board and is seen critically because, at least as the critics fear, decisions on tourism policy are being instrumentalized for political purposes. Traditionally, the Franconian regions are afraid of being marginalized in the activities of BayTM. For instance, in a recent tourist brochure on the Bavarian low mountain ranges, the Franconian Mountains were completely omitted. This led to great turbulence in the tourism community. Likewise, the regional affiliation of political officeholders and their decisions in the interest of their home regions give rise to some speculation. As soon as a county or a region, and thus an election district, is not given the supposedly appropriate attention in external communications, all tourism measures are boycotted. Policies oriented towards real conditions are thus completely disregarded and negated. This holds just as well for the individual tourism regions. Under-representation in the branding and communication strategy always leads to unnecessary discussions. This still holds today for managers, spokespersons or political representatives of tourism interest groups and those of the other interest groups, since the existing structures do not allow responsibilities and interests to be clearly separated.

On the other hand, the BayTM definitely views itself only as a marketing organization and not as the political mouthpiece of the Bavarian tourism business. Its predecessor, the Bavarian Tourism Board, which was disbanded in favour of the BayTM, saw its responsibility not only in marketing, but also in lobbying. Precisely here, then, is a significant gap that has not been closed so far. Thus, it is up to the individual interest groups to become politically active, to represent their own special interests and if possible to push them through. In most cases, however, this endeavour is doomed to failure.

4. Methodology

In tourism research, the topic of lobbying is still a comparatively young field; consequently, in this study we chose a largely qualitative approach. Complex and process-related research fields, in particular, are more amenable to exploratory and flexible methods of qualitative social research. This holds not least when, as already became evident in the preceding sections, the subject is associated in the public mind with a relatively vague and often biased image. A qualitative research approach can be seen here as a form of communication. The resourcefulness, power of observation, manner of questioning and risk proclivity of the interviewer ultimately determine the empirical results (Chia, 2003).

To be precise, we developed a semi-structured interview guide that, apart from structural questions relating primarily to the institution or the interviewed person, consisted largely of open questions. We began with a general question exploring the implications or aspects that the interview partners associate with the term lobbying. The intent of this question was to sensitize the interviewed persons to the subject matter. The subsequent questions delved into the field in more detail both thematically and spatially, in that they dealt specifically with the role of lobbying in the formation of tourism policy as well as with Bavaria as a tourist destination. In this context, we primarily asked questions that were intended to throw light on the perception and/or significance of lobbying in reconciling the competing interests of the tourism business and the makers of tourism policy.

At a general level, we first asked how they would rate the current tourism policies in Bavaria. Then, the interview partners were asked about their opinions on the current role of lobbying in Bavarian tourism policies. Subsequently, they were to assess the extent to which the lobbying that is practised helps to meet the current challenges facing the destination, a question that was closely connected with the adoption of the Bavarian tourism concept in October 2010. We also wanted to investigate to what extent lobbying can ultimately serve as an appropriate link between the tourism industry and the makers of tourism policy.

It should have become clear at this point that a successful project (ideally from the point of view of all stakeholders) requires professional lobbying. In this context, the interview partners were asked to name not only both positive and negative examples of current tourism lobbying, but also benchmark destinations from which Bavaria could learn with regard to tourism lobbying. Finally, the interview partners were asked to assess the factors they consider particularly helpful and/or necessary for strategic and effective tourism lobbying. Particularly, the last question, but also the question as to potential benchmark destinations, was posed in the hope of deriving recommendations for action that ideally should serve as a first step towards meaningful and effective lobbying and contribute productively to the further development of the tourist destination Bavaria.

The participants in the study, which was carried out by the authors primarily in the period from August 2009 to September 2010, included 20 interview partners divided equally between makers of tourism policy (10) and the tourism industry (10). The comparatively large number of interviews for a primarily qualitative study was intended to ensure that the relatively small group of persons who are familiar with the issues was represented in its entire complexity. The representatives of tourism policy included the State Secretary in the Bavarian Ministry of Economic Affairs, Infrastructure, Transport and Technology; the chairman of the Committee on Economic Affairs in the Bavarian parliament; the District President of Upper Bavaria; the spokesperson for tourism policy of the social democratic party of Germany (SPD) in the SPD parliamentary group in the German parliament and the head of the governmental department for the promotion of business and tourism for Lower Bavaria. We were fortunate in being able to win the long-standing chairman of the committee on tourism of the German parliament, who comes from Bavaria and accordingly is closely acquainted with the tourism structures in both Bavaria and Germany as a whole, and whose long-standing activity has made him familiar with the political mechanisms. Most of the persons from the tourism industry were representatives of trade associations and marketing organizations.

5. Tourism Lobbying in Bavaria Between Ignorance, Parochialism and Opportunism

In our empirical study, the experts we interviewed were first asked their opinion about the role that tourism lobbying plays in Bavaria in reconciling the conflicting interests of the makers of tourism policy and the tourism industry, in view of the current challenges to the destination and of the new Bavarian tourism concept. Let us start by citing the managing director of a tourism marketing organization who has campaigned for years to have tourism recognized as Bavaria's leading economic sector, which has occurred meanwhile. In this context, he repeatedly lamented the lack of appreciation of the field on the part of the makers of Bavarian tourism policy:

In Bavaria people do not recognise and comprehend tourism as the leading economic sector. But that's not all: the persons with whom I have to work in the ministries think I am responsible for seeing to it that every Japanese tourist who comes to Bavaria has a rucksack put on his back, is guided over an *alm* a bit, served beer and *weisswurst* [Bavarian veal sausage] and then merrily sent off.

More than any of the other persons interviewed, this director had internalized not only that the makers of tourism policy underestimate the tourism business and its economic implications but also that the small- and medium-sized tourism structures make effective lobbying difficult. This circumstance is reflected paradigmatically in the following quotation:

Tourism has a great deal of potential and is very diversified, but the market orientation is not consistent enough. Moreover, the reaction time is too slow. Even worse, though tourism is an important economic sector, it is not dominated by big companies. Instead it is very much characterised by small and medium-sized companies. That makes for quite a few problems! You see: the Bavarian manufacturers of automobile components do not have the economic might of tourism, but nevertheless things start happening at AUDI or BMW if a supplier of components starts to cough. In tourism I don't know who would have to start coughing before things would change. Unfortunately!

Precisely because small- and medium-sized businesses dominate the Bavarian tourism sector and because they have been contending for quite some time with a considerable investment backlog and a lack of successors (Scherle, 2009), if they are to have a shared political representation of interests they urgently need to join together under a big political "umbrella" (Anastasiadou, 2008; Michalowitz, 2007). The interviewed agents repeatedly called for this. The political actors at the local and state levels still underestimate the significance of these businesses for regional economic development (Dredge, 2006). Moreover, awareness is lacking of the structural changes on the part of tourism entrepreneurships, which have in many cases created an altered conceptual entrepreneurial self-image (Shaw & Williams, 2004).

In addition to the tense general situation for small- and medium-sized businesses, investments in tourism infrastructure are usually voluntary measures, coming under the response of local or county authorities, which they carry out on their own initiative (Weiermair & Kronenberg, 2004). The consequence is that the policy on tourism infrastructure is exceedingly fragmented and depends largely on the commitment of the individual mayor or county commissioner. This, however, leads to some problems, as the following quote reveals:

In exactly the same manner the industry must finally learn to abandon parochial ways of thought and "village emperorship" and to speak with one voice. A crucial problem in this context is that local councils, mayors and county commissioners frequently intervene in tourist affairs without having any professional competence.

As the Bavarian Ministry of Economic Affairs, Infrastructure, Transport and Technology (Bayerisches Staatsministerium für Wirtschaft, Infrastruktur, Verkehr und Technologie,

2010) has meanwhile recognized, the "parochial ways of thought" cited here continue to be one of the main obstacles in many Bavarian regions to an effective and lasting development of tourism. In the opinion of the majority of the interviewed experts, in spite of the diverse challenges, the responsible persons do not consider themselves capable of entering into co-operations between political actors and the tourism business, capitalizing on potential synergies or coming to agreements on joint measures. Differing views of tourism make concerted action for the sake of an issue a difficult undertaking, and diverging interests only complicate this fact.

In the course of the study, we also investigated the question to what extent lobbying could function as a link between the tourism business and the makers of tourism policy. In response to such a question the managing director of a regional tourist board answered:

> For many people Bavarian tourism policy is only an opportunistic platform. Unfortunately, tourism policy does not usually mean that in actuality tourism policy is being pursued. Particularly here in Bavaria this is bad, because in some cases it is merely a matter of activism. We unfortunately have the problem that tourism is like football: everybody thinks he knows the ropes, including politicians. Everybody wants to have a say and everybody knows what should be done, though without having any strategic competence.

This interview partner mentions an issue that researchers and practitioners repeatedly face, but that contradicts the supposedly intensified professionalization of Bavarian tourism. The difficulty is compounded by the fact that tourism is traditionally an enabling industry in which a great number of other branches of industry participate, e.g. finance and real estate, foodstuffs or the sporting goods industry (Oliver & Jenkins, 2005; Tyler & Dinan, 2001a). Generally, the dominant opinion is that people can make comments and decisions on tourism at any time, even without having expert knowledge.

One of the interviewed experts, who serves as the speaker on tourism policy of a party in the state parliament, feels that when it comes to the function of lobbying as a link between the tourism business and the makers of tourism policy, the obligation lies on the part of the tourism interest groups:

> The fault does not lie primarily with the politicians, but with the tourism interest groups themselves. Down to the present day they have not succeeded in presenting a united front vis-à-vis policy-makers. We are always confronted with individual special interests! But the big issues, like for instance promotion of tourism by policy-makers, fiscal issues and many other issues, are not systematically communicated to policy-makers. The interest groups are largely segmented and consequently not very successful. Each time a great number of persons are involved. If only one interest group, which would function as a link between the others, were to contact me, I would be happy to welcome this interest group with open arms!

This quote reflects truly paradigmatically the extraordinary fragmentation of the tourism interest groups in Bavaria. Plenty of special interests are articulated by the interest groups but their diverse or even conflicting interests make co-ordinated and effective tourism lobbying very difficult. Under these circumstances it is impossible to form a strong lobby to encourage political decision-makers to formulate policies favouring a given interest group

(Anastasiadou, 2008). At this point we would like to refer again to Figure 2 in Section 3. As a result of the structures of Bavarian tourism and tourism policy, a large number of different groups exist, each of which pursue their own interests. The result is often stone-walling or collisions of differing interests (O'Brien, 2010; Pforr, 2008). It goes without saying, and this was repeatedly called for in the course of the expert interviews, that the institutions must adopt a uniform stance if they wish to be heard by the makers of tourism policy. Already in the context of the statements made in this study, concerted tourism lobbying by the interest groups should be obligatory if Bavarian tourism is to be equal to the many challenges it will face in the future: increased customer focus and service mentality, a high degree of professionalism on the supply side, continuous training, development of target group-specific products and appropriate marketing (Pechlaner & Sauerwein, 2002).

In conclusion, we wanted to determine which factors could lead to effective tourism lobbying in Bavaria, to be able to act as a successful interest group or as a broker between the actors in question. That there are some hurdles still needing to be taken is made clear by the following statement by the chairman of the commission on tourism in the German parliament:

> [T]he reason why lobbying functions in one case but not in another is that the different interest groups do not speak with one voice, for one thing, and for the other thing that they act so stupidly that the policy-makers do not take the people from the tourism industry seriously. But I also say that tourism lobbying needs to develop first. Networks are very important for this. But the industry must not only lobby the policy-makers; they must also lobby the public. This means that everything that is not transported via the media is not appreciated by the population—that is the voters!

This quote clearly shows that the Bavarian tourism industry has not succeeded in speaking with one voice. All the same, the speaker does concede tourism lobbying a chance, if networks are successfully implemented and the public is sensitized to the issues. In this context, the main element of the Public Choice Theory is clearly demonstrated, namely that lobbying can also be understood as an exchange of goods (see Section 2). When issues are communicated to the public, and thus to potential voters, via the media, ideally pressure builds up on the involved makers of tourism policy. Thus, if there are upcoming elections a change of mindset can begin. Under the influence of external organs (e.g. the media) maximizers of profits and rents (e.g. associations) offer exchange goods to maximizers of votes (politicians); for instance, information on existing issues (Figure 1), in the hope of bringing about a change in behaviour or a decision on their behalf. In return votes are generated (Downs, 1998; Zaugg, 2004).

Successful tourism lobbying by interest groups requires not only concerted actions, the building of networks and intensified sensitization of the public (Greenwood, 2003; Pforr, 2008), but also specific individual dispositions, as demonstrated by the following quote by a mayor:

> A tourism lobbyist is in my opinion doomed to failure if his partner has the feeling, here is somebody with purely egotistic goals that will only benefit a certain clientele and not the public good. Furthermore, he should be a good practitioner, he should be

somebody you know—all the others I would describe as "armchair" lobbyists. He should also know how political structures function and he should be sensitive and with his sensitivity he should recognise trends at an early stage.

Particularly because the interview partners repeatedly mentioned the lack of coordination between the tourism actors or the lobbyists we wanted them to conclude with recommendations as to how the coordination could be optimized in the future. One of the tourism speakers (*Christlich Soziale Union*) opined:

You know, for years I have strongly advocated at both the most important lobby associations and the political level that something happen with regard to coordination because even today the relevant actors act separately more than they do together. The synergy effects that are lost, you can hardly imagine it! When you consider now that the international competition isn't napping, that instead it is getting more powerful all the time and our neighbour, Austria, has a really excellent lobby system in which the individual actors are perfectly interlinked, then I honestly have to say that I really worry about the further development of tourism in Bavaria. What we urgently need now is a central coordination unit that is directly subordinate to the Ministry of Economic Affairs.

With this the interviewee explicitly picks up ideas expressed by Hall (1999), who is one of the very few people working in tourism research who has dealt with the relevance of intensified coordination. Particularly considering how highly fragmented the Bavarian tourism actors are, this would lastingly strengthen the power of the lobby. Nevertheless, in future, it is not only a matter of intensifying the coordination between the individual interest groups, as the following quote by a director of a regional association makes clear; this coordination must be optimized at the intra-organizational level:

To me one aspect of a reformed lobby system in Bavaria (hopefully as soon as possible) seems particularly important, because it is overlooked all too frequently. The point should not only be to increase and optimise the cooperation between the various interest groups in future; it is at least as important that within the organisations optimised coordination takes place. Here much too often an absolutely counterproductive proportional representation mindset still prevails based on the maxim: you Catholic, I Protestant, he from Franconia, she from Upper Bavaria. Everybody has to be pandered to, but what they are actually lobbying for is neglected.

6. Conclusion

With the provocatively chosen title, "Tourism lobbying in Bavaria: between ignorance, parochialism and opportunism", we wanted to draw attention to a topic that has so far scarcely been dealt with in academic research on tourism. To be sure, the term lobbying is familiar to both the scientific community and a broad public, though, as the above remarks have shown, to a great extent it is still associated with vague, but often decidedly biased or negative connotations, which hardly do justice to the true significance of the matter.

As illustrated by the interviews with leading makers of tourism policy and representatives of the tourism industry, tourism lobbying in Bavaria is in an exceedingly weak position, because to a great extent it is unstructured and not well established at an institutional level. Predominantly special interests are articulated, which for the most part fail to find an attentive ear among the makers of tourism policy. By the same token, the different tourism interest groups existing in Bavaria are practically not represented at all in a tourism policy context, have almost no access to the necessary political institutions and struggle with a great number of serious challenges. The diversity and fragmentation of tourism as a sector of the economy, the overlapping activities of some institutions, the competition and the rivalry between different interests are the crucial factors why the industry has still not succeeded in organizing itself better politically (Anastasiadou, 2008). The empirical results reveal a weak representation of interests and a lack of influence of the existing tourism interest groups.

It goes without saying that the outlined lobbying structures are associated with issues of power, a concept that is only beginning to be applied in academic research on tourism (Hall, 2007). Particularly, the existing asymmetries resulting from the divergent interests of the makers of tourism policy and the tourism business itself make it difficult to position a destination successfully. The consequences of the transformation process from modern to postmodern tourism include increasingly complex challenges for those attempting to position a destination successfully and sustainably, challenges that can only be mastered by means of concerted efforts in the tourism value chain (Kachel & Jennings, 2010; Voase, 2007).

As this paper has shown, lobbying can be comprehended not only as a practical activity; but it also definitely has a basis in theory. This refers primarily to the Public Choice Theory, in which it is assumed that so-called exchange goods, in our concrete case information, are exchanged to the advantage of all involved. Currently, this exchange process in Bavaria is based only on the work of a very few association members or politicians who are actively engaged in tourism. Bavarian tourism lobbying is neither structured nor targeted nor efficient. In comparison to other destinations, the general institutional conditions are lacking and most measures are carried out *ad hoc*. In association with the implementation of institutionalized lobbying structures, the following aspects (Pillmayer, 2005; Zaugg, 2004) should be considered:

(1) Establishment of an early-warning system, i.e. integration into communication channels in order to be informed *a priori* of upcoming decisions that will impact tourism directly or indirectly.
(2) Identification of attractive and important tourism topics and communication of the same by means of various public relations measures.
(3) Monitoring or observation, like a kind of radar, of tourist institutions and persons who play an active role in tourism, connected with the establishment of a network of personal contacts plus identification of key figures for tourism.
(4) Measures relating to government relations or government affairs, i.e. cultivating relations to government figures or political representatives who are directly or indirectly associated with and conversant with tourism.
(5) Formation of coalitions and coordination with, for example, professional tourism associations, individuals or pressure groups.

Under the current circumstances successful tourism lobbying cannot be defined, however, by means of a standardized catalogue of criteria. For this the challenges facing the tourism industry in Bavaria are too complex. Tourism lobbying must consequently always be tailor-made, no matter how helpful a glance across borders may be.

Ultimately, the crucial factor is always access to information based on trust (Hommen & Edquist, 2008, p. 464), for the quality and continuity of a cooperation determine whether a partner can achieve credibility or not. This access, however, also requires a mid- to long-term time horizon. In this context, Green and Guth (2007, p. 107) speak aptly of a "struggle for access". In the end, we can only hope that the view of Del Río González (2006, p. 295) that "lobbyism can be regarded as an investment" will increasingly find an attentive ear, indeed as an investment that preferably will lastingly benefit all relevant actors.

Notes

1. I give, so that you might give.
2. Since 2005, new equity capital regulations for banks within the EU have reduced the credit risks by providing for risk-adjusted interest rates and by requiring banks to back their loans with sufficient own capital. This has changed the lending habits of banks. In future businesses without a good equity base or with a poor credit rating will not be able to borrow as much money as before or only at poorer conditions. Tourism companies traditionally do not have much equity capital, which has an important influence on their credit rating. New sources of business financing need to be tapped. These represent a great challenge particularly for small- and medium-sized companies, which make up the majority of the Bavarian tourism businesses.

References

Aglietta, M. (2000) *A Theory of Capitalist Regulation. The US Experience* (London: Verso Classics).

Anastasiadou, C. (2008) Tourism interest groups in the EU policy arena: Characteristics, relationships and challenges, *Current Issues in Tourism*, 11(1), pp. 24–62.

Andersen, U. & Woyke, W. (Eds) (2009) *Handwörterbuch des Politischen Systems der Bundesrepublik Deutschland*, 6th ed. (Opladen: Leske and Budrich Verlag).

Bayerische Staatsregierung (2008) *Koalitionsvereinbarung 2008–2013*. Available at http://www.bayern.de/Anlage8365157/Koalitionsvertrag.pdf (accessed 10 July 2012).

Bayerisches Staatsministerium für Wirtschaft, Infrastruktur, Verkehr und Technologie (2010) *Tourismuspolitisches Konzept der Bayerischen Staatsregierung* (München: Bayerisches Staatsministerium für Wirtschaft, Verkehr und Technologie).

Bennett, R. J. (2002) Factors influencing the effectiveness of business associations: A review, in: J. Greenwood (Ed.) *The Effectiveness of EU Business Associations*, pp. 15–29 (Basingstoke: Palgrave Macmillan).

Berry, J. M. & Wilcox, C. (2006) *The Interest Group Society*, 4th ed. (New York: Longman).

Binderkrantz, A. (2005) Interest group strategies: Navigating between privileged access and strategies of pressure, *Political Studies*, 53(4), pp. 694–715.

Boessen, S. & Maarse, H. (2009) A ban on tobacco advertising: The role of interest groups, in: D. Coen & J. Richardson (Eds) *Lobbying in the European Union: Institutions, Actors, and Issues*, pp. 212–232 (Oxford: Oxford University Press).

Boyer, R. (1990) *The Regulation School. A Critical Introduction* (New York: Columbia University Press).

Bramwell, B. (2006) Actors, networks and tourism policies, in: D. Buhalis & C. Costa (Eds) *Tourism Management Dynamics Trends, Management and Tools*, pp. 155–163 (Oxford: Elsevier Butterworth-Heinemann).

Chia, R. (2003) Organization theory as a postmodern science, in: H. Tsoukas & C. Knudsen (Eds) *The Oxford Handbook of Organization Theory. Meta-theoretical Perspectives*, pp. 113–140 (Oxford: Oxford University Press).

Coen, D. & Richardson, J. (Eds) (2009) *Lobbying in the European Union: Institutions, Actors, and Issues* (Oxford: Oxford University Press).

Coles, T. & Church, A. (2007) Tourism, politics and the forgotten entanglements of power, in: A. Church & T. Coles (Eds) *Tourism, Power and Space*, pp. 1–42 (London: Routledge).

Del Río González, P. (2006) Implementing the EU emissions trading directive in Spain: A comparative study of corporate concerns and strategies in different industrial sectors, in: R. Antes, B. Hansjürgens & P. Letmathe (Eds) *Emissions Trading and Business*, pp. 293–312 (Heidelberg: Physica-Verlag).

Dewhurst, H., Dewhurst, P. & Livesey, R. (2006) Tourism and hospitality SME training needs and provision: A sub-regional analysis, *Tourism and Hospitality Research*, 7(2), pp. 131–143.

Downs, A. (1998) *Political Theory and Public Choice (Downs, Anthony. Essays. V. 1.)* (Cheltenham: Edward Elgar Publishing).

Dredge, D. (2006) Policy networks and the local organisation of tourism, *Tourism Management*, 27(2), pp. 269–280.

Dredge, D. & Jenkins, J. (2003) Federal-state relations and tourism public policy, New South Wales, Australia, *Current Issues in Tourism*, 6(5), pp. 415–443.

DRV (Deutscher ReiseVerbands) (2010) *Fakten und Zahlen zum deutschen Reisemarkt 2009. Eine Übersicht des Deutschen ReiseVerbands (DRV)*. Available at http://www.drv.de/fileadmin/user_upload/fachbereiche/DRV_Zahlen_Fakten2009_01.pdf (accessed 10 July 2012).

Edgell, D., Allen, M. M., Smith, G. & Swanson, J. R. (2008) *Tourism Policy and Planning. Yesterday, Today and Tomorrow* (Burlington, MA: Butterworth-Heinemann).

Eising, R. (2004) Multilevel governance and business interests in the European Union, *Governance: An International Journal of Policy Administration and Institutions*, 17(2), pp. 211–245.

Feltenius, D. (2002) Pensioners organizations in the Swedish policy process: From Lobbyism to corporatism. Paper presented at the Conference 30th Joint Session of the European Consortium for Political Research (ECPR), Turin, Italy. Available at http://www.essex.ac.uk/ecpr/events/jointsessions/paperarchive/turin/ws21/feltenius.pdf (accessed 10 July 2012).

FUR (Forschungsgemeinschaft Urlaub und Reisen e.V.) (2010) *Die 40. Reiseanalyse RA*. Available at http://www.fur.de/fileadmin/user_upload/RA_Zentrale_Ergebnisse/FUR_Reiseanalyse_RA2010_Erste_Ergebnisse.pdf (accessed 10 July 2012).

Graziano, L. (2001) *Lobbying, Pluralism and Democracy (Advances in Political Science)* (Basingstoke: Palgrave Macmillan).

Green, J. C. & Guth, J. L. (2007) Big bucks and petty cash: Party and interest groups activists in American politics, in: A. J. Cigler & B. A. Loomis (Eds) *Interest Group Politics,* 7th ed., pp. 91–113 (Washington: CQ Press).

Greenwood, J. (2003) *Interest Representation in the European Union* (New York: Palgrave Macmillan).

Hall, M. C. (1999) Rethinking collaboration and partnership: A public policy perspective, *Journal of Sustainable Tourism*, 7(3&4), pp. 274–289.

Hall, M. C. (2003) Politics and place: An analysis of power in tourism communities, in: S. Singh, J. T. Dallen & R. K. Dowling (Eds) *Tourism in Destination Communities*, pp. 99–114 (Wallingford: CABI).

Hall, M. C. (2007) *Tourism Planning. Policies, Processes and Relationships*, 2nd ed. (Harlow: Longman).

Hall, M. C. & Jenkins, J. (2004) Tourism and public policy, in: A. Lew, C. M. Hall & A. M. Williams (Eds) *A Companion to Tourism*, pp. 526–540 (Oxford: Blackwells).

Haller, M. (2008) *European Integration as an Elite Process. The Failure of a Dream?* (New York: Routledge).

Homan, M. S. (2007) *Promoting Community Change: Making it Happen in the Real World*, 4th ed. (Belmont, CA: Brooks Cole).

Hommen, L. & Edquist, C. (2008) Globalization and innovation policy, in: L. Hommen & C. Edquist (Eds) *Small Country Innovation Systems: Globalization, Change and Policy in Asia and Europe*, pp. 442–485 (Cheltenham: Edward Elgar).

Hula, K. W. (1999) *Lobbying Together: Interest Group Coalitions in Legislative Politics (American Governance and Public Policy)* (Washington, DC: Georgetown University Press).

Kachel, U. & Jennings, G. (2010) Exploring tourists' environmental learning, values and travel experiences in relation to climate change: A postmodern constructivist research agenda, *Tourism and Hospitality Research*, 10(2), pp. 130–140.

Kavanagh, D. (2006) Pressure groups and policy networks, in: D. Kavanagh, D. A. Richards, M. Geddes & M. Smith (Eds) *British Politics,* 5th ed., pp. 417–440 (Oxford: Oxford University Press).

Kollman, K. (1998) *Outside lobbying: Public opinion and interest group strategies* (Princeton, NJ: Princeton University Press).

Lambsdorff, J. G. (2007) *The Institutional Economics of Corruption and Reform: Theory, Evidence and Policy* (Cambridge: Cambridge University Press).

Leif, T. & Speth, R. (2003) Anatomie des Lobbyismus: Einführung in eine unbekannte Sphäre der Macht, in: T. Leif & R. Speth (Eds) *Die Stille Macht: Lobbyismus in Deutschland*, pp. 7–32 (Wiesbaden: VS Verlag für Sozialwissenschaften).

Lessing, L. (2006) *Code: And Other Laws of Cyberspace, Version 2.0* (New York: Basic Books).

Michael, E. (2001) Public choice and tourism analysis, *Current Issues in Tourism*, 4(2–4), pp. 308–330.

Michalowitz, I. (2007) *Lobbying in der EU* (Wien: Facultas Verlag).

Müller, H. & Zaugg, B. (2005) Lobbying im Schweizer Tourismus, in: T. Bieger (Ed.) *Jahrbuch der Schweizer Tourismuswirtschaft 2004/2005*, pp. 29–41 (St. Gallen, Switzerland: IDT-HSG Verlag).

O'Brien, A. (2010) Beyond policy-making: Institutional regimes, the state and policy implementation in the Irish case, *Current Issues in Tourism*, 13(6), pp. 563–577.

Oliver, T. & Jenkins, T. (2005) Integrated tourism in Europe's rural destinations: Competition or cooperation? in: E. Jomes & C. Haven-Tang (Eds) *Tourism SMEs, Service Quality and Destination Competitiveness*, pp. 25–38 (Wallingford: CABI).

Palazzo, G. & Scherer, A. G. (2008) The future of global corporate citizenship: Toward a new theory of the firm as a political actor, in: G. Palazzo & A. G. Scherer (Eds) *Handbook of Research on Global Corporate Citizenship*, pp. 577–590 (Cheltenham: Edward Elgar).

Pechlaner, H. & Sauerwein, E. (2002) Strategy implementation in the Alpine tourism industry, *International Journal of Contemporary Hospitality Management*, 14(4), pp. 157–168.

Pforr, C. (2008) Tourism in the northern territory: Caught in an intergovernmental quagmire, *Public Policy*, 3, pp. 159–174.

Pies, I. (1996) Public choice versus constitutional economics: A methodological interpretation of the Buchanan research program, *Constitutional Political Economy*, 7(1), pp. 21–34.

Pillmayer, M. (2005) *Tourismuslobbying—Fluch oder Segen? Wirkungs- und Effizienzanalyse sowie Schlussfolgerungen für Tourismusakteure in Bayern* (Trier, Germany: Förderkreis Tourismusmanagement Universität Trier).

Rommetvedt, H. (2000) Private and public power at the national level, in: H. Goverdi, P. G. Cerny & M. Haugaard (Eds) *Power in Contemporary Politics: Theories, Practices, Globalizations*, pp. 112–131 (London: Sage).

Scheff, J. & Gutschelhofer, A. (Eds) (1998) *Lobby-Management—Chancen und Risiken vernetzter Machtstrukturen im Wirtschaftsgefüge* (Wien: Linde Verlag).

Scherle, N. (2009) *Project Report Tegernsee* (Eichstätt: Chair for Cultural Geography).

Schneider, V., Lang, A., & Bauer, J. M. (2006) *The adaptation of complex associational systems: Coordination and lobbying strategies of business associations in the context of globalization, and Europeanization.* Available at http://www.uni-konstanz.de/FuF/Verwiss/Schneider/ePapers/CAS_VSALJMB041906.pdf (accessed 10 July 2012).

Sedlenieks, K. (2004) Rotten talk: Corruption as a part of discourse in contemporary Latvia, in: I. Pardo (Ed.) *Between Morality and the Law. Corruption, Anthropology and Comparative Society*, pp. 119–135 (Aldershot: Ashgate Publishing).

Shaw, G. & Williams, A. M. (2004) From lifestyle consumption to lifestyle production: Changing patterns of tourism entrepreneurship, in: R. Thomas (Ed.) *Small Firms in Tourism: International Perspectives*, pp. 94–114 (Oxford: Elsevier).

Svaleryd, H. & Vlachos, J. (2009) Political rents in a non-corrupt democracy, *Journal of Public Economies*, 93(3), pp. 355–372.

Svendsen, G. T. & Svendsen, G. L. H. (2010) *Handbook of Social Capital. The Troika of Sociology, Political Science and Economics* (Cheltenham: Edward Elgar).

Timothy, D. J. (2007) Empowerment and stakeholder participation in tourism destination communities, in: A. Church & T. Coles (Eds) *Tourism, Power and Space*, pp. 199–216 (London: Routledge).

Tyler, D. & Dinan, C. (2001a) Trade and associated groups in the English tourism policy arena, *International Journal of Tourism Research*, 3(6), pp. 459–476.

Tyler, D. & Dinan, C. (2001b) The role of interested groups in England's emerging tourism policy network, *Current Issues in Tourism*, 4(2–4), pp. 210–252.

Voase, R. (2007) Individualism and the 'new tourism': A perspective on emulation, personal control and choice, *International Journal of Consumer Studies*, 31(5), pp. 541–547.

Weiermair, K. & Kronenberg, C. (2004) Stuck in the middle: The future of small and medium sized tourism enterprises, in: P. Keller & T. Bieger (Eds) *The Future of Small and Medium Sized Enterprises in Tourism*, pp. 125–140. 54th Congress 2004, Petra, Jordan. AIEST International Association of Scientific Experts in Tourism (St. Gallen, Switzerland: Ed. AIEST).

Woolcock, S. (2005) Trade Policy, in: H. Wallace, W. Wallace & M. A. Pollack (Eds) *Policy-Making in the European Union,* 5th ed., pp. 377–400 (Oxford: Oxford University Press).

Zaugg, B. (2004) *Lobbying im Schweizer Tourismus* (Bern: Berner Studien zu Freizeit und Tourismus).

Index

Entries in **bold** denote tables; entries in *italics* denote figures.

For Product Safety Concerns and Information please contact our
EU representative GPSR@taylorandfrancis.com Taylor & Francis
Verlag GmbH, Kaufingerstraße 24, 80331 München, Germany